bless our workforce

Changing The Way We Manage Our People

Mark S. Young

©2021 – Mark S. Young
ISBN: 9798702154091
Independently Published
1st Edition - Paperback

praise for bless our workforce

Mark S. Young's *Bless Our Workforce* provides an aspirational examination of the promise of the emerging Jewish professional talent network. His thoughtful approach, blending anecdotes, experiences and hard data, offers content and context for those of us committed to building a more robust and engaged field. The work complements so much of what we see within the Leading Edge, JPRO, SRE sphere of influence. Ultimately, the book humanizes our field and the personal and professional journey each of us experiences in our profession. I look forward to seeing how this contributes to the communal landscape as we process the opportunities and capacity of our field.

– Brian Schreiber, CEO
  JCC of Greater Pittsburgh

Mark S. Young's new text is the long awaited blessing for all professionals working in the many agencies of the Jewish Community, He has successfully mastered the art of the "talking book" on the printed page: each of the cogent and upbeat chapters will have you feeling this wise counselor, educator and trainer is your best friend sitting on the sofa next to you. A joyful and eminently readable text for all who journey in our field. A most practical gift from a supervisor/manager to her/his hard-working staff to practice 'Learning Never Ends'.

– Steven Rod, Vice-President
  Professional Development Services, *JCCs of North America (retired)*

As someone who has worked in traditional Jewish institutions for over 30 years, I can honestly say that his book is essential. It's the kind of book employees should read and gift to their employers and lay leaders!

– Barb Gelb, Director of Development
  United Jewish Federation of Tidewater, Virginia Beach, VA

Mark has truly blessed us with this articulate and cogent message. We are fortunate to have so many passionate, committed and smart professionals in the field, including those on whom he has shined the light. It behooves us to really hear Mark's message and constantly consider the many factors that motivate them and drive them so that the Jewish communal field continues to thrive, and that a career of a Jewish Communal Professional will be one that children aspire to and not just fall into because of happenstance. I will use Mark's 15 blessings as reminders, as I work to develop professionals every day, to ensure that our colleagues are motivating and valuing each other, that we are championing new talent, empowering them in their work and amplifying their strengths. Thank you Mark for elevating our field and giving us a "playbook," one based on Jewish values, from which to raise up our professionals.

– Cindy Goldstein, Executive Director, Darrell Friedman Institute for Professional Development
  Na'aleh: The Hub for Leadership Learning- Baltimore, MD

Bless Our Workforce is an invaluable tool for Jewish communities big and small. As the leader of a synagogue, Mark's book helped me better understand what I need to do to motivate and inspire my staff to work at their best. As I read the book, I often thought of ways I could improve in my work. This is an invaluable resource not just for Jewish communities but as a study of the way we treat those that work for us and how we can help them to reach their highest potential.

– Rabbi Marc Katz, Rabbi
  Temple Ner Tamid, Bloomfield, NJ

dedications

To Noah Sadie and Asher Russell, how blessed I am
to be your Dad, you light up Mommy and my life
every day. Stay silly.

To Mara, for blessing me with unconditional love
and partnership. I love you.

To Rosalie Young, z'l, for blessing me with guidance
to "keep my head on my shoulders," "be safe, be
careful," and to "get my rest." I miss you, Mom,
and love you dearly.

contents

INTRODUCTION	Why I Wrote this Book	7
PRE-BLESSING	Preparing the Canvas	11
BLESSING 1	Challenge Our Talent	19
BLESSING 2	Build Around the Talent	29
BLESSING 3	Foster the Relationships	41
BLESSING 4	Feed Their Creative Drive	55
BLESSING 5	Show Them the Fruits of their Labor	69
BLESSING 6	Promote Collaboration, End Exclusion	81
BLESSING 7	Cut the B.S.	95
BLESSING 8	Empower Them to See the Big Picture	111
BLESSING 9	Bringing their Whole Integrated-Selves to Work	121
BLESSING 10	It is Not About Them	135
BLESSING 11	Make it All About Them	145
BLESSING 12	Champion The Relentless Pursuit	157
BLESSING 13	What Success Can Look Like	173
BLESSING 14	Amplify Our Strengths	179
BLESSING 15	Adjust Our Imperfections	189
POST-BLESSING	Mah Tovu	199
In Gratitude, Appendix, Resources and Works Cited		204

why i wrote this book

I feel blessed to be a Jewish community professional. I wasn't always planning to be one, and for a long-time, I didn't realize how wonderful this profession is.

When I was 18, a recruiter from the Mandel Jewish Community Center (JCC) of Cleveland, Ohio paid a visit to the JCC's summer camp, Camp Wise, where I was the head song leader. The recruiter pitched us working full-time for the JCC after college. I was a prime candidate. I loved working and put my heart and soul into working at camp, it never felt like a chore. Yet, I wasn't inspired, why not?

At the time, I thought working for the Jewish community, at camp or otherwise, didn't seem to me like a real job. I also thought I couldn't raise a family or make a decent living this way. In addition, I foolishly thought that I wouldn't be respected by my peers.

But I was wrong! Two decades later I am a proud Jewish community professional, and working in fact for the JCC Movement as I finalize this book. I remain and am committed to this profession because I have been blessed to work for great people, assigned interesting projects, on the whole have been well-compensated, and have caught a few lucky breaks. But my journey has also been convoluted and, at times, challenging. My work environments haven't always felt supportive and rewarding, and the ability to elevate to new roles hasn't been as clear as I think it could have been. I began to wonder, could the journey to feeling like a blessed Jewish community professional be easier? What have been the experiences of my peers? What was their journey and what continues to motivate them?

I began this project in response to these curiosities, well before COVID-19 massively began to disrupt our society. Beginning in fall of 2017, I interviewed 13 colleagues in an effort to complement the growing quantitative studies on the Jewish community professional workplace in recent years. I wondered if narrating a portrait of each of these colleagues might reveal a "big idea," to how we can better motivate and show value to our staff. This would then help inform how we — leaders, managers, and participants in Jewish organizational life — can best inspire, invest, and retain our talent. I completed the book manuscript in summer of 2019, with aspiration to publish in early 2020.

Then COVID-19 changed our world and set my timeline back a few months, yet allowed me to make a few adjustments in light of our new reality. As I publish *Bless Our Workforce* at the end of 2020, we find ourselves at a time of immense challenge. We are now dealing with the crisis of a lifetime and still at a time when Jewish life has been mobilizing for several years to ensure strong community leadership for the future. While we are forced to make difficult staffing decisions to keep our organizations afloat, now is also the time to ensure we have sufficient high-quality talent in our workforce for today and the future. We must inspire young people both to become Jewish community professionals and our current talent to stay, so they thrive in our field for years, if not decades. A compelling set of strategies can help us achieve these goals. What might these strategies be though, and how do we go about uncovering them?

Though each interview I did indeed uncover a big idea. I call each a blessing. My initial curiosity morphed into a core purpose and goal of this book: for us to change how we manage our Jewish community professionals so each feel honored, valued, and blessed.

Many of these blessings may already be widely used, while some less so. Each is supported with a brief narrative portrait of the professional I interviewed. I also support each idea both with research and practice from the secular world of management and leadership and with the wisdom of our Jewish tradition. Each aims to uncover a deeper understanding of our professionals' intrinsic motivations, desired career path, motivation to remain in the workforce, and reasons they might consider leaving; finally, I explore how we can apply each idea to inspire and retain our talent.

I feel blessed that you are reading this book. I hope *Bless Our Workforce* helps us to inspire more talent to join the work of strengthening Jewish life, including those young camp counselors to join up early, grow their potential, maximize their impact, and help them feel joy in their work. I also hope this book will help Jewish community professionals at all levels to lead and innovate, take control of their own destiny, and advocate for themselves and their colleagues.

If you are a Jewish institutional leader, either lay or professional, because of your title, your actions, or whom you influence, I hope this book helps you lead our critically important institutions towards long-term success.

If you are a manager of staff, I hope this book provides you with a concrete and applicable guide to inspiring, valuing and blessing your staff.

If you are a Jewish community professional at any point in your career journey, I hope this book gives insight to your own journey, what motivates and excites you, and how you would like to be valued.

To all readers, I hope this book motivates you to have the *kavanah*, intentionality, to act by deeply getting to know the journeys and motivations of those you work with, who work for you, and for whom you work for. Let us ensure our entire workforce feels blessed. We've got some important work to do. Let's get started.

preparing the canvas

My first Jewish community professional paying gig was as a *B'nai Mitzvah* Tutor at my childhood synagogue. The first prayer I would teach my students was the pre-blessing to the chanting of the *Haftorah*, a selection from the Biblical book of Prophets. I always enjoyed teaching the pre-blessing. It established a working rapport with my student, helping me learn how best the student likes to learn and practice. Once we got past the pre-blessing, we were ready to dive into learning the *Haftorah* blessing with increased confidence and energy.

The pre-blessing is like a pre-game ritual. It's the wisdom of preparing ourselves so we are properly ready to chant the Biblical passages. Building on and applying this Jewish wisdom to our discussion, I offer this pre-blessing, defining our terms and providing important background information to help "prepare the canvas" for the professional portraits and big ideas we will encounter.

DEFINING OUR EXPLORATION

I selected a small diverse group of 13 Jewish community professionals who inspired me. I asked each of them a series of 10 questions that you can find in the appendix to this book. I wanted to learn about each of their career paths and personal journeys, and uncover whether their journey, though unique, could help inform how we all might better:

- Inspire the current and next generation of professionals to make an intentional career choice to become and remain a Jewish community professional.

- Properly and rigorously motivate, inspire, and support our talent so they want to stay, because they feel they can reach their full potential by working in our field.

Choosing the Individuals: A Focus on Diversity

Each person was comfortable speaking to me about their compensation, career transitions, implications around DEIJ (diversity, equity, inclusion, and justice) in their work situations, and other sensitive and personal topics. These narratives also represent a mix:

- Religious movement backgrounds and current practices

- Types and categories of Jewish organizations (both legacy and start-up)

- Gender identification

- Geographic location

- Those who have held executive roles and those who have not

- Racial and ethnic background

These professionals are also neither at the very beginning nor anywhere near the end of their careers. Each has significant experience, yet they still have hopes and dreams for their career journeys, where our field can go and grow, and how they hope to experience it in the decades they have left to serve.

From the standard questions I asked each participant, each conversation took on a life of its own, and this is in part why each blessing, while focused on a strategy with narrative support, not the other way around, may have a different structure or tone. At the same time, each narrative provides insights into key questions that permeate this book. I also put these narratives into conversation with each other that addresses the following:

- Who are these professionals, their origin stories, what makes each tick?

- Why do they work for the Jewish community and what continues to motivate them?

- What strategies would they prescribe so they and their peers would feel more valued?

Lastly, these narratives are largely a snapshot in time, conducted two to three years prior to the publishing of this book. Where applicable, there are updates.

SHARING IDEAS THROUGH STORIES

The 2013 Pew Research Center study on the North American Jewish Community, along with Leading Edge's *Leading Places to Work* surveys, have informed us that Jewish community professionals are inspired by their organizational missions yet often dissatisfied by many aspects of their jobs. These data points are instructive. Yet behind this data are the narratives, individual journeys, detailed experiences, inflection points, and broader stories of our Jewish community professionals who can help us understand how those who are emerging as the professional leaders of today and tomorrow choose to enter, remain, leave, and in some cases return to, our workforce.

These narratives can provide deep understanding of what our professionals want to accomplish, what they want in return, and how each truly desires to feel valued. I was inspired by this approach during my time working at the Jewish Theological Seminary (JTS). I had the pleasure of learning from my colleague Rabbi Dr. Sarah Tauber, z'l. Building off the work of her dissertation, Dr. Tauber published *Open Minds, Devoted Hearts: Portraits of Adult Religious Educators*, which examines the work and life of three Rabbis, noting that Rabbis are more than spiritual leaders; they take on many forms: community leaders, educators, and, facilitators to name a few. By using portraiture as a form of research, Dr. Tauber came to many compelling conclusions, and "helped reveal how constructing personal meaning and building sacred community through study situates adult learning as a dynamic centerpiece of an energized congregational life. (*Tauber, Open Minds, Devoted Hearts*)." Dr. Tauber's work inspired me to use portraiture for this exploration. Dr. Tauber departed from this world just as I finalized this book. I am indebted to her wisdom, creativity, and kindness in helping me with this project (thank you Sarah).

In this text, we will similarly use portraiture to reveal the big ideas on how best to motivate and inspire Jewish community professionals.

DEFINING OUR TERMS

Who is a Jewish Community Professional?

Let us also clarify our terminology. For example, when we say, "Jewish community professional," what do we mean? In 2009 and 2010, the Jewish Communal Service Association (or JCSA, which is now JPRO Network) surveyed 2400 self-identified Jewish community professionals, and none were able to agree on a singular definition. Rather, the exploration of the term leads to additional questions:

• Does one have to identify or be identified as Jewish to be a Jewish community professional?

- Does one have to occupy a classified (as per government or union labor standards) professional role (instead of say clerical or maintenance role) to be considered a Jewish community professional?

- Does one have to be actively working for a self-described Jewish organization to be a Jewish community professional?

- Is one required to earn a certain credential to be considered a Jewish community professional, whether it be a specific academic degree or certificate, or must one have a Jewish educational background?

This is to say nothing of the organizations one must work in, or how to discern whether an organization is considered a "Jewish organization." Is their Jewish "status" tied to the mission statement or whom the organization serves? What about professionals who are independent consultants and don't work for particular organizations yet see themselves working for the Jewish community and Jewish people broadly? The conversation can be dizzying.

For the purposes of our work, I suggest my own definition of Jewish community professionals with the following criteria. A Jewish community professional is an individual who:

1. Chooses to identify as one.

2. Has a specific expertise or skill-set that can serve an organization or fellow individuals that self-identify as "Jewish" or "primarily serving the Jewish community."

3. Is intentional about serving a self-identified Jewish organization or the Jewish community.

This tripartite definition implies a few things. One, if an individual works for a Jewish organization but does not consider themselves a Jewish community professional, in my view, we should not force the label onto them. While we may wish they identify as a Jewish community professional, I see no value in coercing them into the category. For example, a CFO, programming or marketing professional, or maintenance director at a JCC might not want to label themselves a Jewish community professional. We might like them to. Yet, if we forced the issue, it would be like saying that a hospital CFO or maintenance worker works in the field of medicine. To be clear, this principle applies regardless of whether or not they self-identify as Jewish. People of all faiths or no faith can be and are Jewish community professionals.

Two, if an individual's intent is to serve Jewish life, they ought to want to grow in their knowledge and understanding of Jewish content and the skills they view as applicable to their work. Similarly, they should see their contributions, whether as a Jewish educator, development officer, marketing professional, or administrator, as serving their Jewish organization in a way that reflects their own growing expertise and interests.

For our purposes, I chose to profile individuals who fit within this definition. My aspiration is that this definition does not forcibly include individuals who don't want to be labeled thus, nor forcibly exclude individuals who want to be included.

What are we trying to change?

In my two decades working in Jewish organizational life, I have observed many Jewish community professional peers state that they happened to fall into Jewish community professional work. I occasionally, yet rarely, encounter a Generation X or Millennial Jewish professional who began aspiring to this career path when they were a teen or college student. I have also observed that many Jewish community professionals who supervise others do not necessarily have the training or skills to do so effectively, or, their methods may no longer fit in today's workplace.

Let me be clear, I believe our hearts are in the right place and that most of us strive to promote a work culture that helps employees thrive. Yet, relative to keeping a balanced budget and our end-users satisfied, we may not always prioritize the career motivations and personal health and well-being of our workforce as much as we could be.

As I finalize this chapter during COVID-19, we are learning that staff's mental health and well-being are being impacted. According to the June 2020 pulse survey by Leading Edge, only 69% of professionals feel that their organizations support their health and well-being. In a field north of 80,000 Jewish community professionals, that's a lot of talent who may not feel adequately supported.

Even before COVID-19, the results of the Leading Places to Work Studies by Leading Edge indicated that 47% of employees do not receive a meaningful performance review. The studies also indicated that employees do not always have the proper skill sets to effectively offer regular meaningful feedback to each other, and an alarming number of new Jewish community professionals leave their organizations, and often the field as a whole, within five years of taking their first Jewish community professional job.

How might we then learn from the stories of our professionals in order to strengthen how we demonstrate value to and therefore bless our talent? As we read through the stories and big ideas in this book, I encourage each of us to take more time to deeply get to know our staff, by actively listening to them and understanding what makes them tick.

This is worth stating twice: **If we deeply get to know who we work with, we can better motivate, inspire and demonstrate value towards them so they feel blessed at work.** It is analogous to Rabbi Hillel and his articulation of the golden role: "What is harmful to you, do not do unto any person. That is the whole Torah, the rest is commentary, go and study." Consider truly getting to know our staff as our *Bless Our Workforce* golden rule, the rest of this volume is commentary for us to study.

PART OF A LARGER MOVEMENT

Of course, the important and sacred work of blessing our workforce isn't occurring in a vacuum. In recent years, dozens of continental agencies, including Hillel International, Jewish Federations of North America, JCC Association of North America, Foundation for Jewish Camp, JPRO Network, and Leading Edge, have been addressing staff investment and leadership development, endeavoring to strengthen the Jewish workplace experience, cultivate and retain talent, and reduce the perceived professional leadership gap in Jewish organizational life. The work up until now has shown tremendous promise. We have, for example, seen an increase in professional leadership programs, some of which I have had the honor to either develop and lead or participate in. We have slowly begun to see significant wage increases, more clearly crafted job descriptions, more Jewish organizations adopting paid parental leave policies, and at least a stated desire for our field to be more gender and racially equitable. I hope *Bless Our Workforce* can support these field building efforts with continuous focus on the individual Jewish community professional and consider each of their needs and interests so we can best value, support, nurture, and guide each of them.

WHAT LIES AHEAD

I hope reading the journeys and big-ideas from each of these impressive colleagues will help us shift many of our assumptions, amplify practices that prioritize our talent we are already doing well and adjust practices that are not properly serving our workforce.

Following the 13 narratives, chapters 14 and 15 will help us reflect on what we have learned, extrapolating major lessons. These sections will highlight what we are already doing right and should amplify, along with where we need to adjust. Finally, just as we got ready with this pre-blessing, there is a post-blessing, closing with learning from our Jewish tradition that allows us to take our learning into practice with confidence, curiosity, care, and an updated game plan so we can truly bless our workforce each day.

challenge our talent

Blessing Summary — If we challenge our talent with meaningful and exciting projects that speak to employees' drive for autonomy, competence, belonging, and purpose, they will feel valued and motivated to work hard and meet the audacious goal.

"If I gave you one million dollars to benefit the community, what would you do?" Before a local philanthropist asked David Cygeilman this question during a chance meeting in college, he wasn't planning on becoming a Jewish community professional, let alone establishing and growing one of the most influential Jewish engagement institutions of this generation.

Yet it was this *challenge*, or invitation, to craft a vision and see it through, to both address and resolve what appeared to be the intractable problem of engaging post-undergraduate young adult Jews into Jewish life, that excited and motivated David. This challenge, that David ultimately accepted, led to the development of Moishe House. Moishe House engages the largely unengaged Jewish population in their twenties and early thirties into active Jewish life. Back in the mid-2000's, no program or institution was successfully engaging non-Orthodox Jews primarily in their 20's on a large scale, and it was of increasing concern among community leaders and funders working towards maintaining and strengthening a healthy and engaged Jewish community for the future. There are of course Taglit-Birthright Israel experiences, which have been shown to increase a young Jew's connection to Israel and bolster Jewish identity, but unclear if this connection lasts, given that the experience is a one-off without consistent follow up. Moishe House is thus a game changer in today's Jewish education and engagement landscape. A decade and a half after this challenge was made, 200 communities throughout the world, both big and small, now host a thriving Moishe House.

Let's pause for a second. Who has given you a challenge in your work? Did that person's challenge motivate you? If it did, how might this challenge have contributed to your motivations? This first blessing is about how a challenge, one that is meaningful and appropriate, can motivate our workforce and, as they achieve, allow them to feel blessed in their work.

David's first real connection to Jewish life was on his teen trip to Israel. The destination turned out to be far less important to him than the people he met. As a child, there were no other Jewish students in his school. He went to a Catholic high school and never attended Jewish summer camp, yet on his Israel trip he was surrounded by eighty other Jewish sixteen-year-old peers. An immersive setting that was "all Jews" was a new experience for David. He liked it and wanted more.

As an undergrad at UC Santa Barbara, David attended programs at Hillel, joined a Jewish fraternity, and taught religious school. It was through Hillel that he met Morris Squire, the philanthropist who would ultimately pose to David this very real million-dollar challenge. The challenge came with a few caveats. One, David couldn't spend it on himself. And two, David must use the money to benefit the Jewish community in a meaningful way.

He accepted the challenge and made several proposals to Morris, who rejected many of them. But after working on several ideas together on some initial smaller grants, David was eventually awarded the promised one million dollars to launch Moishe House, followed by additional support as Moishe House gained traction and early success.

Still, at this point, becoming a Jewish community professional was not a part of David's career plan. He was a business and economics major in college and, even as Moishe House began, David thought he would ultimately pursue a career in the private sector. Yet as Moishe House took off, he noticed that the demand for this type of young adult Jewish engagement far outweighed the supply. David knew that if he didn't say yes to meet the challenge of effectively serving young Jewish adults, then he would be missing a meaningful opportunity to build and strengthen Jewish life and be further motivated and professionally nourished by this idea of challenge.

Our Jewish texts also include stories motivated by challenge. In the book of Genesis, Noah is challenged by God to build an ark to save the human race from both the ensuing flood and their own self-destruction. Also, in Genesis, Joseph is challenged to escape from prison and reclaim his life by helping re-make Egypt, serve the Pharaoh and interpret his dreams. Beginning in Exodus, we encounter Moses, who perhaps had the ultimate challenge of our Jewish historical narrative from God at the burning bush: to save his own people by leading them out of slavery to freedom and their eventual promised homeland.

Also, in Genesis Chapter 12, the first patriarch of the Jewish people, Abram, who would later be renamed Abraham, is given this challenge by God, "Go forth from your land, your birthplace, your father's house, to the land that I will show you. I will make of you a great nation, and I will bless you; I will make your name great, and it shall be a blessing."

Abraham did not know whether to trust God or where this journey would lead him. The road ahead was unknown, and to be asked to go forward without a clear destination, to push oneself beyond what he thought he could achieve, likely felt scary. Yet this was a blessing for Abraham. He was given an opportunity to shine. Here, a challenge was placed before him, to lead, and to, in the words of our text, make a great nation. He seized it.

I see a bit of the Abraham story in David's. When many of us are presented with the challenge to do something innovative, interesting, and perhaps, most importantly, "good" for a people we care deeply about, we become eager, excited, and motivated to accept the challenge. Morris Squire gave David such a challenge, and he then ventured on his journey, not unlike Abraham's in a way, to support the Jewish community as a key part of his life and career – to advance and "make great" the Jewish people for the next generation and beyond.

It is also here that an inherent challenge lies for those who manage other people in Jewish organizations. How might we challenge our staff in a way that can inspire them to both pursue a vision and achieve great things for our organizations that enhance the greater Jewish community? How do we offer these challenges so that they will be accepted? If and when they do, how do we continue to nurture these motivations, fostering their and their projects' growth?

If we are successful, we can imagine playing a key role in forwarding our professionals' journeys in a manner that strengthens their passions, productivity, and achievements both for our organizations and the Jewish community as a whole. Put another way, as our staff achieves victories, so do we. Or, if they try their best and fail, they will learn and grow, as will we.

To challenge the professionals among us who are motivated by such challenges and feel valued when presented with them can be a win-win-win for Jewish life: a win for the Jewish community professional, a win for our institutions, and a win for Jewish life *b'gadol* (writ large). We can look at this visually through the following schematic:

THE CHALLENGE SCHEMATIC

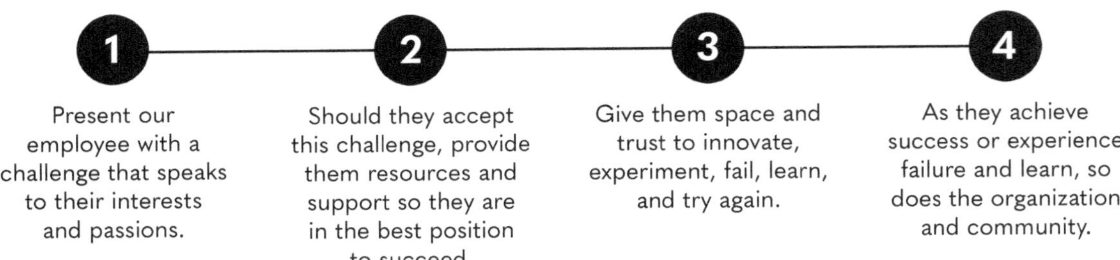

With this schematic in mind, we can further dissect this concept. Challenge, as a motivational tool, rests on three legs:

Leg 1: Empowering Professionals' **Creativity**

During Moishe House's infancy, Morris presented David a challenge that allowed David to be the innovator and idea generator, coupled with the freedom to create and iterate. David was not offered this challenge and then told what to do, nor was he micromanaged in the process. This suggests that challenge must come with autonomy and trust in order for this motivational tool to work.

Leg 2: **Financial Means** *that Instill a Sense of Feeling Valued and Supported*

The challenge to David came with meaningful resources. Had a professional been told to create a new idea that could change the world yet not have had sufficient funds to bring his vision into reality, the challenge could lessen how the professional feels valued. If, for example, David's challenge was supported only by $1,000 or even $10,000, Moishe House wouldn't have gone very far. This was not because it wasn't a superb idea. Rather the challenge may not have been properly resourced in order to succeed, or felt like a meaningful or valued challenge. As result, David may not have been as engaged and felt supported enough to truly to go for it.

Leg 3: Opportunity to Respond to an **Emerging Relevant Demand**

David accepted a challenge that was speaking to the concerns and anxieties of the times. As a result, the challenge is more motivating. David knew that there was an appetite in the Jewish world for a creative and pragmatic vision to engage young adult Jews and their friends.

Even with Moishe House's enormous success, there is so much more work to do, including expanding Moishe House to more communities, further strengthening the quality of Jewish learning in Moishe House settings, and sustaining a culture of innovation and connection building among and beyond the Moishe House network. Multiple Jewish foundations, lay leaders, and fellow Jewish community professionals are supporting Moishe House, and David feels the on-going nature of their challenge to him and his staff. He does not want to let them down. He is motivated to continue to accept the challenge aspiring to deliver an outcome that both he and the stakeholders around him can truly be proud of.

How to Implement the "Challenge Our Talent" Motivational Tool

Investing in the challenge our talent formula is both easily replicable and can lead to a strong return on investment. Engaging employees at all levels through challenge allows them to:

- Honor their own ideas, insights, and perspective on the world

- Allow staff to own the problem and thus be motivated to design and own the solution

- Nurture creativity and empowerment, risk-taking, and learning from our experiences

- Promote critical thinking and problem-solving skills

As we will also see in later blessings, many of these big ideas connect to three key components of internal motivation, which, along with the three-legs model, provide the basic framework to motivate and value our employees through challenge. Psychologist Edward L. Deci has explored the nature of internal motivation in his book *Why We Do What We Do*. Let's define our terms in light of Deci's work:

- **Autonomy:** The universal urge to be causal agents of one's own life and act in harmony with one's integrated self; this does not mean to be independent of others.

- **Competence:** To seek to control of the outcome and experience mastery.

- **Relatedness:** The universal desire to interact, be connected to, and experience caring for others. (Deci, *Why We Do What We Do*).

The challenge that fueled David's internal motivations hit upon all of these elements. First, he was given autonomy to figure out the concept that eventually became Moishe House. He was not micromanaged or beholden to strict standards. Second, he was able to experiment with his idea, learning from each iteration and thus being able to feel increasingly competent in his work, especially as the Moishe House concept caught on. Third, he was working on this project in relation with Morris, as well his own peers, whom he saw Moishe House benefiting, which added a sense of *relatedness* and belonging to the challenge.

As we put the pieces together, we see the following plan of action:
Step 1: We must ensure that any challenge we provide our staff fits the criteria of all three legs: *empower for creativity, provide sufficient financial means, and ensure challenge meets a demand and is of emerging or ongoing relevance* to them and those the project will serve.

Step 2: We must ensure that our staff, both individually and in teams, have the autonomy to do their work. This includes giving the person or the team *space, time, and trust* to play with and complete the challenge, so they feel empowered and free to be creative and make the necessary mistakes in order to learn.

Step 3: Create an environment in which they can feel competent in the challenge, which includes providing resources, training, or professional development to obtain or strengthen the skill sets needed in order to properly address the challenge.

Step 4: Nurture an environment in which the staff is working to be in relation to others. Even if the individual prefers to work independently, they should minimally be in connection to another's work, including that of their supervisors or lay-supporters, to feel that they belong to something bigger than themselves. We will discuss fostering relationships further in Blessing #3.

Step 5: We must check in regularly. No person works well without accountability and connection. The magic here is in both making sure the challenge fits certain criteria, that the environment breeds success, and that the conversation is ongoing. In the early years, Morris worked frequently with David, and in subsequent years other financial supporters have been in conversation with David and his staff to reinforce the environment, working collaboratively and creatively together to further nurture and grow the Moishe House success story.

Beyond being motivated by challenge, David shared with me that the key to his happiness is maintaining low financial expectations and maximal freedom. Put another way, David doesn't need very much. He sees himself as very fortunate in his job, and there is nothing beyond his immediate financial grasp because he chooses to live in Charlotte, NC and does not have expensive hobbies. Thus, David's feelings towards, for example, his compensation, are not the same as many other narratives presented in this book. David believes that he is fairly valued at his current salary given the size and scope of Moishe House today, and because he feels his compensation adequately covers his life needs.

Clearly, having the financial means to carry out one's potential solution to a challenge must include a discussion of how we compensate our employees. We will discuss the role of compensation and how they interact with many of these blessings throughout this book. For now, it's sufficed to say that if we pose an exciting challenge to an employee, who otherwise is motivated to meet this challenge, yet they constantly worry about their financial situation because their salary is non-competitive or not what they feel they need, this will detract from the efficacy of the *Challenge our Talent* motivational tool.

For *Challenge Our Talent* to work, David points out several other areas of his life that allow him to stay motivated and focused on the challenge.

For example, much has changed for David since he and his wife Myka had their first child, Jordan, in 2017. Upon realizing how difficult it is to work outside of normal business hours, David does not schedule more than four hours of meetings a day, or three hours of meetings on a Friday. He is able to build the job around his needs, a concept we will explore further in Blessing #2.

He also believes deeply in work-life integration, which we will highlight in Blessing #9 and in Blessing #14, where we examine the overall practices that require adjustment, including work/life balance for our employees. David has recognized that, in order to have time away from work with his family, he needs to be flexible, judicious, and efficient.

David also studies one-on-one with a Jewish educator each week and goes to Israel every year to explore and learn. Both his personal Jewish study and reading for pleasure help with his self-care, providing him with new ideas, new challenges to pursue, and new context for his work, and allowing him to feel centered and whole. He sees in himself an enormous growth need to improve in his Jewish knowledge, so he prioritizes such learning. Recognizing the value of these practices, Moishe House staff and board are also now offered personal Jewish learning as a work benefit.

David is also committed to having work time outside of the Jewish social sector. He works part time in real estate to keep his skills sharp and to be up to date in the latest corporate business practices, which further feeds his "challenge our talent" orientation to work.

Finally, part of our responsibility when motivating our employees through challenge is to set them up for success, helping them to navigate the inevitable frustrations that come from trying to accomplish something difficult. Thus, both for our ourselves and those we manage, we must be intentional about creating structures or otherwise incentivizing our employees to get their aggression out and energy flowing so they are in the right headspace when they are at the office or otherwise focused on work. For,

David, that means playing basketball early in the morning, sometimes arriving at the gym before 6:00 a.m.

CHALLENGE ACCEPTED

Abraham's journey led him to a new home, a family, and the opportunity to lead a great people with a tradition, heritage, and set of *mitzvoth* (commandments) that continue on to this day, all because he accepted the challenge presented by G-d.

David accepted a challenge, too, and in doing so, he feels extremely fortunate. He's enjoyed the work, and he appreciates the individuals in the Moishe House network. He and his team are constantly ready to meet the challenges ahead of them and make great things happen.

He relishes the many challenges of his work, the challenge of engaging the next generation of Jews, the challenge of taking advantage of our unique opportunities and blessings, and the challenge to create transparency and consistency so we can notice all the opportunities that may exist in our midst. We just have to be ready and daring enough, like David was, to accept the challenge, and to appropriately and effectively challenge our talent.

QUESTIONS FOR REFLECTION

1. How can we further a sense of autonomy in our staff in the challenge projects we assign them?

2. How can we assign work that speaks to a staff person's competencies and allow them to grow in areas they are excited about, furthering their skill sets and competence?

3. How can we ensure that the work of our staff connects them to others, increasing the "relatedness" of their work experience?

build around the talent

Blessing Summary — This blessing is about building the job parameters around their needs and interests of our talent, instead of the opposite, following a philosophy of happy staff → happy camper → happy camp.

How do we measure success? Whether it be a synagogue youth program, a big JCC event, or a Federation fundraiser, it is often about the numbers: the "tushies in the seats," as it were, the kids registered for camp, or the number of dollars raised in the campaign. On the surface, this makes perfect sense. Our institutions cannot function without stakeholders participating in our experiences and paying for what we provide. Yet, it is not in our mission statements to simply count the beans.

Alyson Bazeley, our next portrait, doesn't thrive as a Jewish community professional by counting beans, nor could she perform her work either previously as a youth educator and engagement director at a synagogue, or currently as Assistant Director for the Union for Reform Judaism's Crane Lake Camp, in the typical work box: 40+ hours a week, defined inflexible schedule, with only quantitative goals such as "how many events occurred," "how many teens attended," or "how many campers recruited."

Alyson exemplifies the Jewish community professional who thrives when her needs are considered and baked into how the job is built. Thus, our managerial strategies for motivating professionals like Alyson should follow suit. We must take our sights solely off the goal posts of the numbers that too frequently guide our decision making. Rather, our goal must be to hire the superstars, make whatever job we create with them work for them, and then support and nurture their experiences.

In this blessing, we will consider how we motivate and value of our staff by making the context of work – *work* — for them. This is not to imply that Jewish community professionals are selfish and needy. Far from it. When I think of Alyson, for example, my colleague, friend, and fellow rabbinical spouse, descriptions of selfishness don't even enter into my mind. Alyson gives incredible amounts of her time and energy to work, designing engaging experiences for her youth, camper, and teen learners. At the same time, Alyson and others like her want to have a life outside of work as well. Though our field encourages "work/life balance," these discussions still often put the needs of the organization first. In this blessing, we flip the equation.

Alyson's introduction to Jewish community professional life started young. Growing up actively in the Reform Movement in South Florida, Alyson describes her childhood as "never having the option of opting out of a Jewish education." She doesn't recall complaining about that and, as Alyson puts it, she went "all the way through" formal supplemental Jewish education from early childhood to high school. In college, she rushed a sorority and was astonished when she found herself in a sorority with only a small percentage of Jewish women, including a few women in her sorority that had never met a Jew.

Alyson, recognizing her knowledge, background, and growing interests in teaching, made herself the "de-facto Jewish educator" of her sorority house. When her sorority initially scheduled a sisterhood retreat at the same time as Rosh Hashanah and Yom Kippur, Alyson took it upon herself to educate the sorority about the high holiday Jewish traditions so they could intentionally avoid the conflict and thus not marginalize their Jewish sorority sisters in future years. Later that year, Alyson hosted her first sorority's Passover Seder, introducing some of her new friends to the rituals of and history behind the traditional gathering. It was then Alyson realized that the role of Jewish educator fit her well.

Alyson continued this adventure into Jewish education, working summers during her undergraduate years at Crane Lake Camp. While at Crane Lake, she met a friend who convinced her to leave sunny Florida for New York City and interview for a position as a youth director at a Reform synagogue on Long Island.

During the course of her five-year tenure there, she met her husband, Phil, a Rabbinical Student at Hebrew Union College (HUC), and was encouraged by her boss at the time, the senior rabbi of the congregation, to apply to be the head Jewish educator as the current educator was planning her retirement.

Alyson was flattered, yet she felt she did not yet have the skills and experience to be successful in this role, nor at the time did she feel the position's schedule worked for her. Upon sharing this reflection with her rabbi, Alyson was encouraged to apply to HUC and their MA in Jewish education program. HUC invested in Alyson, understanding her need to finish the program in four years as a part-time student so she could maintain her full-time director role, while the synagogue invested in Alyson by keeping her on staff in the youth engagement role with appropriate accommodations in her hours and responsibilities. Importantly, both her employer and her academic institution built her job and study around Alyson, which kept Alyson both in the field and feeling valued.

Alyson didn't fit the box of a full-time student, which would have also included a one-year study in Israel. While Alyson knew that there would be significant experiences she'd miss, she also knew that her study experience had to align with both her financial needs and personal need to continue to work with youth. Upon reflection, she doesn't think she would have completed the program and advanced in her Jewish community professional career without this flexibility and support.

Like David and his work with Morris from Blessing #1, it is not surprising that Alyson's origin story included helpful guidance by a mentor, in this case the senior rabbi, as well as investment and flexibility from her school. During my own years on staff at the William Davidson Graduate School of Jewish Education of JTS, I can recall many examples of talented individuals who needed accommodations to make their studies possible. The school tried to make study work for them, and thus, to the extent possible, it built the program around their needs, especially for the students who displayed unwavering commitment to a career in Jewish education. Similarly, students often shared with me that they entered this field because a mentor, supervisor, or previous employer believed in them and encouraged them to pursue it. Mentorship plays an essential role in nearly all of the portraits in *Bless Our Workforce*. It is something we in Jewish community professional life, whether consciously or by accident, do very well, and I discuss how to amplify this practice in Blessing #14.

Maimonides, often referred to as the Rambam, the medieval philosopher and scholar, suggests in his Mishnah Torah eight levels of charitable giving, one more holy and righteous than the next. Maimonides' top level of charity is commonly described as "one whose donation should be provided either as a gift or a free loan with nothing expected in return so the recipient will no longer need the giver's assistance."

One can look at Alyson's involvement with HUC and with her synagogue at the time through this lens of charitable giving. One might characterize this partnership as investment instead of charity. It is quite possible that had one or both of the institutions had not shown the appetite for flexibility and a creative solution, Alyson's work and study might both have suffered. Worse, in the words of basketball great LeBron James when he moved from his home town of Cleveland to Miami in 2010, she may have "taken her talents elsewhere," not merely away from her employer and HUC, but from Jewish life altogether. At this point, Alyson already had earned a master's degree in Social Work and was marketable in other industries. Yet, because of this investment, and by building the job and school work around Alyson, she felt valued, motivated to stay in Jewish life, and eager to grow and thrive.

Alyson's story and this illustration of the benefit of building work around the needs and interests of the talent really is a blessing for us to reflect upon. It asks us to consider how we might view our workforce differently, not solely as workers who serve the leadership and in service of our mission statements, but as valued human resources whom those in leadership must serve so our missions are best met. We are called to accept the charge to apply the Jewish wisdom of Maimonides and his highest level of charity as additional rationale from our tradition.

What does this investment do for us? Simply put, it enlarges our network of resources, revenues, and returns. I once had a conversation with a CFO who had recently implemented a paid parental leave policy. He shared that he felt that implementing the benefit was the right thing to do but that it would cost the organization by adding salary expenses for temporary workers or putting important work on hold, cutting up the pie of resources and reducing revenue. I responded to the CFO that the outcome of the new policy is the direct opposite, and that he was considering only the short term consequences. In fact, such a policy that invests in employees, allowing them to contribute meaningfully to the workplace and, moreover, increasing their satisfaction at work, encourages longer-term commitment, and, as we will talk about later in this book, increases productivity, revenue, and fulfilling mission — enlarging the pie.

I learned about this success equation, or schematic, long ago at my own Jewish summer camp, and it's a simple one:

THE SUCCESS SCHEMATIC

My supervisor and the camp director at the time, Jodi Sperling, shared with me that early on in her tenure she had the opportunity through grants from the local federation and other fundraising to make capital improvements to camp, including more cabins, a new swimming pool and tennis courts, and winterizing the dining hall. My director had these improvements in her plans as well, but not before her first priority, a new staff lounge.

I had been a camper for six years and a staff member for eight years. Our "staff lounge" was in truth a smelly and gross room in the back of the dining hall. The room had stained old couches, smelled like smoke (even after they prohibited smoking in the lounge, it still smelled like cigarettes), and only had the illusion of privacy, being so close to where campers ate their meals and held both drama and rainy-day activities. It was one example in which the message was clear: campers come first.

Jodi had a different philosophy. She knew that the guardians of the tradition, *ruach* (spirit), and joy of camp were the staff. She knew that the exceptional program originates with the staff's creativity and dedication. She knew that campers loved camp in part because they adored their counselors, program specialists, and supervisors. If she was going to invest millions of new dollars in camp infrastructure, how could she show that what mattered most to a successful camp was its staff?

She would show them by funding a new building just for them as the first capital improvement, close to the front of camp and on the other side of the parking lot from the camp office, all away from the campers. It was a place that the staff could call their own – with nicer couches, several rooms, and working high-speed internet. It was also a place for staff to either connect with their families, finish school projects or apply for academic year jobs. It was also a place to hold programs just for staff. As Jodi shared with me, there were members of her JCC leadership who initially believed that this was not a solid investment strategy. They believed that a new staff lounge would not bring in new camper families and raise additional revenue. But Jodi stood firm and built the staff lounge first.

Camp doubled in size over Jodi's tenure, notably after the staff lounge was built and put into use. It was just one of many examples of overt staff investment that wasn't about counting the beans or making the staff fit into the box of what leadership wants and thinks it needs. At the same time, the strategy helped catapult revenue and profit both for camp and the JCC.

Jodi examined what the staff needed including where and when they needed flexibility and support in order to have their own best experience at camp. Subsequently, staff would be able to do their best jobs keeping campers safe and curating an exemplary camp experience. Jodi and many of her camp director peers today recognize that staff often work at camp to pursue a dual ambition. They hope to be great role models and programmers for their campers, often giving back to the camp they enjoyed immensely as campers, and to grow and have fun for themselves. This second ambition must be nurtured in order for the first to reach its full potential. I would argue this dual ambition is present for most of our Jewish community professionals, certainly for Alyson and many of the professionals portrayed in this book.

In a sense, Jodi and Camp Wise followed Maimonides top level of charitable giving, or investment strategy. The partnership Maimonides speaks about recognizes the "dual ambition." Invest in staff and their own desire for an enjoyable experience by building the work around their needs, and the staff will feel motivated to work towards an amazing camp experience. This is also sound business strategy. We are not seeking ways for the staff to "fit in" to the organizational box. Rather, we need to look at the staff needs first to make our larger endeavor more set up for success.

When I drafted this chapter, Alyson held the position of Director of Youth Engagement at Congregation Temple Bnai Jeshurun (TBJ) in Short Hills, NJ, another employer who, for Alyson, applies the success equation. Alyson's supervisor asked Alyson what she needed to be successful, they outlined together the goals of the role, and then they allowed Alyson to do what she does best, mostly on her terms.

Alyson's own synagogue youth director, when she was a child, taught her the philosophy of moving beyond numbers, that if we focus too much on "how many tushies are in the seats," we neglect the quality and care needed for each child and the importance of developing a relationship with each to spark their own unique interest in Jewish tradition, ritual and community. A few years later, while still in Miami, Alyson had the good fortune to work as colleagues with her old director. Alyson says confidently today that this, along with her sorority experiences, is where she got her true start as a Jewish educator, developing her skill and love for this work.

Like Alyson, the Youth Director who mentored her also had children early into her career. She advised Alyson that the first few years of a child's life are critically important for their development and well-being. Alyson still feels challenged in the work that she is doing, yet she doesn't feel overly burdened by her work because the job is built around her needs, so she can in part spend significant and meaningful time with her husband and two young sons.

So how do we manage by not counting the beans and putting "happy staff" at the start of the success equation and center of the conversation? We can delineate this idea into five components: strong content, flexibility, clarity, relationships, and matterness.

Strong Content – Plainly put, the talent needs to enjoy and find meaningful the work they have been hired to perform. Alyson, for example, was hired in her synagogue roles to specifically to help build on an educational philosophy that combines signature (on-going) programs and one-off (or episodic) programs that model the best of experiential Jewish learning for these teens. This is also much of her work for Crane Lake Camp, designing experiences during the year and in the summer, especially during COVID-19 when in-person camp was cancelled and experiences were virtual. This allowed Alyson to be creative in the design of her programs whether they were field trips to engage teens in experiences outside of their typical Jewish learning environments or innovative within the synagogue space or on zoom. Performing work that one genuinely loves leads to feeding their creative drive, a motivational tool we will examine further in Blessing #4.

Much of the actual work drives Alyson: corresponding with parents, overseeing all aspects of the programming, and managing staff. Alyson lights up, as she did during our interview, when she talks about her work because she both loves the tasks and what they are trying to achieve. The results in fact, are not in the numbers at all. At her most recent synagogue role, she observed teens, as well as their parents and her congregational leadership, beginning to see the important connections teens are making during each social action or skill-building program and its connection to Jewish ideas and values. Judaism is no longer "the thing that they do one day a week;" rather, it's something that permeates their lives. This "happy camper" effect is due in no small part to Alyson as a "happy staff" buoyed by her strong connection to the job content.

Flexibility – If we provide our Jewish community professionals flexibility in how they design their hours and get their work done, they will feel trusted, empowered, and valued to be able to complete the work on their terms. Alyson, to a large extent in her current and previous roles, has gotten to design her hours, especially around when she needs to be home with her boys, and she rarely has ever received pushback. On the contrary, they have promoted flexibility because they know it will make her happier and more productive, and thus more successful.

Clarity – Designing a job around one's talent must include working with the Jewish community professional to design a clear job description that is continually reviewed and updated as an employee grows and job circumstances change. Alyson has felt valued and empowered in part because she has known what her job goals have been and how her work fits into the larger organizational mission. We will talk more in depth about the importance of our clear defined and co-created job description in Blessing #15.

Relationships – If a Jewish community professional's work puts them in relationship with others both within the organization and outside it, they will feel part of a broader community and thus more valued. Alyson loves that this work empowers her to work with partners throughout the tri-state area to create engaging experiences for her learners, which keeps her engaged and connected to a purpose that goes beyond, yet still is connected to, her own work.

Part of the relationship's ingredient to the "Happy Staff" part of the success equation is Alyson's drive to partner. There is often, as Alyson has personally experienced, a mentality in organizations that if we partner, then the organization may become anxious and territorial: "is this place going to steal our teens or campers away from us?" Alyson and those she has worked for see it differently. If a partner is providing a service that the organization doesn't, why not partner with them and enable our learners to have a unique and amazing Jewish experience that can be a part of both the partners and our own organization's name and brand with them as well? By giving first, we will ricochet success back to us.

Matterness – Taking the action of putting staff at the beginning of the success equation, such as building a staff lounge first for the staff at camp rather than capital improvements for the campers, delivers a simple and direct message: "you matter, and we care about you." Creating a role for Alyson that recognizes her talents and life-needs gave her the same message. To make clear to our Jewish community professionals that they matter. We must put actions to our words. This will benefit not only Jewish community professionals but those in leadership directing their work.

Over the past 15 years since Alyson started this work professionally, Alyson's acknowledges, perhaps with a bit of dismay, her compensation hasn't jumped considerably. The Jewish community professionals who work often closest to the learner, patron, or client, receive lower compensation relative to the value we place on senior fundraising, programming, operational, or executive professionals. We explore this further later in the book, but suffice it to say here that spending less on the professionals who work closest with those we serve is antithetical to the success equation. For Alyson, her salary at the time of our interview was only approximately $20,000 per year more than her entry-level position over ten years earlier. While noting that she was technically part-time (if we can call 35 hours per week part time), even in her previous full-time roles, her salary wasn't much higher.

In examining her entire career, Alyson acknowledges that she has not been paid at the same level as her colleagues. The few studies available indicate that direct-service professionals make less then administrators, and that women in similar roles make less than men.

It is no surprise, then, that Alyson's salary is lower than her counterparts. According to the New York salary survey of Jewish community professionals from 2012, she could theoretically be making anywhere from $60K-$120K per year depending on the role. Leading Edge suggests similar data, with lower salary levels in areas where costs of living are lower.

If we look at position and time allocated, the market might demand a lower salary for Alyson than many of her peers. Yet if we look at the value of Alyson's talents, what she can offer and accomplish for the institutions (even with slightly less than full time hours), then the determination of her salary should be less dependent on what the market says and more on the value Alyson brings to the organization. Suffice it to say, like with challenge our talent, the efficacy of building the job around the talent may be muted if the professional's compensation feels inadequate to them.

This said, Alyson looks back on inflection points when she could have made the compensation jump and has no regrets. She looks into her two young boys' eyes every day and knows that for her, she made the right call. It is also worth noting that when Alyson was at her synagogue, her compensation package included free pre-school and summer camp for both her children for the entire year, which translates at least to a five-figure value per year, tax free. Today, working for Crane Lake, she receives complementary summer camp for her children. This is a massive part of the package that keeps Alyson pleased with how she is valued financially – and it didn't cost the congregation, or doesn't cost camp much more to have one more child in the room or bunk.

OFFERING SOLUTIONS

Once Alyson manages to build relationships with her learners and sees them enthused, engaged, and curious about Jewish life, the value she feels is immeasurable and reflects themes from our first two blessings: competence, belonging, strong job content, and clarity. She feels that, as an educator, programmer, and direct service provider, this may be the most important and meaningful value she can feel.

Alyson reminds us that often when individuals first dip their toe into Jewish community professional work, they may be really young, often a teen or emerging adult themselves, either a camp counselor or unit head at camp, or an entry-level Hillel engagement professional right out of undergraduate studies, for example. Our goal as stewards of Jewish community at the leadership level is to encourage them to consider this work as a career and then keep them on board the Jewish community professionals train for decades. Alyson's story, complemented by my own summer camp experience, and the resulting success equation, gives us a roadmap which starts at putting our talent's needs and interests at the center of the conversation.

Clare Balding once said, "fitting in is boring." Requiring even the most adaptable, flexible, and eager talent to fit in to our systems without putting equal or more focus on making sure our organization can fit with them can be counterproductive to the success of the role and for our constituents and institutions. What we must do is fit the work around our talent, encouraging creativity and quality of experience over bean counting; considering strong job content, flexibility, clarity, and relationships as part of the "happy staff' part of the equation; and delivering the clear message that it's the Jewish community professional is at the heart of our success.

If we allow our talent to focus on the creative and qualitative aspects of their work, the people will come anyway. By giving first, we are investing in a partnership with staff giving them the gift to be successful on their own terms, and in the spirit of Maimonides' top level of "charitable" giving, we will be rewarded with a handsome return on investment.

QUESTIONS FOR REFLECTION

1. What actions might our organizations commit to demonstrate investment in our staff, putting their needs first in order to drive organizational success? Reflecting on what Jodi did for Camp Wise, what might be a similar action to building a staff lounge?

2. How might we have a conversation with each of our staff ask how their role is structured and work together to includes the 5 elements that make up a happy staff (strong job content, sufficient flexibility, meaningful relationships, clarity in objectives, and feeling a sense that they matter in the organization)?

3. When designing compensation structures, how might we think generously and creatively. Alyson's example is helpful because, while her compensation has not always been competitive, she has been offered flexibility and pre-school for her children and opportunities to add value outside of her current role. Where can we get creative?

foster the relationships

Blessing Summary — Jewish community professionals will feel more valued when they are encouraged to foster meaningful relationships within the work place and throughout the field. By applying the "relationship schematic," and leading from a position of Oneness and empathy through a strong, supportive community, each will feel part of something bigger then themselves and be able to thrive.

In Blessing #1, we introduced Deci's framework that drives internal motivation, featuring the concepts of autonomy, competence, and belonging. One might argue that it was a desire to achieve that encouraged David to accept Morris Squire's challenge and that his achievements at Moishe House have since fueled his internal motivations through an increased feeling of competence. In Blessing #2, one could argue that autonomy plays the lead, as Alyson enjoys the freedom to design her schedule and the way she approaches the work, as well as her employers designing her position around her needs and talents rather than fitting into a certain position box. The increased flexibility and self-confidence led Alyson to feeling autonomous, which has allowed her to more easily find meaning in her work.

Yet in my experience many Jewish community professionals I have engaged with are not solely in this work to feel autonomous and competent. After all, we serve the Jewish community, with its core function to bring everyone who wishes to engage in our community space to do so. In his recent book *The New American Judaism*, Dr. Jack Wertheimer, Professor of American Jewish History at JTS, confirms today's reality especially in non-Orthodox Jewish communities: a primary driver of engaging in Jewish life, whether it be attending a synagogue, community function, or social action event, is to be around friends. Ron Wolfson, Professor of Education at American Jewish University, in his book *Relational Judaism* confirms this as well. Wolfson implores us to focus on the relational aspects of our community in order to make it both more appealing to the unengaged and strengthen the ties among those already active. For our purposes, we can learn from Wertheimer's and Wolfson's research and apply the relational motivations for becoming an engaged Jew to the desire to become and remain a Jewish community professional.

In addition, to be in relationship with others is not only a source of motivation; it is also a matter of Jewish tradition and, to many, an obligation. We are commanded not only to pray, but to pray as a people, a congregation, a community with each other. The Rabbis of the Talmud require us to chant Torah and sing our liturgical prayers in a *minyan* (a minimum group of ten worshippers). Our relationships with each other, an obligation or not, foster a deep sense of belonging to something bigger then ourselves which can fuel us and our work deeply. We see this firsthand as we get to know our next portrait, Ezra Shanken, the current CEO of the Jewish Federation of Vancouver, BC, and a long-time Jewish Federation professional.

Ezra loves to be around people. It drives him, fills his emotional reservoir, and keeps him focused and balanced. The relationships he has cultivated in the Jewish community have been both the source and the result of his success. There is then a benefit for us to deeply understand how relationships may fuel the motivations of our Jewish community professionals so we can best foster these relationships as part of their work. This blessing argues that doing so will advance a Jewish community professional's commitment to our organizations and to thus remain a part of this workforce.

Ezra's journey to becoming a Jewish community professional was modeled to him from a young age. Ezra's grandfather was a Rabbi, his father was a Jewish community professional, and his family was very active in Jewish life. Ezra was also surrounded by dedicated and vibrant Jewish activists and thinkers throughout his childhood and teenage years. In addition, Ezra recalls each participating individual of his childhood community contributing to the caring, support, and guidance of the whole, by working to help them find personal and professional growth. "They were all my family," Ezra shared with me. "Each cared about my future and worked to foster my growth." The community also modeled for Ezra that the importance and impact of these relationships took place in an active Jewish communal context.

Through the tight-knit relationships that served as the foundation of his community's strength, Ezra learned the importance of engaging with those around him. He also learned that these relationships were naturally intertwined with Jewish tradition and practice. Ezra quickly internalized that Jewish life and community equaled a sense of family, which gave Ezra exceptional personal satisfaction.

We can break this down with our relationship schematic:

THE RELATIONSHIP SCHEMATIC

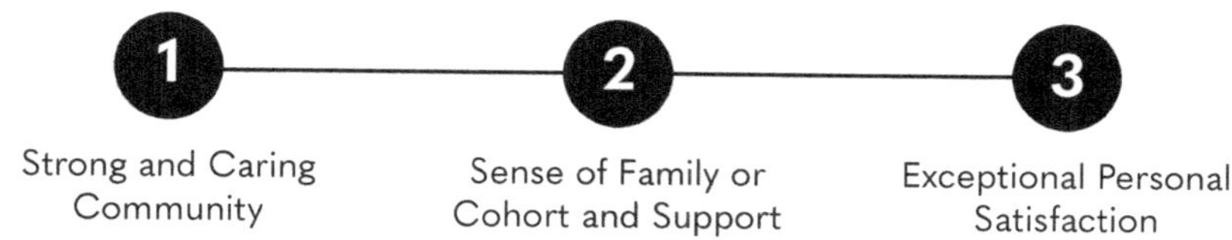

If we know that a happy worker is a productive worker, one way to ensure strong productivity is to make them feel that they are surrounded by those who care about them, support them, and give them the sense of family that makes them feel loved and, thus, personally satisfied.

It is core to Ezra's identity that "Federation is family" to him (Federation referring both to the local Jewish Federation organizations in each Jewish Community in North America and the continental Jewish Federation movement). It is then hardly a surprise that Ezra's career has almost exclusively been as part of the Jewish Federation system. Ezra has come to be certain that the collision between private life and work that often feels inevitable when working in a senior role of a Jewish community institution, especially a Jewish Federation, is a formula that works for him and, we'll suggest here, can work for many other Jewish community professionals as well.

This also suggests a natural blend of personal and professional life that may cause a conflict or threat to the coveted "work/life balance" desire. Yet, as we will examine further in Blessing #9, many Jewish community professionals desire a blend of their personal and professional souls, and that there can be a healthy integration. This scheme also is perceived as attainable whereas a true separation and balance between personal and professional lives may not be so realistic for many Jewish community professionals, especially as most Jewish community professionals work from home during COVID-19.

Yet for all the modeling and love of Judaism Ezra experienced, he initially planned a career in politics. Incidentally, politics is also built on relationships. Yet, for Ezra, political relationships often felt more transactional than transformational. Pursuing this desire, though, Ezra moved to Washington D.C. and completed government internships while in college. The political environment, in his words, "didn't feel right to me to stay;" there was something missing for him. He had experienced success running a winning political campaign, yet he felt compelled to depart the nation's capital afterwards. Ezra cited the culture and stress of political life. It may have been that the authenticity of the relationships that he grew up with were not visible or present enough in the political landscape.

Ezra thus embarked on a new adventure, traveling west with friends to Colorado. He worked odd jobs and eventually pursued a graduate degree in non-profit management. As he started his degree, he also realized that he still needed to work, and he noticed the local Jewish federation was hiring. Ezra remembers clearly the day he walked into the Jewish federation of Colorado building in his tan leisure suit. According to Ezra, they took one look him and said, "you belong here."

There it is again, the word "belonging." Deci also interchanges belonging with the term relatedness. It is worth reiterating the entire thesis of Wolfson's book: Jews return to Jewish spaces not solely out of obligation, tradition or the desire to learn – though these are often present. Rather, they return because they feel a sense of home, of "I belong here," of oneness. It is where we surround ourselves with other people who can relate to us. This oneness is a result of the relationships we build with each other.

We see oneness in perhaps the most recognizable part of Jewish liturgy. The Shema:

שמע ישראל יהוה אלהינו יהוה אחד

Shema Yisrael Ado-shem Elo-keinu Ado-shem Echad.
Hear O Israel The Lord is Our God the Lord is One.

There is, of course, an entire theological discussion and contemporary political discussion about Jewish community and oneness that I won't broach here. If you are interested, Jack Wertheimer's book is one well-researched perspective of the unity, or lack of thereof, in North American Judaism today. Yet, if we examine just the beginning and the end of the prayer's translation, "Hear O Israel", and "One" … we notice that the prayer is not only an affirmation in a religious belief that there is one God, but that the people of Israel, are One. As participants and as professionals, we are individuals that are part of something bigger and are commanded by this daily prayer to be in relationship with each other.

As many of us who chant the *Shema* close our eyes, and some of us stand, to both concentrate and show reverence to the prayer, we can also take the moment to reflect on the relationships we cultivate and manage in our areas of work. I wonder which ones our professionals most enjoy fostering each day, and how might they be increasing both our and our staff's personal and professional satisfaction.

The results of the Leading Places to Work surveys are clear on this point. Jewish community professionals, like professionals at large, cite a primary reason for leaving their jobs as an unhealthy relationship with their supervisor. In other cases, Jewish community professionals may stay because of healthy and rewarding relationships with their boss. If we took time during our moments of reflection and planning, not unlike when many Jews recite the Shema twice each day, to consider examining how we nurture the working collaboration between manager and employee, then we too may be able to foster the same kind of "you belong here" relationship that has retained and grown Jewish community professionals such as Ezra all this time.

Ezra's professional journey suggests that the relationships he has built with his colleagues and supervisors have sustained his interest and passion for serving Jewish community. He actually identifies three intertwining variables that he looks for in any professional experience, all based on the power of fostering relationships.

Relational Work — Ezra wants to be in a political job. Of course, he mentioned this to me mere moments after sharing that he explicitly left US politics. He explained that politics is the nature with which we interact, debate, make decisions, and then institute policy that effects and hopefully benefits others. This is the part of politics Ezra most enjoys, as long as the process means engaging with people and a community he cares about and when the community promotes healthy and mutually respectful relationships. I believe that when Ezra says political, he means relational.

Meaningful Work — Ezra wants what he does to matter. He put this to me another way: "Every time I go to bed at night I want to know, believe, and have confidence in that the world may now be a bit better because of what I did that day." One can make the argument that while political campaigns can be in service to that larger purpose, the *tikkun olam* or "repairing the world" feel of that political work may not be so prevalent or even present on many of these days. Ezra's work serving Jewish community, however, and specifically within a Jewish Federation, feels quite different. His daily impact feels real and palpable to him. I'll suggest here that this is also about being in relationship and fostering relationships to the world around us, for what we do is more meaningful and matters to us when we are in relation to those we are serving. Again, his motivations are relational in nature.

Spiritually Nourishing — Ezra doesn't consider himself overly religious, yet he and his wife Rachel, who have three young children, consider themselves active practicing

Jews. Ezra admits to me that "my work needs to fill and nurture my soul." Ezra felt it was clear to him that this need was not going to be in Washington, or even in state or local government. Recognizing the soul-fulfillment he so naturally was nourished by growing up in the belongingness of a Jewish community space, he wanted to pursue professional work in the Jewish space as well. Ezra's work must also help foster and nurture his relationship to himself and to the divine. For Jewish community professionals like Ezra, devoting one's professional time to the community is more than passion— it is spiritual fulfillment. It is a form of spiritual or religious practice, akin to prayer and following the *mitzvot* (commandments). Our work, as it has an impact on the world, can also foster our sense of spirit, of *shlemut*, wholeness, often achieved when we have healthy and active relationships to our souls and to God, or however each of us may choose to believe in or conceptualize the sacred presence.

Fortunately, each of these elements appeared at Ezra's first Federation position in Denver and in every Jewish community professional position since. But how do these multiple layers of fostering relationships to our peers and communities, to the world, to ourselves and to the divine play out within each of us and within our staff? One might begin by asking our staff directly (or asking them to journal) to respond to the following prompts:

1. How does being in relationship with others at work influence my motivations?

2. In what ways am I motivated to do my work understanding how my efforts support a better, more just, or more prosperous world?

3. How, if at all, does my work nurture me spiritually and may connect me to a more sacred holy presence, either God or another conceptualization of the divine?

The data we gather will be helpful as we consider how to best approach both our work and managing those of our staff with a healthy dose of optimism, purpose, and belonging, and give us a road map to how to best motivate and make them feel valued. If our staff are at all similar to Ezra, then there is an opportunity to place them in more meaningful working relationships with each other, the people they are serving, their own souls, and their relationship to something holy.

Ezra's journey mirrors the three components he laid out for me and allowed him to be ambitious, driven, and determined in writing the script of his career. During his first days at Jewish Colorado Ezra had the opportunity to meet the CEO. He looked at him, and he said to himself, "I want to be him, yet faster than when he got to where he's at now." Ezra gave himself his own *challenge to accept*. In addition to his desire for his work to have a sense of belongingness, Ezra is a driven individual, with a strong desire to succeed.

Yet when Ezra talks about being "driven," he is referring to the more standard definition of Drive, that Daniel Pink writes about in his book, *Drive*, which is to be "motivated by or having a compulsive quality or need. (Pink, Drive). Put another way, Ezra is driven because that is simply who he is. Yet it is important to note being driven was not enough for Ezra; he needed to also be in an environment where his skills, talents, and interests were aligned to a place that fostered the relationships that allowed him to succeed. Jewish Federation as a highly relational workspace spoke to him and reinforced his innate desire to be a driver for steering the collective Jewish experience.

Ezra has worked hard to be present, engaged, and actively involved during every workday, in every meeting, and at every event. He recognizes that the Jewish people have an outsized effect on the world around them and thus attributes a sense of honor to be working for a Federation, fueling his excitement to help repair this world while surrounding himself with building relationships across the Jewish community.

Wolfson's thesis gives us plenty to consider about the power of relationships in forming, strengthening and maintaining healthy communities. We can also drill down to what specifically works about relationships and how we can apply in the workplace and to foster motivation and a sense of value – leading to more personal satisfaction, higher productivity, greater retention, lower turnover, and stronger meeting of our mission, all the positive outcomes we in leadership desire from our human resources, and feeding a virtuous cycle that we will discuss more deeply beginning in Blessing #7.

In this light, we can examine research from the Society for Human Resource Management (SHRM), which identified six factors that have the most impact on knowledge worker productivity.

1. Social cohesion

2. Perceived supervisory support

3. Information sharing

4. Common vision, goals and purpose

5. External communication

6. Trust

Many of these factors involve working in relationship to others including, social cohesion, sharing, common, communication, and trust. Echoing this, a Harvard Business Review study also indicates a significant role of friendships on our level of satisfaction and engagement at work. This study revealed that "camaraderie promotes a group loyalty that results in a shared commitment to and discipline toward the work. Camaraderie at work can create 'esprit de corps,' which includes mutual respect, sense of identity and admiration to push for hard work and outcomes. So it is, fostering healthy relationships in the workplace translates not only for our employees to feel valued – they are also more motivated to 'push for hard work and desired outcomes.'" (*Harvard Business Review,* "Friendships at Work," Sargent, 1/2017).

The Leading Places to Work studies also help us better understand the current level of social cohesion and trust in our Jewish organizations. According to the 2018 survey 82% of employees at Jewish organizations feel like the mission of their organizations makes them feel they are making a true difference at work. Yet, alarmingly, only 53% feel there is open and honest two-way communication within their organization.

What might this say about the trust people have for the people they work for? A lack of trust can erode people's motivations. Scheduling regular coffee or meal dates with our staff are then all the more critical as a relationship-building tool that builds social cohesion and trust and nurtures transparency. It also fosters a sense of empathy in those we work with as we become aware of each of their vulnerabilities and real-life issues.

We are part of something bigger when we get to our work stations. Ezra understood this when he was at Jewish Colorado during the economic downtown in 2008. There, he felt responsible for those who lost their jobs in the Jewish world as a result of massive cutbacks. He remembers driving to the office during these darker times and began saying to himself, "what am I going to do without my colleagues?" He felt both blessed and guilty that he was among those who were spared. Ezra felt he had to do more with his time and advantageous position to make a difference.

That is when two of his lay leaders, along with Ezra, started hosting local art space events aimed at bringing Jewish community professionals together. They modeled their vision on a café in Budapest. There would be live music and innovative programming, with Jewish symbols on the wall. Ezra wanted to create a space where people would come in and say, "wow this is amazing, wow this is a great teaching, and wow this is Jewish and Jews in relational community with each other."

It was called E-3 events. He saw this as an initiative to benefit individuals and community organizations a like. People could share contact lists to get everyone involved. It found its market. People kept showing up, and Ezra observed that he was building relationships among his peers that were solid and palpable. We will see more of this entrepreneurial spirit and discuss how to champion the relentless of pursuit of entrepreneurs in Blessing #12.

Ezra's work developing E-3 events helped him become a young leadership director at Jewish Colorado, where he had 200 coffee dates a year with young adult Jews, tasked to learn more about this age cohort and encourage them into roles of young leadership with the Federation. He was doing what he always loved doing – talking to people and building relationships with them. He later assumed a similar role as the director of Young Leadership for UJA-Federation of New York, which covers the five boroughs of New York, Long Island, and Westchester County. He loved interacting with all of these different people. He also developed a mentoring relationship with Dr. John Ruskay, the CEO of UJA-Federation of NY at the time, learning from him the importance of building strong relationships with both donors and staff to achieve key objectives. Ezra believes he wouldn't have been successful in New York if it were not for his time growing and focusing on the relational aspect of his work while in Denver. He believes he certainly would not have gotten to his current role, if it not were for his time in Denver and New York.

Ezra recalls his most important and memorable learning during his tenure in New York: there were a lot of personalities involved – lay leaders, professional colleagues, grantees, and community partners among them -- each with a myriad of priorities. He told me that he came to realize a hard lesson, that "not everybody is you – thinks like you and wants the same for your work as you do. Not everyone is on the journey that you are on."

Organizational theorists Lee Bolman and Terrence Deal in the iconic work *Reframing Organizations* discuss the four frames of work and examine this notion in their human resources frame: Ezra's learning underscores that our direct reports, peers, superiors or lay leaders do not have the same thoughts as we do, and are not on the same journey as we are. This sounds obvious, yet it is difficult to recognize in real-time. In order for the relationships we build in the workplace to be healthy and motivating, we must not rely on this assumption. Rather, we must engage in active engaged listening (coffee dates!), intentionally build relationships, and work toward consensus to meet our position objectives and larger work goals.

As a Jewish community, we may be more productive and successfully better if we acted with empathy when we raise money from individuals, attract them to our events, or hire, manage, evaluate, and nurture the professional growth of our staff. We may have to admit that sometimes we manage others the way we want to be managed. Yet those who work for and with us are not us. We must devote the same relationship building to those within our workforce we already do to our donors and patrons.

Part of fostering relationships for a healthy, valued workforce is to build relationships with each person to better understand how each person's work style, motivations, and aspirations differ from ours, reflect on each of their responses, and then apply this learning in order to manage them more successfully – benefiting them, us and the organization as a whole.

When Ezra was in New York, he collaborated with multiple departments to push the message of the Federation. Each department had a director, and he worked hard to build a relationship with by learning their journey and discovering how each was driven to be successful and achieve their stated department objectives. Ezra sees this parallel when he works with the executives of Jewish communal agencies in Vancouver. Among them are the professional and lay heads of the Vancouver Jewish Community Center (JCC) and the local Jewish Social Services Agency. Ezra sees as vital to his role building and strengthening relationships with these organizations' CEOs, Executive Teams, and lay leadership, and he recognizes that he needs to be invested in the JCC's success in order for him to expect that the JCC will help push the Federation's message. This is seeing our work and challenges from the journeys and perspectives of our partners.

This methodology speaks directly to the work of Curtis Ogden's and his principles of shared leadership and network theory, including the concept of "giving first". To give first and act in someone else's best interest will, according to Ogden, ultimately serve our own interests. Ezra sees his role as instilling that culture of Oneness throughout the Jewish Community of Vancouver. Like the *Shema*, we are separate individuals who are all part of *K'lal Yisrael* (people of Israel) and are part of a larger whole. To lead by "giving first" allows for shared ownership and further fosters belonging and the collaborative spirit.

The Jewish Federation system has given Ezra nearly everything he has wanted in life: a sense of autonomy, mastery, and purpose, all ingredients for a perfect drive, a desirable career, and his most important personal relationship. Ezra and Rachel met at Tribefest, a national gathering of young Jewish lay leaders the Jewish Federation of North America (JFNA) held twice in the early 2010's. A similar feeling of relationship and family for Ezra comes to the foreground when he attends the JFNA's General Assembly (now Fed Lab), the annual gathering of Federation system professionals and lay leadership. Ezra describes it as feeling like a family reunion, fostering relationships among Jewish federation CEO's and JFNA professionals and others, all of which are strong and a vital lifeline for Ezra. He shares with me that fellow CEOs "are truly present to support and guide each other," reflecting back to a key ingredient of our relationship equation. Ezra is fueled not only by the relationships built within his current employer and the organizations and people it serves, but in the larger system. Relationship building is abundant in Ezra's professional life.

During my conversations with Ezra, we talked a lot about our responsibility to the future as a result of the relationships and promises we make to our colleagues and family today and those in our past we are hoping to honor. We must embrace the teaching from Perkei Avot 2:21 (the Ethics of our Fathers) who charge us.

לא עליך המלאכה לגמור ולא אתה בן חורין להבטל ממנה

Lo alecha ha'me'lacha ligmor, ve'lo ata ben chorin le'hibatel mimena.
It is not your responsibility to finish the work [of perfecting the world],
but you are not free to desist from it either.

To be in a relationship means we care about those we are in a relationship with include future generations of Jewish life. Fostering relationships with those we seek to serve, and by allowing our staff to foster their own relationships with each other, themselves, their past and the sacred, furthers our empathy. Empathy is the motivational driver behind relationships. Ezra recognizes that change is something we must own. If he sees a gap that needs filling, he has empathy for it and is thus motivated to go out and do something about it. This reflects his desire for change, a desire to be successful, and a desire to build relationships within that success – so he feels a part of a whole.

It is important to note the relationships we build must not remain at the surface level. They must be deep and meaningful connections. Ezra also told me a story of a co-existence camp with Palestinians, Israelis, and Canadians he has been involved in. One morning, all the flags were raised, and each "faction," as it were, objected that both flags that were not given an equal honor. The resulting firestorm led to campers and staff defaming each other's characters. Ezra observes the lack of relationships that were being fostered between the groups, those relationships that could have built empathy, motivation, and feeling valued by their peers. In Ezra's words, our "sense of false intimacy sometimes gives us perceived flexibility, too much flexibility, in speech."

This is not how we build community. When people show a lack of empathy toward others, a lack of focusing on the importance of building strong relationships built on kindness, social cohesion, and trust, we might instead slander each other in the face of the values that we hold dear in the Jewish tradition. This can happen in the Jewish community professional workplace too if we are not careful. A lack of empathy can creep in to the relationships we have with our fellow Jewish community professionals. We can consider the improper yet all too common practice of *l'shon hara*, (gossip) as one example. There are also times when we are so focused on the bottom line that we neglect the needs and care of the staff and our relationships with them that are primary to our success. It may be our lack of understanding, not giving the space and opportunity for our employees to truly be heard, that diminishes their motivation and capacity to be productive. Put another way, it could be our own leadership style that puts a low priority on building relationships with and among our workforce that plays a key role on our high turnover rates, lack of productivity, and lower institutional morale.

As we have explored Ezra's journey and the research that supports it, we learn that we can choose to prioritize understanding the internal motivations of our staff at their core and pay attention to nurturing these relationships with the empathy that they require.

As Wolfson explains, "The vision of Relational Judaism is to strengthen Jewish consciousness and commitment by encouraging individuals to build relationships with nine levels of Jewish experience: self, family, friends, Jewish living, community, peoplehood, Israel, world, and God." (Wolfson, *Relational Judaism*). Perhaps it is embedded in "community," but I would have added another category: our professionals. As Jewish community professionals build relationships, they foster empathy and can therefore manage these relationships with kindness. Our workforce thus becomes better equipped to tackle the most challenging programs of the day.

The word empathy comes from the German term *Einfühlung*, meaning "feeling into." If we can "feel into" other people's lives and experience the world as they do, we can improve our relationships and create a better society. "A recent State of the Workplace Empathy study in 2018 by Businessolver found that 87% of CEOs see a direct link between workplace empathy and business performance, productivity, retention and general business health. Also, 87% of CEOs believe a company's financial performance is tied to empathy in the workplace, as do 79% of HR professionals. Empathy motivates workers and increases productivity."

Empathy must be coupled with a culture of fostering relationships and inclusion in the work place. Studies in the *Journal of Applied Developmental Psychology* have suggested that "empathy can increase liking and care for others, whether they are part of one's in group or not, only if a group has a norm of inclusion." In the relationships we foster, empathy must be an active presence, the glue that allows these relationships to motivate our employees, which will again boost morale, productivity and performance.

Ezra's story reveals to us that context matters. Ezra wasn't fulfilled in politics, there was no *Shema* or Oneness connecting his work to the community around him, and the relationships were not worth fostering for him. There was important work to be done, but he didn't feel it was this work he wasn't free to desist from. There was also little empathy within the relationships for him in the political sphere, which was a disconnect to the community who raised him. Yet, Ezra found the right place for him is as a Jewish community professional, and he continues to be in the Jewish Federation system because of the relationships he gets to be a part of, with others, to those he serves, to himself, and to his own connection to the divine.

We all need to build the relationships for ourselves and for our staff, and answer that call to throw oneself in what we are passionate about. At the end of the day we must use our relationships to both motivate ourselves and raise the feeling of value in others. This opportunity must be given to our staff, and we must see ourselves in the role of helping to foster these incredibly powerful motivating relationships.

So, what are the relationships we can foster between our staff and us, and among our staff to excite and ignite them? I would suggest that we bring this question to our professional and lay colleagues: how would they like to foster stronger relationships with each other, with us, and the professional and volunteer teams that support them? To involve others in the design process increases their own ownership and motivation to pursue this important relationship fostering, motivational building, and value building strategies.

QUESTIONS FOR REFLECTION

1. From earlier in this blessing, how might we bring these 3 questions to each of your staff, and have a discussion about their response?
   a. How does being in relationship with others at work influence my motivations?
   b. In what ways am I motivated to do my work understanding how my efforts support a better, more just, or more prosperous world?
   c. How, if at all, does my work nurture me spiritually and may connect me to a more sacred holy presence, either God or another conceptualization of the divine?

2. How might we use team meetings as an opportunity for everyone to share one relationship from their past that motivates them today? Each can then dedicate their current work to this person. This activity alone will further strengthen the relationships among your team and connect them to those who inspire them, creating further value for their work today.

3. How might we seek to build empathy for those around us? Consider having everyone on your team share something that they care about or have experienced outside of work, and begin to make connections with other staff members who have had similar experiences.

feed their creative drive

Blessing Summary — Many of our Jewish community professionals are driven by the opportunities to display their creativity in the work place. Our role, then, is to identify strategies to feed their creative drive by employing the ideas of Flow, managing to our employee's strengths, applying the ideas of Deep Work, and that all of their gifts are *tov* (good), or "of use" to others.

"Do you see someone skilled in their work? They will serve before kings; they will not serve before officials of low rank." – Proverbs 22:29.

When I started on staff at JTS in 2010, I was the Program Coordinator of the Experiential Learning Initiative in the William Davidson Graduate School of Jewish Education. Oddly, I didn't know what experiential education was when I was hired. Much of my career up until that point used the techniques of experiential learning; I just didn't know the language and theory of it quite yet. In the months before I coordinated my first cohort of experiential education graduate students, I audited many of the classes my future students would soon take, including the Experiential Jewish Education seminar taught by my colleague and friend, Dr. Jeff Kress.

In the class, Jeff taught the concept of *Flow* by Mihaly Csikszentmihalyi, a Hungarian psychology professor who authored the idea in 1996. Csikszentmihalyi suggests that learners learn the most and are fully in engaged in their learning when they are in *Flow*, a state of experience that exactly meets the skills and interests of the learners. Put another way, the challenge is just hard enough that it isn't boring, but not too hard to become frustrating or anxiety provoking. The content also exactly matches the intrinsic interests and curiosity of the learner. The task or experience is familiar, yet there is always more the learner wants to learn and engage with. *Flow* is different for everyone. When I was in college, I felt *Flow* when I lead a loud and raucous song session at Jewish camp. I both loved every moment leading the songs and cheers while feeling challenged to keep the campers and staff engaged: again, not too easy, not too difficult.

For, Miriam Brosseau, *Flow* comes when she gets to exercise her creativity. This has included performing a self-described Jewish bubble-gum pop song or producing a slick and compelling 10-minute online talk. Miriam is motivated when her creative drive is fed. By nurturing her natural interests and curiosities and giving her related work challenges that meet her skill level, Miriam, and Jewish community professionals like her, can achieve *Flow* at work, an incredibly enjoyable and rewarding state of being that, naturally, strengthens motivations and makes her feel more valued.

I first met Miriam eight months into my job at JTS, at a conference on experiential Jewish education conducted by her employer at the time, The Jewish Education Project. Miriam had pink hair and played a rockin' guitar. She and her full-bearded husband Alan were the duo of their self-described Jewish bubble-gum pop-group *Stereo Sinai*. I marveled at Miriam, at her energy and her intentional mix of seriousness and silliness. It was clear to me that she was in a state of *Flow* when performing and embodying her identity as a "creative type," and that she was feeding off her creativity while she was performing and teaching the conference attendees. I was inspired by her creative drive, and it was clear it was completely feeding her that weekend.

Miriam grew up in Racine, Wisconsin, a small Jewish community in the shadows of the larger Jewish community of Milwaukee twenty-five miles to the north. She recalls during her childhood being schlepped unwillingly up to Milwaukee by her parents once a week for Sunday school. Her experience, in her words, "was terrible, because Sunday school is often terrible." Miriam's journey into Jewish life sadly wasn't off to a strong or inspiring start. Luckily, her family switched synagogues to a place closer to their home and with both a Rabbi and Cantor who noticed Miriam's talents and interest in singing. They took her under their wing. They taught her to chant, to read *haftorah* (a section from the Prophets of the Bible that is assigned to accompany the weekly Torah portion) and gave her a youth leadership position. Miriam went from being completely disinterested in Judaism to having a genuine excitement and eagerness to participate.

Miriam's story begins with the lessons from our previous blessings. Miriam was inspired by the mentoring relationships she fostered with her clergy. Miriam's experience also notes the importance of pointing out others' talents. Often individuals do not recognize their own potential until someone else can point it out. Perhaps among our holiest obligation as managers and leaders is to point out the strengths, talents, and interests in our staff, especially those with creative skill sets, and help amplify them in a work context.

Adam Simon, the director of the AVIV Foundation, has a fantastic ELI Talk (which Miriam helped produce) on identifying and nurturing one's strengths. He argues that we must manage from people's strengths rather than prioritizing areas of improvement. As people like to do more of what they already enjoy and are good at, this management approach will motivate them, demonstrate value, and boost their productivity, creativity, and satisfaction. This, of course, encourages us to schedule time to examine the strengths and interests with each of our staff by taking each out to coffee and learning more about them, another blessing reminder to schedule those coffee dates!

Miriam's life-changing experience with her clergy, who pointed out her talents and encouraged her to amplify them, gave her the initial thought to pursue a career in the rabbinate. She enrolled at the University of Wisconsin at Madison for her undergraduate studies and majored in Jewish Studies with the assumption that she'd go on to rabbinical school upon graduation. She dropped that quickly, though. She had fallen in love with the Jewish Studies and the academic environment, yet she dreamed of other creative ways she could serve the Jewish community.

After college, Miriam moved to Israel and pursued further Hebrew and Jewish Studies learning. She also worked in the campus service division of the World Zionist Organization, followed by working for non-profits both within and outside the Jewish world before deciding to earn her Masters in Jewish professional studies from Spertus College in Chicago. Her creative heart was leading her somewhere, but not yet to a place where it was being fully fed and nourished.

Then came a turning point when she was hired by the Jewish Education Project. By this time, she had met and later married her husband Alan and with him formed *Stereo Sinai*. She began her journey of writing and singing Jewish "pop-bubble gum" songs. They had also worked for a friend who was running a small organization to help Jewish artists with their social media promotions. Alan and Miriam fell in love with the world of social media and technology and began integrating communications into everything they did both in the work and in their music. They had begun performing with several Jewish organizations and were building up a repertoire of work, feeding their creative souls in the process.

This weaving of Jewish learning, music, and technology brought her to the Jewish Education Project, which serves Jewish educators in New York City, Long Island, and Westchester County by, in her words, "doing digital media stuff." 20% of her time was devoted to special projects working with the organization Darim Online and their executive, Lisa Colton, with freedom to connect back to her main work at Jewish education project.

When Darim Online merged with See3 Communications, which then signed a contract with the AVI CHAI Foundation to launch ELI Talks (ELI stands for Educating, Literacy, and Identity) Miriam transitioned out of the Jewish Education Project and into developing and leading the ELI Talks team which, as of the initial writing of this book, has well over 100 talks online. Her position at ELI Talks was a culmination of the creative outlets Miriam had been building until this point: digital media, Jewish education, music, and innovating/creating in the professional world. It was an ideal fit.

For much of her time prior to and while with ELI Talks, Miriam experienced *Flow* routinely in her work. She felt completely immersed in the experience, strongly interested and passionate about each talk and the growth of the ELI Talks franchise, and optimally challenged to make each ELI Talk as innovative and well-received as possible.

In our professional environments, we can translate *Flow* into creating work experiences in which we manage to ensure the work is engaging — of optimal skill-level and optimal interest to the person doing the particular job. This produces not only the best learning for our staff but the most creative productivity and results. To be clear, I am not talking about making work simply fun and placing games everywhere like they do in a Google or other Silicon Valley inspired office, though this can also lead to more creative inventions and deliverables. Rather, we should examine directly the work itself and designing work, so it isn't either boring or overwhelming and speaks to each employee's creative interests. The best way to start this design is in partnership with the staff we are managing, asking them about their passions and interests, designing work with these ideas in mind, and putting this data at the center of the conversation.

The goal, especially in light of Miriam's narrative, is to consider how to connect people's work to people's creative interests and desires and make sure we pay attention to the things that call to them. As Csikszentmihalyi put it, "If you are interested in something, you will focus on it, and if you focus attention on anything, it is likely that you will become interested in it. Many of the things we find interesting are not so by nature, but because we took the trouble of paying attention to them (Csikszentmihalyi, *Flow*, 1996)."

Miriam's journey to reaching a point of *Flow* during her time with ELI Talks was largely due to the transformational mentors she had along the way. One, as we mentioned before, was her clergy team back in Wisconsin who gave Miriam her first leadership role. She also had amazing teachers in college who were, in her words, "super-inspirational." The colleague who introduced her and Alan to the world of digital media and technology helped Miriam integrate her creative love to the rest of her life, mission, and work. Lisa Colton, who encouraged Miriam to focus on the digital media arena, was essential for Miriam's growth and career trajectory. Lisa's leadership at See3 encouraged Miriam to shift out of solely ELI Talks to get involved in other projects.

Our mentors and managers can help each of our staff become the right person in the right seat for their role. Miriam was the right person for ELI Talks at the right time and was supported in a manner that allowed her to be creative in the way she wanted to be, which fed her professional soul and had her feeling blessed in her work.

We must also recognize when a seat is no longer right for a person and when it is no longer feeding their creative drive. Mentors have also helped Miriam recognize that the slightly outsider consultancy seat is where Miriam can be most capable and where she is best positioned to help the Jewish community. When Miriam is unhappy, it is often at least in part because she is not interested and challenged to fulfill her creative outlets. Of course, when she feels blessed, the opposite is true. This is in part why as of this book's publication, Miriam is the Principal and CEO of her own company, Tiny Windows Consulting, that in her own creative way helps other non-profits with their strategy, digital communications, and storytelling.

Let's take a moment to view our first four big ideas and Jewish community professional profiles from the balcony, or from 30,000 above this discussion, for a moment (we will discuss the concept of going to the balcony as itself a strategy to bless our workforce more in depth in Blessing #8). Each of these blessings builds off the others. Like David, Miriam received many "challenges" notably, the challenge to make ELI Talks a success and driver of conversation in Jewish spaces, that she was eager to accept. Like Alyson, the positions in which Miriam was most successful were fit around Miriam's needs, and though the quantitative results were important, such as the number of ELI Talks produced, or number of hits and views online, the creative and mission-driven aspect of the work mattered more to her and to the team. And, like Ezra, it has been Miriam's relationships that have helped her stay motivated and thrive. These all complement this new blessing of feeding her creative drive — pursuing roles that speak to her creative skills and desires — and making necessary changes so the *Flow* can be rebuilt.

If we were to return to our earlier blessings, we could also have highlighted further the examples in which David, Alyson, and Ezra were fueled when their creative drives were fed. The point here is that each of these blessings is more potent and powerful when they are mixed creatively. We can by inspired by this "motivational tool mixing" from Jewish tradition. When Jews pray each morning, afternoon, and evening, we don't just say one prayer and then stop. We say many prayers and blessings in a highly coordinated service of liturgy. Each of these blessings has its own merit. Yet, taken together, they have real power to help us grow and thrive as professionals, organizations, and as a community.

Miriam views her career journey through the story framework of what she and her colleagues often refer to as the Hero's Journey. The Hero's Journey, found in mythology and literature from the likes of Homer to Joseph Conrad, "is the common template of a broad category of tales that involve a hero who goes on an adventure, and in a decisive crisis wins a victory, and then comes home changed or transformed." Miriam may not quite have completed the journey, but certainly her career and life path feels like an adventure, with decisive crises, many victories, and constant transformation.

The role of the mentor in the Hero's Journey is to name for the hero what the hero doesn't see in themselves. By the end of the journey, the hero begins to see it and begins to own that narrative. As Miriam pointed out to me, in *The Wizard of Oz*, Dorothy wore her red sparkly shoes the whole time. Similarly, Moses was on a Hero's Journey as he was transformed from the adopted son of the Pharaoh to a runaway to a prophet leading his people from bondage to freedom. The lesson for us is to examine those we work with and for in the Jewish community professional context as each being on such a Hero's journey and helping them along the way. In doing so, our organizations reap tremendous benefits.

Thus, there is a clear connection between working with a mentor, or manager who provides mentorship, and identifying and achieving one's creative soul and eventual state of *Flow*. Many Jewish community professionals already do a fairly good job of utilizing mentoring and coaching to advance professional growth, strengthen employee motivations, and enhance a feeling of value. From the camp counselor to the executive, we relish the idea of mentoring others and being mentored ourselves. We discuss this positive practice further and how to amplify it in Blessing #14.

So how do we help our staff feel valued by feeding their creative drive? We break down Miriam's narrative to identify multiple concrete action steps:

Shift Our Staff's Focus Back to Their Core Mission
When Miriam was still a part of the ELI Talks team, she would often be at the tail end of what they called "red-team" meetings with each of the ELI Talks speakers.

Each speaker works with a coach for several weeks to get their ELI Talks in order, and Miriam's role was to hear the speaker's talk during this preparation and suggest changes so each sentence would directly speak to and support the Talk's core message. Through Miriam's guidance, the speaker may then shift their narrative so the ELI Talk can be the best version it can possibly be. Often that means bringing the speaker back to their original mission and vision. The speaker is almost always be energized by and appreciative of this shift back to their core. It re-ignites their purpose and allows them to re-connect to their task at hand with more confidence.

Miriam shared a vignette of working with a speaker on a talk about Jewish meditation. He had beautiful stories to tell, yet he was dancing around the core of his talk: the uniqueness of the Jewish meditation practice. Through his conversation with Miriam, the speaker was able to shift back to his original focus. The speaker was appreciative and relieved that he was given guidance to refocus his message and felt the *creative* flow to continue. This was also exciting for Miriam and an experience of creative flow for herself. As she shared with me, "to be able to work with somebody and help them see how interesting, compelling, powerful and important their purpose is to themselves and to the world at large is unbelievable and a huge source of motivation for me." She felt driven, in full flow, motivated, valued and "ridiculously blessed" to be in this position.

Shifting one's focus back to their core is a core responsibility for each of us who manage, mentor, or otherwise influence a Jewish community professional. Miriam sees that its "everyone's job in the Jewish community to help others in their own hero's journey so they come out mentors. We are here to support one another in our respective journey's so we can be mentors for each other, in whatever format." I wholeheartedly agree.

Enable Staff to Feel of Use
It is not enough to give someone a project that allows them to be creative in the way they want to, it is also important to show that their work has utility for the organization and community they are serving. When Miriam and I discussed her related motivations that help feed her creative drive, she naturally gave her response to me through a Jewish lens. "In the beginning," she declared, "God creates the world and declares things to be good." We thought together during my interview with Miriam about the Hebrew word, *tov*, for good, and she sees in the translation much more than the English word "good." Rather, she suggests that *tov* should be translated to, "of use," or utility.

Miriam wants to see her work advance the cause of the organization and the lives of its constituents in a meaningful way. When she was with ELI Talks, she would see empirically how many hits, social media likes, or comments were given to each talk and hear anecdotal testimonials from field professionals and lay leaders sharing how a given talk inspired them. Miriam also invoked the translation of the *Kiddush* blessing Jews say over the wine, which includes the word *La'asot*, meaning "created to do:" the wine is of use as it can instill in us a sense of joy during the day of rest. Miriam, too, wants to see the utility of her creative efforts, and when she can see this in plain slight or through feedback it feels her with joy and fuels her creative drive.

Empower Our Staff: Advise that Saying NO is OK

A Jewish community professional's creative drive can feel stymied when they are given tasks or projects that prevent them from utilizing their creativity and pursuing a passion. Of course, sometimes when the boss assigns a project or task and says, "you must take care of this," one says yes out of obligation, because they trust the boss or out of fear of being accused of insubordination. Yet, as managers, we must not abuse this power, which risks diluting our staff's natural passions and talents.

Miriam acknowledges that while desiring to be of use is generally a healthy motivation, especially when one's creative work is the focus, it could be detrimental to her and her fellow Jewish community professionals at times. There is value in saying no even though we want to be useful. If by always saying yes Jewish community professionals become overwhelmed and overextended then they may actually be more of use to the organization when they sometimes say no management. We must find the balance when our talent feel that they can meaningfully contribute to a problem's resolution, which can be motivating, and when they are given work that doesn't have obvious utility, is not core to their passions, or is simply too much, all of which can dilute their motivations and productivity.

Prevent Our Staff from Feeling That Their Work is Meaningless

Perhaps a direct converse to feeling "of use," Miriam feels frustrated when she exerts a lot of effort without seeing measurable results. She doesn't want to look back on her professional efforts and see them as a waste. No worker wants work to be or feel meaningless. By being transparent with the "why" behind what projects or tasks we are asking our employees to complete, we can often mitigate this feeling.

It is also important to point out that there is a difference between work feeling meaningless and feeling like our work is a failure. Failure, as has been written about by Mike Robbins in his book *Bring Your Whole Self to Work*, which we delve more deeply into in Blessing #9, is a great resource for managers and can actually be something quite meaningful. When we create and try something new yet do not achieve the result we had hoped for, we can examine this as an opportunity to learn and grow. The idea of "failing forward" has long been a hallmark of Silicon Valley and has, in the last decade, been pushed in Jewish life by the Jewish Education Project's Dr. David Bryfman, for whom Miriam used to work for, and by Upstart, the organization that fosters start-ups in the Jewish sector and other social entrepreneurship and intrapreneurship ventures.

Miriam stresses that when she felt her work was simply meaningless, when there was no tangible impact nor opportunity to learn and grow, it was her biggest *de*-motivator and would make her want to *jump ship* from that particular employment situation. Luckily, Miriam's mentors not only helped her make a name for herself, but also to help her locate where her creative skill-sets could be best applied. This must be a key role for all of us in leadership and management. We need to help name each of our employee's talents and interests for themselves, and then "manage them," by finding the best use for them and making it clear how their contributions are meaningful. We can ensure that the individual continues to be "the ideal fit" for that seat by adhering to the guidance stated thus far in this blessing, that the work: 1) speaks to the employee's core 2) that the work is of use 3) is not meaningless and 4) allows them to learn and grow if they fail.

Making Sure One's Creative Drive Connects with Others

We know that no one person completes their work in a vacuum. Leadership must take heed of how each employee's talents and interests connect to their colleagues, and how these connections can nurture everyone's creative soul, which can also enhance organizational collaboration, efficiency, and effectiveness. When managers devote their time to increasing the creative Flow of the team, that creates new energy and excitement. Gathering data on the specific nature of each team member's creative drive and making intentional decisions to help each team member work well with others by creative collaborative work teams will go a long way to reducing wasted energy in an organization, strengthening team productivity, job satisfaction and a feeling of blessing.

Creative Jewish Community Professionals Don't Want to Fret Over the Funds

Miriam, "doesn't want to worry about money." There are a growing number of studies, including the *Leading Places to Work* study for the Jewish community, showing that professionals in the not-for-profit sector are motivated to make just enough money so they don't have to worry about it, and beyond that the compensation is not a primary source of motivation. Studies published by the Society of Human Resources Management and *Harvard Business Review* have found this as well. More compensation beyond what already generously demonstrates value doesn't fuel one's creative job any more, but a compensation or salary level that does not feel adequate, competitive, or fair can reduce or detract feeling of *Flow* in one's work. Miriam's wants to be doing purposeful work that makes her feel useful and to feel flow, but only if she makes enough money for Alan and her two young boys to feel reasonably comfortable. Jewish community professionals like Miriam who are incredibly creative, talented, and accomplished should not have to feel that these are unreasonable asks.

In the 2016 ELI Talk *Mah Tovu* that I was fortunate enough to write and produce in concert with Miriam (and that I speak more about in our post-blessing at the end of this book), I argue that Jewish community professionals must be paid well, slightly yet significantly above the market rate for their role in a non-profit, so their compensation is not reason for them to leave. We must acknowledge that our talent is not "in it for the money" but that they also don't want to worry about living a reasonably comfortable life. Miriam, for instance, desires to have meaning, soul, and purpose to her creative work, and not being able to afford a middle-class lifestyle should not have to be a dilemma that she faces.

Can We Always Give Them What They Ask For? Of Course Not!
We only have so much revenue, and we can't simply upend current established salary levels. Yet, both more transparency in the compensation process and merely being asked, "what do you need?" will make the employee feel more valued AND, if you find that you could provide them a bit more financially so they don't have to worry about the money, then we've already made headway in addressing the concern.

Employees may also think their superiors are being paid a lot more than they are, and in some cases, they are not. Any amount of money can feel too low or too high; it's all relative, and if an organization provides clear, transparent, and reasonable salary levels that are placed slightly above the market rate for these positions folks will also feel well enough about their compensation that they won't worry about it so much, feeding their creative drive. We will discuss salary transparency further both in Blessing #7 and Blessing #15.

How We Manage Our Creative Professionals Matters
Miriam's ability to exercise her creative process and feel truly "fed," is reflected in the way that she is managed. Early in her career, she felt she was poorly managed. She'd have insights and get excited about things and rarely see results because there was no clear process to the creativity, no documentation, no regular conversations with managers to improve, which meant it was much harder to replicate or scale anything she produced.

Miriam has since been blessed with many supervisors who direct her energies and holds her accountable. Miriam can then best plan out her own time. She takes her cues from the book *Deep Work* by Cal Newport, which teaches us to focus on the work that is meaningful and is of greatest use. These cues also include, 1) blocking out time for deep thinking, strategizing, and writing, and 2) building in points when she is connecting with colleagues, collaborating, learning a lot, and listening a lot, and checking her assumptions, a lot. That may include receiving critical feedback, which often may feel like failing, yet it is an opportunity for learning; it almost feels like she is experiencing mini-failures in her creative work, so she can fail forward and be set up for more success during the project's next iteration.

She also feels that her work ethic contributes to the value of her organization when she is able to capture the daily learning that organizations do. This has a lot to do about how work works, and for those who are most motivated by feeling their creative drives fueled and fed. There is something about the concentric circles of how work works that Miriam had to learn, practice, and refine. She notes that:

1. There needs to be the practice of the inner work ethic, the combination of blocking out time between deep work and shallow work.

2. There needs to be connecting to others, experimenting, collaborating, failing (a lot!) and learning and growing from it.

THE CREATIVE SCHEMATIC

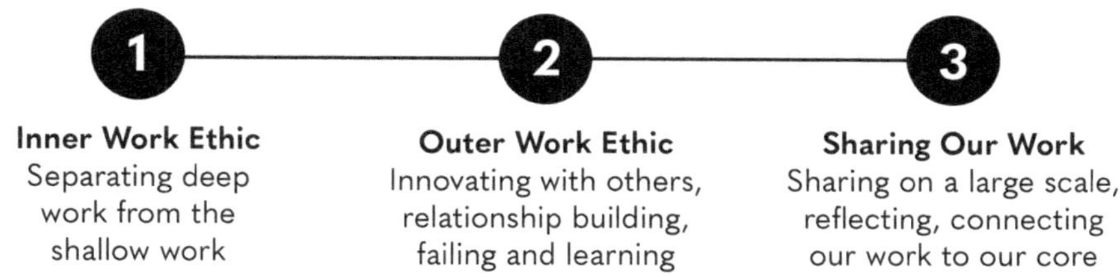

3. There needs to be sharing out the work on a large scale, being reflective about what we learned, and connecting to the larger mission of the organization we are serving.

This leads us to our fourth schematic of *Bless Our Workforce*, the creative schematic.

This results in a fueled and fed creative drive that allows professionals to work harder, smarter, and feel valued while doing so.

The challenge for us is to craft work experiences so our creative workers are able to regularly practice and master these three steps, notably actively connecting their iterative work to the larger mission of the organization. Simply asking them to engage in this process and training your managers to facilitate this process can do wonders to ensuring our creative Jewish community professionals feel motivated and valued.

Acknowledging, Pushing (But Not Breaking) The Creative Constraint

Miriam wouldn't be engaged in this work if she didn't believe in the power and potential of Judaism and what the Jewish community can offer the world. What Miriam loves about Judaism is its structure and its boundaries. There are few things more exciting for her than exploring and challenging these boundaries with a sense of humility and genuine love and passion for Judaism and the Jewish community. She observes that this most often happens through the creative artists among us. Including, "Bulletproof Stockings," the Chasidic Alt Rock Girl Band based out of Crown Heights, Brooklyn, who worked within creative constraints and pushed past boundaries.

The ultimate creative constraint for Miriam is Shabbat. We are commanded to stop our tasks and experiences that are classified as work according to Jewish law for an entire 25 hours each week. The Jewish organization Reboot has turned this into a personal practice in the liberal circles of Judaism with their national weekends of "unplugging," completely turning off our myriad devices. As Miriam puts it, "it is not a surprise that people often come up with their most creative ideas 'in the shower,' or on Shabbat, or during other times of pause or when we are not stimulated or over-stimulated, this is certainly built into Judaism."

Just as we don't want to put up walls, we do want to give our Jewish community professionals direction, and this includes providing them at least some constraints when we assign projects and tasks. Often this can be determined through a S.M.A.R.T. Goal framework made popular by management guru Peter Drucker. While S.M.A.R.T. goals can be used in simple goal setting, it can also be used to provide clear direction while allowing for an employee to have autonomy and creativity in their work: We should be sure to give creative constraints that state:

- The **Specific** aim of a project or task: what is it trying to achieve?

- Can we **Measure** what the project will accomplish?

- Is what we are trying to achieve and create **Attainable**?

- Are the projects we are assigning **Relevant** to our work?

- Is there some kind of **Time-Boundedness** to the project?

While creative workers may want infinite time to be creative in their process, and occasionally it makes sense not to be so constraining, it is also important to keep eyes on the goal, and often at least timed check-ins are helpful to drive work forward.

REFLECT BACK AND LOOKING AHEAD

For much of her life, Miriam has sought after finding her Flow, which to our benefit has often been working for Jewish community, and thus has bent towards leaning in to serving Jewish life. There are times when she feels an interest to tilt out as it were, to feed her creative drive outside Jewish life, and that is of course ok, our talent must not always feel bounded to our field. Yet, our desire should also be that our Jewish community professionals find a home in serving Jewish life, in part because their creative interests and drive are welcomed, nurtured, and aptly fed. As long as we can take heed of the lessons in *flow, Deep Work*, the creative schematic work ethic, *creative constraints*, and in feeling *tov*, of use that are key to driving those in our workforce who excel when their creative drives are being fed and nourished, our talent will continue to *tilt in* to the Jewish workforce.

QUESTIONS FOR REFLECTION

1. How might we identify the creative skill-sets and desires of our staff? Perhaps we can discuss with them and work together to design work leading them to feeling *Flow*.

2. How can we encourage our staff to shut some of their work off from time to time so they can have 100% attention to their own creative process, generating and playing with new ideas? Schedule "creative" or "brainstorm" time each week with staff inviting them to explore their creative selves and not be distracted by other tasks.

3. How might we examine the work portfolio of our staff — is all of their work particularly useful to the organization? If not, how can we amend work so it is, and if so, ensure that we communicate how their work is useful, and meaningfully contributes to the operations, mission, and success of the agency?

show them the fruits of their labor

Blessing Summary — By helping our Jewish community professionals see directly and frequently what their work produces and it how it helps others, they will be more motivated to perform the work well, feeling valued and blessed realizing the impact of their work on their community.

Throughout the five books that are defined by his name, we find Moses on his own Hero's Journey to rescue his people from slavery and deliver them to a promised land. He delivers to them a code of law, the 10 Commandments, to live by, and he leads his people in battling with tribes that seek to destroy or deter his people from reaching their destination. Working with God, he keeps them fed and hydrated, largely exercising strong leadership. There is, however, one exception, when his temper gets the best of him and he strikes a rock instead of talking to it so water and manna would arrive.

That one incident, according to the text of the Torah and various *Midrashim* (stories around the text that help illuminate the text's potential meanings) is why Moses is prohibited by God from entering the promised land of Canaan. He dies looking out at the land before his people cross the Jordan River. He gives over his reigns to his successor, Joshua, who has been deemed worthy to take the mantle. Joshua will see and inherit the fruits of Moses's labor, leading the Israelites into the promised land.

Moses was not motivated to lead his people to freedom and a new home solely because he wanted to see that vision become a reality. One has to wonder, however, after working his entire life for this vision, whether he would have appreciated seeing the fruits of his labor. Perhaps I am superimposing my own wishes onto our great prophet. Perhaps he knew his time had come and that it wasn't in his destiny to see his mission fulfilled. Perhaps coming this far satisfied him. If that is the case, more power to Moses. However, I would venture that many Jewish community professionals today who work diligently for a cause would feel blessed if they were able to see the fruits of their labor: their work benefiting the end-user and the next generation.

What is the impact of seeing the end game of our work? To know that "I made that happen," or perhaps more indirectly, "I played a role in making that happen!" For those in direct service, for example, a social worker, classroom teacher, camp counselor, even our clergy, we often see the fruits of our work daily: our families' situations improve, our students learn, our campers have fun and thrive, our congregants grow and express gratitude.

Yet many Jewish community professionals, especially but not exclusively those who have risen up the ranks of management or work in the back offices that our learners, patrons, and consumers don't often encounter. When do they see the result of their efforts? These Jewish community professionals make important decisions and play a key role in determining the direction of our Jewish organizations, yet they may not already be privy to seeing first-hand what their work is leading toward. They aren't often in or observing the classrooms, adult learning programs, social justice events, or social service projects. Might making the fruits of the labor explicit and evident increased their motivations and help them feel blessed at work?

Jon Shapiro, a long time JCC, camp, and not-for-profit professional who at the time of our initial interview held the position of Vice President for Programming and Operations at the JCC of Indianapolis, talked in detail with me about this notion of "seeing the fruits of our labor" to feel more motivated and feeling more valued at work. It seems a simple idea, yet it is one we could be more intentional about with everyone on our payroll. This blessing will in part lay out how and with whom we can have more *kavanah* (intention) as we manage and support our staff.

Jon grew up involved in his synagogue youth group, in part-time Hebrew high school during his teenage years and started going to Jewish overnight camp at the age of 12. He became hooked on all that Jewish camp could offer — friends, accessible connection to Jewish ritual, and opportunities to assume roles of leadership — so much so that he returned to staff Jewish camp, at the Union for Reform Judaism's Camp Eisner in the Berkshires. At Eisner, Jon had a specific identity and felt beloved by the campers and staff. Jon went back to camp simply because it is "what Jon knew." Yet examining his motivations reveals a mix of much of what we have already presented in this book and what we are introducing in this blessing.

First, he felt an enormous sense of autonomy, competence, and relatedness in the environment of Jewish camp, echoing Blessing #1, As Jon shared with me, "I realized that at Camp I learned how to be dependable, responsible, accountable, and how to effectively plan programs and manage staff." Second, echoing Blessing #3, Jon was able to foster relationships with his campers and co-staff that kept him returning to the Berkshire mountains each summer.

Thus is not surprising why staff at Jewish camp can be a prime breeding ground for future Jewish community professionals. At camp, there is a constant feedback loop to check-in on the efficacy of our work. Are our campers happy? Did they like our programs? Do they feel welcome and become more eager to engage with Jewish content and ritual? At Camp, almost all positions don't have to wait for an annual report or performance review to come out to see if their labor has borne fruit; it's right in front of us at each meal, at the lake, art shack, and in the cabin.

This may be the most straightforward schematic yet in presenting a formula that can help us better motivate our staff and have them feel valued and blessed at work.

THE FRUITS OF THEIR LABOR SCHEMATIC

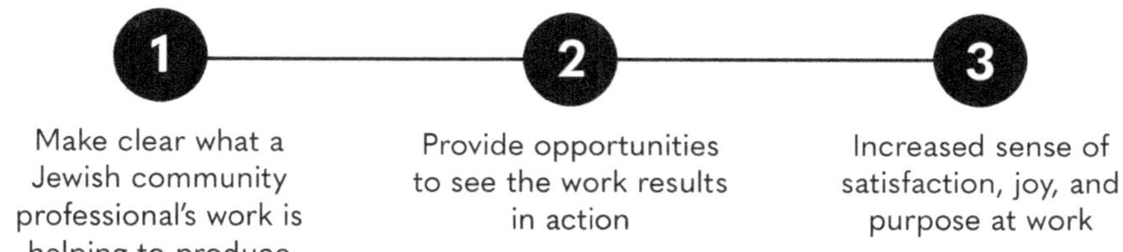

We've already talked about purpose and its potency to fuel motivations. Being given a challenge provides purpose. Producing work that is of high quality and not just to fill "tushies in the seats" can fuel purpose. To be in relationship with others and understanding that our efforts affect those we care about fuels purpose. To be given creative deep work that is "of use" fuels purpose. And now we add that when we actually see what our work produces, we feel joy and purpose as well.

Seeing the fruits of his labor at camp, Jon had a light bulb moment. "I can do this kind of work as a career!" he thought. It was an insight that guided him to Indianapolis, his wife's hometown of and where there was an opportunity to take on a Vice President role at the local JCC. Yet until this moment, Jon felt like he "fell into the Jewish professional field," as he put it.

The Fruits of Our Labor Blessing as Means to Recruit Jewish Community Professionals from a Young Age

This blessing offers us an opportunity to counteract the trend of those who feel that it was all an accident that they are now unexpectedly pursuing a career serving Jewish life. Perhaps Jewish community professionals, myself included, have seemed to think that it was an accident simply because we didn't say, "I want to be a Jewish community professional," when we were in Kindergarten or even in high school. We have other answers during these life stages: astronaut, actress, doctor, chief Justice of the Supreme Court, or the President.

Yet, what most often happens is that these lofty dreams often are not based in reality. Many children grow up, these dreams tend to dissipate, and they become most influenced by the experiences around them. What the professionals we have gotten to know thus far have in common is that all had powerfully meaningful and positive experiences in a Jewish educational context during their formative years. They see first-hand the work of a camp counselor, religious school educator, or Hillel professional and the impact they can have, guiding the next generation into well-rounded, Jewishly informed adults.

Thus, I now think about what the recruiter could have said to me and my fellow camp staff when she visited Camp Wise while I was in college. She could have made explicit what was right in front of us the entire time. She could have said, "Jewish community professionals make an enormous difference in people's lives for the better, and you can see the fruits of your labor with your own eyes regularly and often. This work is holy and is incredibly fulfilling, and it could be for you as well. Join us in this incredibly rewarding career."

Had she framed her pitch like this, I would have been hooked in that moment and can imagine that many young people who have already experienced deeply engaging and meaningful Jewish experiences would be as well. If we dial up the explicitness of what a Jewish community professional's efforts lead to, especially to those who may not see it every day in their work, then I believe we will do a much better job of recruiting and retaining talent, as long as we keep our *kavanah*, our intention, to maintain this explicitness throughout a Jewish community professional's career.

We also gravitate to work in arenas aligned to the experiences and people that have inspired us. The experiences and people of Hillel and his trip to Israel inspired David, Alyson was inspired by her youth group director, Ezra by his family and community around him, and Miriam by her youth rabbi and cantor. Jon, who had interests and skills that could have taken him in any number of directions, was inspired by his friends and campers at Eisner, feeling a sense of belonging and competence at Jewish camp, which morphed into a larger professional purpose. Jon had this light bulb moment relatively early on.

During college, Jon reached out to a rabbi from his youth and shared that he was looking for part-time work. The rabbi, shortly after meeting and getting to know Jon, offered him a job as a youth group manager at North Shore Synagogue in Syosset, NY. Jon soon settled into a yearly routine of working in this part-time youth director position during the school year and staff at Eisner during the summer. Year after year, he moved up the professional ladder in each institution. Jon's synagogue role eventually became full time, yet he was still encouraged to continue working at Camp. Jon also juggled undergraduate work, which didn't come easy. He had to work hard to both build his resume and pay his way through school. But he kept with it in part because he kept seeing the importance of his work each day both at North Shore and at Eisner. As the years progressed, he also gained enormous confidence in his abilities and freedoms handling both jobs and his studies. He developed a strong sense of autonomy which added to his feeling of competence and belonging that he already felt, completing the Deci trifecta of ingredients that support one's internal motivations. He continued to accept the challenge he posed to himself to work both jobs that he immensely enjoyed while completing his college education.

After five long and sometimes difficult years of juggling, Jon received his degree and was hired as the Assistant Camp Director of Eisner, a full time role, shifting his career to full time Jewish camp, which he continued for 12 more years. Jon was known as "Shappy," and with autonomy, competence, belonging, and purpose in hand, along with seeing the fruits of his labor daily, Jon recognized even more deeply the larger impact his Jewish community professional work could have. In our interview, he remarked, profoundly, that:

> *"I saw at a deeper level the kind of work that I was doing, seeing the direct line from my work planning programs, recruiting new families, supporting operations with the director, leading meals, and managing staff translating in front of his eyes every summer to smiley faces, campers learning new skills and gaining confidence, and being instilled with a positive, interesting, and engaging Jewish experience and identity — from Shabbat, to Israel, to the Jewish values we permeated throughout the camp each day."*

It is perhaps then no surprise that Jon was the assistant director for 6 years. Seeing the fruits of one's labor is an incredibly potent retention tool, especially when supported by the other motivational strategies we have already discussed. I can relate strongly to Jon's narrative working at the senior level at Camp Wise, for many years. Each day, whether playing my guitar, leading a Shabbat service, running a program, or training a staff member, I could observe nearly every moment the positive feedback from my efforts. The positive feedback loop was a constant source motivation for me.

The loop is a virtuous cycle. We will examine the idea of the virtuous cycle more deeply in Blessing #7 when discussing Dr. Zeynep Ton and her *Good Jobs Strategy*. This particular cycle is also reflective of the Kolb Learning Cycle developed by David Kolb, writer of the recent volume the *Experiential Educator*. Kolb's learning cycle's basic premise is that as we have experiences, we have the opportunity to reflect on these experiences. From these reflections we learn, and with that new learning we can then experiment and try to new things, leading to new experiences, and thus the cycle continues, as we see below.

FRUITS OF OUR LABOR VIRTUOUS CYCLE

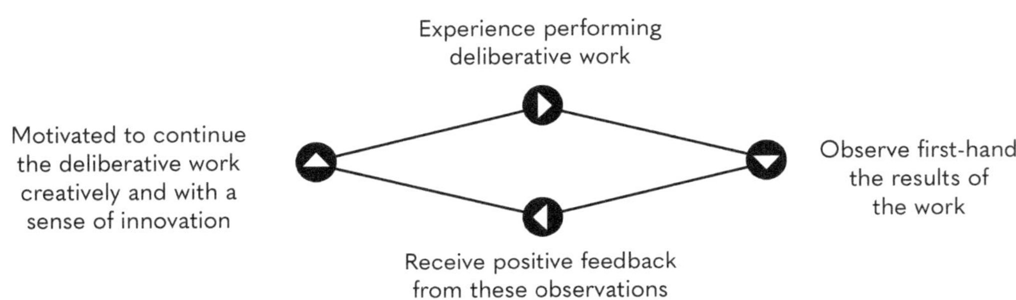

A Jewish community professional's deliberative work is an experience that they can reflect upon as they observe the fruits of their labor first-hand. When Jon is noticing happy campers are learning new skills at camp as a result of his own efforts he is reflecting on his experience, which to him learning how is actions benefit others and makes him more motivated to work harder and better. Armed with this learning, Jon continues with the deliberative work with more energy and creativity," which leads to him creating new work experiences and so forth. This is a powerful way to see the blessing of seeing the fruits of our labor in action.

The Power of "Pay it Forward"
Reflecting on the fruits of our labor adds an additional motivational component — the satisfaction in paying our work forward. Instead of paying-someone back for a favor or service, we, *pay it forward* to someone else. We see counselors at camp provide meaningful enriching experiences to us, and we want to do the same for the next generation.

Pay-it-forward reminds professionals that the work is not all about us, it is for those we are serving, a concept we will go into more deeply in Blessing #10. For here, it is worth highlighting that professionals like Jon do this work largely not to receive more pay, more accolades for ourselves, or more goodies for us. Professionals do this work to be in service to the Jewish values and principles of *g'milut hassadim, tzedek, and tikkun olam* — to provide acts of loving kindness, to pursue justice, and to help repair and strengthen our world, respectively. These Jewish values are the religious embodiment of paying it forward.

In a 2016 piece on the science of paying it forward, the *New York Times* reported: "The good news was that receiving help reliably increased the likelihood of being generous toward a stranger, and that participants who benefited from generosity had they themselves observed high levels of helping in their group (motivating them to pay it forward)" Professionals like Jon had memorable positive Jewish experiences growing up. Our roles as managers and leaders can be simply to help them pay-it-forward to a new generation as part of their work.

One way is through mentorship which, as we have already explored and will do so further in Blessing #14, is one of the motivational tools in Jewish life we do well and should amplify. It is difficult to pay a mentor back in an equivalent way that the mentor has helped their mentee. Often, the only comparable way a mentee can honor the gifts from a mentor is to provide the same meaningful wisdom and guidance to a new mentee. The original mentee is *paying it forward* to the new mentee, honoring the original mentor and feeling valued themselves because the original mentee now sees the fruits of their labor mentoring someone now. For both the original mentor and the original mentee in this example, seeing their respective mentee for both can be incredibly gratifying and *motivating*, each feeling more valued seeing the result of their efforts paying-it-forward.

Both Jon and I were enriched and grateful for the experiences we had in Jewish spaces that helped us grow and thrive, feeling both a sense of belonging and competence. It is not a surprise that decades later we find ourselves doing similar work and hoping to see the fruits of our labor so we can inspire others to pay it forward and follow in this tradition. I imagine many of you reading this book chose this field to make lives better in a manner that honors the professionals who worked tirelessly to bring these experiences to life for you. Consider this diagram, the pay-it-forward schematic, which can help us visualize how we can recruit new talent into our field from a young age and retain them throughout their career:

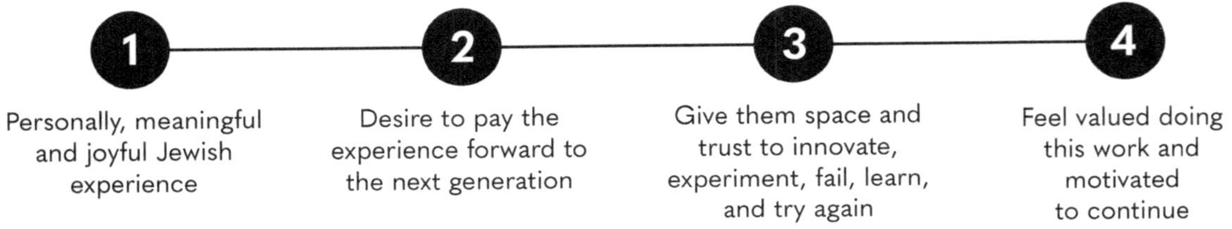

Our goal as managers is simply then to channel our professional's past positive experiences into a desire to provide these experiences for others, and then give them the proper autonomy, flexibility, and freedom to experiment and fail, and they'll continue to be motivated to pay it forward.

Helping Professionals do to BETTER, not MORE, Work

After many years at camp, Jon desired to become a camp director and thus headed to Capital Camps in Waynesboro, PA where he was director for 6 years. Four years in Jon and his wife had their first child, Micah. Though he continued to love camp, Jon quickly felt a challenge he wasn't prepared to continue to accept: how to be a present dad and also giving his 100% to his camp director role. He didn't feel he could give his full self to both roles.

As a result, he made the choice to leave camp to be able to have time to focus on family, while still pursuing the fruits-of-our-labor and pay-it-forward work that motivates and makes him feel valued. While at the IN JCC, Jon supervised and facilitated youth programs for the Jewish community. In this role Jon hoped to ensure the JCC provided safe and meaningful experiences for the children in their programs, and when people walk through the halls of the Indy JCC they feel a part of this community and want to keep coming back.

Reflecting on this learning from his camp director roles, Jon focused on doing better work instead of merely planning *more programs or projects*. He took a deep dive with his staff into the quality and mechanics of each of the JCC's youth programs. Jon follows the philosophy of his own former mentor: "we can't be everything to everyone, and so what are we going to choose to be excellent at?"

His philosophy is not only compelling and true as we strive to value our patrons; it is also true for how we can value our staff. We learn this from what may be my favorite discussion in the Talmud.

In the tractate or chapter *Bava Metzia*, Chapter 7, Mishnah 1, there is a *Gemara* discussion about the hours employers should set for their employees to work. This includes considering whether commuting time is work as well as the number of hours employees ought to be working on a given day. The Rabbis also argue about the setting of an employee's wages. One rabbi in the argument believes that if the employer raises the wages of an employee, then the employer is allowed to extend the employee's hours. The other rabbi rejects these arguments. He suggests that employers should not extend the hours when raising wages but should keep the hours as they are and allow the employees to continue their work *better* because the employees have to worry less about their compensation.

Again, we are faced with the struggle around compensation and time, and the value of creating more opportunities for employees to see the results of their work may be mitigated or go unrealized if employees feel under compensated or overworked. What they observe may not have quite as much resonance to them. Seeing the fruits of their labor may retain employees for a short time. But if their pay is too low or if they are working too much, eventually Jewish community professionals will burn out and leave.

We see this in our most entry-level workers who work very hard in their mostly direct service roles, so they see the fruits of their labor frequently yet are being asked to work longer hours while receiving low compensation. If they receive more compensation yet this comes with longer hours, it can still reduce their motivations. We see this clearly in the Leading Places to Work surveys which shows an exodus of entry-level professionals leaving after their first or second year in the field, with a low overall retention of early career professionals. Retention only increased among those professionals who are able to reach 5 years in the field. Only then do we have a better chance of retaining them for the longer term.

This *Gemara* text is thus instructive for us and our compensation discussions throughout this book. Our past profiles have suggested that Jewish community professionals need only enough money to not dwell or worry about their compensation so much. The *Gemara* reinforces this. We can pay them plenty enough while not adding onerous additional responsibilities when we do, so Jewish community professionals can properly appreciate the fruits of their labor and do better work.

Yet it is also instructive here that often Jewish community professionals may feel they have to prove their worth by producing more deliverables and results rather than focusing on a few particular projects are roles and completing them exceptionally well. We have a role as leaders and managers to counteract these feelings with an explicit managerial approach that includes generous compensation, work/life balance, and ample opportunities for employees to experience first-hand the fruits of their labor without distraction. To have Jewish community professionals focus on performing better work if it's not of a higher volume empowers them to live by the pay-it-forward schematic presented earlier. If the projects are of top quality and they aren't distracted by multiple other projects, or wondering if they can make rent, the pay-it-forward experiences will become ever more-clear and motivating.

Early in 2018, the Indianapolis JCC experienced a change in leadership and thus a restructuring of positions including Jon's position which was eliminated. Shortly thereafter, Jon found a new professional home outside of the Jewish community as the Associate Director of Programs for the Simon Youth Foundation, which helps vulnerable youth populations earn their high school diplomas, operating in 15 states across the US.

In his current role, Jon notes that his fruits-of-their-labor motivation shows up a little differently. "I'm definitely a layer removed. At the JCC I supervised people that perform the direct service but physically in a space where I can sense in all ways what was happening. Now I have to leave my building and go to program sites around the country to see the fruits of my labor or hear or read about them through stories and interactions."

The Authentic and Specific Thank You
Jon relishes the small tokens of appreciation. Even simple responses such as "Thanks a lot; I appreciate the follow up" from his CEO helps Jon feel valued and helps him see why his work matters to his colleagues and constituents. Jon also takes significant time to engage with his direct reports, helping them think through issues. He facilitated one of these meetings with two of his reports from his time at the JCC just before our initial interview and, again, received a simple yet elegant response: "thank you for so much for leading this meeting for us and helping us grow." He appreciates the specificity of these expressions of gratitude.

Jon also appreciates the intangible "thank you" when programs that he directs are successful and he gets to observe his success in action. Yet, Jon wants to be clear. He likes the tangible rewards beyond the "thank you." If his success leads Jon's superiors to offer him, for example, an excellent professional development opportunity which can further his growth, he will gladly accept it and see this as a further marker that he is being valued for his work.

Jon notes the specific importance of the, "authentic thank you" and believes it needs to be ongoing. He has learned that, when giving feedback, not just constructive but also positive, it needs to be specific, timely, and relevant, akin to a S.M.A.R.T. goal that we discussed in Blessing #4. As our goals must be Specific, Measurable, Attainable, Relevant, and Timely, so too must our feedback be to our employees. To receive a "good job," if he doesn't know what the "good job" is for can often feel devaluing, especially to an employee motivated by "paying-it-forward". Jon prefers the model of, "**describe it, label it, and praise it**," in which a manager will describe what the positive or constructive feedback is for, label its significance, and then say the "good job, well done, or *kol ha'kavod* (all the honor)" so it has meaning and context.

The "authentic thank you" is also important because Jon can easily start finding all of the things that are going wrong in a situation, which can demotivate Jon and prevent him from being motivated. It is a not a healthy cycle for any of our Jewish community professionals to fall into especially because there are always tasks we could have done better. Jon aims to stay positive both in the details and the big picture. To harness this need to feel valued, Jon, while at the JCC, and even today at the Simon Youth Foundation, often leave his office and walk around the building or heads to a program site, see first-hand the smiling kids or eager young adults at their programs. Jon has learned "not to sweat the small stuff," and appreciate the big picture of what all his efforts help lead to.

QUESTIONS FOR REFLECTION

1. Is there a motivator for you to pay it forward in your work? Can you track the experiences that may have inspired you and how you are honoring them by the work you are doing now? How can we make this link apparent to our professionals, nurture it and strengthen it?

2. What do we ask of our staff? Do we ask them to produce more in order to demonstrate their worth/effectiveness, or might we re-focus our expectations, so they do better — higher quality work — even if that means they produce fewer deliverables?

3. How can we provide more "authentic thank yous" to our staff as a result of specific tasks, and encouraging our non-direct-service staff especially to walk around the building (literally or metaphorically) so they can be reminded of the importance of their work?

promote collaboration, end exclusion

Blessing Summary — Jewish community professionals feel more valued when they feel included at work. This occurs when they are invited to collaborate and work in cultures in which there is a dedicated practice of inclusion. We explore inclusion and exclusion through a discussion of social identity theory and how to approach our work through an "abundance mindset," that promotes a culture of transparency, a healthy relationship with risk, and furthers equity.

הנה מה טוב ומה נעים שבת אחים גם יחד

Henei Ma Tov UmaNayim Shevet Achim Gam Yachad
Behold, how good and how pleasant it is for brethren to
dwell together in unity (Psalm 133)

This text reminds me of the values of *Am Yisrael*, the idea that we are a nation that stands together and supports one another, *Kol Yisrael Aravim Zeh La Zeh*, that all of Israel is responsible for one another.

This text of course represents an ideal, an aspiration, not always reality. Certainly, there are times when we aren't supportive or collaborative. Instead, we make assumptions or ignorant statements which foster a feeling of exclusion or otherness. A light-hearted example: new acquaintances often say that my wife and I are intermarried. For the record, we are not. We were both born into Jewish families and self-identify as Jewish. Yet while Mara was raised in the Reform movement, I was raised in the Conservative movement. When individuals suggest that we are intermarried, they (I assume) are making a joke and mean no harm. I, however, find these folks' assertions misguided at best. At worst, their comments misuse an already emotionally-charged term. They also may make us feel "othered," that for some reason one of us doesn't belong or that we don't belong together.

Human beings can develop nasty habits of practicing otherness or exclusivity within our *Am Yisrael*, our greater community that includes Jews and people of all faiths, and this certainly can extend to our workplaces, promoting a culture that opposes what, at least I have found though my many conversations, many Jewish community professionals today want to feel: a sense of inclusion to feel valued at work.

The Jewish people have felt "othered" in their communities throughout history. We were othered during our centuries of slavery in Egypt, when we were exiled to Babylonia after the destruction of the first temple in 586 B.C.E. and during the diaspora, or Jewish communities outside of Israel, starting in 70 C.E. and even through today. Otherness leads to Antisemitism, and we have experienced the worst Antisemitism in our history only within the last century. In North America, Jews have largely succeeded in fully integrating into society, yet we can still feel "othered." The alarming increase in Antisemitism of the last several years has been a sobering reminder.

As a Jewish community professional, I have little tolerance for othering, and the Jewish community professionals I know have little appetite for exclusion either. Exclusion, otherness, or even more mildly feeling left "out of the loop," has enormous effects in the work place. A recent study from the journal, Psychological Science found that upwards of 70% professionals felt excluded at work, which can lead to embarrassment or anxiety, reducing one's organizational and communal commitment and sense of belonging. Belonging, as we discussed starting in Blessing #1, is a key variable to build an employee's internal motivation. Perhaps unsurprisingly, the study also found that, "compared to victims of harassment, people who reported feeling ostracized were significantly more likely to have suffered health problems and to have ultimately quit their jobs." (*Psychological Science*, January 2014).

Aliza Kline has no patience for otherness or exclusion in the workplace, or anywhere in the Jewish community, for that matter. In fact, Aliza is actively working to promote the opposite. Aliza is the CEO of OneTable, whose mission according to their website is to "empower people who don't yet have a consistent Shabbat dinner practice to build one that feels authentic, sustainable, and valuable, and where guests of any and all religions and cultures are welcome. It is where people join together, share stories, build new connections and moments of meaning."

OneTable combats the "otherness" in our midst. Her leadership and passion strengthen Jewish community by nurturing innovative Jewish engagement. This directly correlates to her belief that the Jewish community must have no patience for the practices of exclusion. Instead, Aliza argues, we must foster collaboration, inclusion, and sincerely practicing *Am Yisrael*, which would be a blessing to our community and, for our purposes, to our staff, who will be more motivated, and valued in their work serving a Jewish community that promotes *b'yachad* – togetherness. Helping us get to this point and using Aliza's journey as a guide is the focus of this blessing.

Unlike several other of our portraits, Aliza is no accidental Jewish community professional. On the contrary, there have been several moments beginning when she was young when she aspired to work in the non-profit mission-driven sector, and realized the Jewish community was her platform to having the greatest impact. Consequently, each of her experiences included the opportunity to bring people together, open doors rather than shut them, and promote a larger feeling of Oneness or *Am Yisrael*.

Her first moment was as a teen in BBYO, when she learned to "grab the microphone." She planned events, ran for chapter and regional office, and become involved in important issues. The BBYO platform enabled Aliza to assemble 500 Jewish teens to take action around social justice and community issues. By bringing people together, she developed her leadership. Aliza reflected that Jewish spaces were much more of an opportunity to practice active citizenry than her high school in Colorado Springs. She felt the real opportunity to do something that would make significant impact on the world in a Jewish context by collaborating and being inclusive.

Aliza had her first major experience with otherness during her time at Washington University in St. Louis. She was attracted to Wash U. in part because of its Jewish presence. It's student body is approximately 35% Jewish. Yet, Aliza learned that being Jewish where there are a lot of other Jews wasn't going to shield her from exclusion. During her senior year, David Duke, the former grand wizard of the Ku Klux Klan, was running for senator in Louisiana where, incidentally, her parents had recently relocated. Aliza's Hillel Rabbi said that, as the Jewish student from Louisiana, she needed to speak at the upcoming rally on campus.

Aliza was motivated to accept this challenge, a nod to Blessing #1, not just because it was outrageous that a KKK leader was running and had a chance to win a Senate seat. She noticed that this was an issue the whole campus cared about. While there were secular organizations rallying against David Duke on campus as well. Perhaps most important to Aliza, she felt "othered," yet she found strength, and power in the distinctly Jewish platform she was offered and used it to oppose a white supremacist movement whose mission was, in part, to "other" the Jew in America.

Fostering Collaboration Through Social Identity Theory

During my own undergraduate studies, at McGill University in Montreal, Canada, I studied social identity theory with Professor Don Taylor, a prominent social psychologist of our time. Taylor's book, *Theories of Intergroup Relations*, discusses the power of groups and explores theories that govern our group behaviors and norms. I found the most powerful to be *Social Identity Theory*, from British social psychologists Henri Tajfel and John Turner. It proposes that an individual's evolving sense of self depends on the groups to which they belong.

Taylor expands on this, saying specifically that as we feel more part of an in-group and begin to identify more closely with this particular group, we can feel increasingly motivated to see this in-group become successful. We can view this as a positive outcome to leverage in our work situations. We can add here to our series of schematics that can help us foster relationships, community, trust, appreciation, and care of those around us, leading to more motivated, productive and blessed employees. Let's call this the inclusion schematic.

THE INCLUSION SCHEMATIC

Turner and Tajfel have studied these effects in the workplace and shown that "individual employees may exert increased effort and experience greater motivation if working on tasks for their collective group rather than in working for his or herself or themselves (Taylor, *Theories of Intergroup Relations*, 1994). Aliza, as an executive, knows this. At various times the OneTable website has shown each employee's picture wearing the same t-shirt, simply labeled, "FRIDAY." OneTable, like many organizations, has staff retreats and tries to promote staff bonding. But with this particular statement, they are one group, and they are working together to accomplish the same goal.

Yet social identity comes with potentially negative outcomes in which members of the "in-group" may eventually feel antagonistic toward the "out-group." We may even outwardly demonstrate our disdain for the out-group to strengthen our ties with the in-group. Turner and Tajfel cite a classic study that created two groups of boys at a summer camp who had no significant differences upon arrival, yet had created an in-group feel among each through bonding and simply giving them each a different group name. They quickly found that each group would artificially reward their in-group and punish their out-group. "Their belongingness to each group was meaningless, yet they always tended to favor their own (Taylor, *Theories of Intergroup Relations*, 1994)."

Just as promoting belonging and an in-group feeling can foster workplace motivations, it can also fuel the beginnings of prejudice and discrimination within the workplace and broader society. In the workplace, we aim to form teams within departments and connect co-workers so they can discover new friends or like-minded individuals among their ranks – fostering the relationships and sense of belongingness that we introduced both in Blessings #1 and #3. Yet while fostering inclusiveness, others can feel left out. Sometimes this can be a galvanizing force for motivation. It is incumbent upon all of us in charge of managing staff, creating culture, and assigning work teams to foster a sense of inclusion among staff without also fostering any sense of otherness or exclusions for any individual or between staff groups.

 Shortly after speaking at the rally against David Duke, Aliza was offered a fellowship with Hillel International as the public policy fellow. Suddenly, Aliza was meeting many extraordinary people who were committed to working on social justice issues — and she had a platform to reach an enormous constituency of people. She could easily write an email to 20,000 students to encourage them to advocate for pressing issues.

Having this platform was pivotal for Aliza as she considered and began to craft her career path. She also typically says YES to opportunities as they come. Aliza was taught by her high school history teacher not to be "milquetoast," which she meant to be bland and un-opinionated. Her teacher rather advised Aliza to have an opinion and bring people together. Aliza isn't sure if this teacher was simply giving her permission to be who she already was or challenging her to be and do more then she had been doing. It is perhaps not surprising, then, that the jobs Aliza has been most drawn to are those where she can share her ideas and gather others in the process. These have been the most transformational, when her ideas are welcome, celebrated, and enacted.

Nurturing an inclusive environment can also help Jewish community professionals speak out and speak up. As we see with Aliza, it increases their confidence within their in-group. As managers, we may be more comfortable sharing our vision in the work place than our staff are. For our staff to feel this way as well, they must not only feel individually that they have the autonomy, competence, and belonging to feel internally motivated but that they also feel a part of the team. It may behoove us to ask our staff if they do feel comfortable enough to speak up. This in-group phenomenon moves beyond belonging; it is core to a person's social identity to feel either in or "othered." We can foster a feeling of being in the in-group to deepen our staff's internal motivations

Have No Patience for Exclusion

At the same time, we must be wary that social identity theory practices can also foster exclusion or otherness in our Jewish community and specifically in the workplace. If Aliza's feelings about exclusion are an exemplar for her fellow Jewish community professionals then there is simply no patience for foster or tolerating practices that exclude people, both in our community writ large or in the workplace. She doesn't believe, for example, that the Torah or the rabbis of the Talmud believed that there are "levels" of Judaism, that one Jew is more holy or special than any other, or that a person of another faith or no faith is more or less special. To even suggest such a thing diminishes all of our efforts. It creates ignorance, confusion, and resentment, not unlike the joke about my wife and I being "intermarried."

To make categories that feel exclusive to one another inhibits our ability to come together and achieve *Am Yisrael* or a cohesive work culture. Thus, Aliza fulfills her passion by opening up access to Judaism to as many as she can. She exemplified this when she was the executive director of Mayyim Hayyim Living Waters Community Mikveh and Education Center, a project for establishing and promoting a community *mikveh* in communities across the country, and now in leading OneTable. Judaism, in Aliza's view, can teach that there is a universe much greater than each of us, and it is thus each of our duty to act justly, slow down, be cognizant of the needs of those around us, including those we work for, with, and who work for us, and stop and be present with their needs even for a moment. This reflective practice will help lead us to all to lead healthier, more balanced, happier and blessed professional lives.

How We Apply Promoting Collaboration to Blessing Our Staff: Stop and Reflect

To stop and reflect is a key step in the process of learning experientially and popularized by the educational scholars John Dewey and David Kolb. To use experiential education in order to promote inclusion and collaboration, we can allocate meaningful time in each of our days to:

- Stop, reflect and ask ourselves, as managers, if we act justly with our human resources
- Stop and slow down our work so we can be more present and better observe our actions and the actions of those around us

- Stop and be cognizant of the people around us to ensure they feel that they are being paid attention to and included in the various aspects and operations of the organization

- Stop and notice when we may be inadvertently or intentionally excluding others and when our actions do not reflect our Jewish values of Oneness, of *Am Yisrael*

These practices can be simple. Are we including the proper staff in organizational communications and meetings? Are we allowing everyone on the team to share their input and be heard? Are we providing sufficient growth opportunities to each team member and not acting in anyway biased toward a certain individual or part of the team? These are important reflective questions to address and review regularly to ensure we are enjoying the benefits of promoting collaboration and avoiding the consequences of allowing for exclusion.

A Consequence of Exclusion — The Equity Gap

One place, as a community, that we haven't yet completely figured out how to stop, reflect and make change is the gender equity gap in our organizations, though thanks to recent efforts from the Gender Equity and Hiring Project, Leading Edge, and the Safety, Respect, and Equity Coalition, we are making progress. We will return to gender equity and bias again in Blessing #15 when we discuss making adjustments to our managerial behaviors, as this issue permeates throughout many of our portraits.

For here, we will focus on Aliza, who recalls her one-and-a-half year gap between leaving Mayyim Chayim and starting at OneTable. Aliza had been emotionally invested in Mayyim Chayim, and it took her a long time to transition. She completed multiple consulting and volunteer projects, notably working with Shifra Bronznick and her team at Advancing Women Professionals (AWP) on gender equity in the Jewish community, particularly in the professional workplace. She also studied design thinking, which has also changed the way she thinks, creates, communicate, functions, and leads. She had also been consulting with Upstart, an organization that supports Jewish start-ups and other entrepreneurial ventures, and the Jewish Education Project in New York.

She was building up an even more stellar resume. Yet during this time Aliza had also interviewed for several executive positions at Jewish legacy organizations. She was excited for each interview and brought her enthusiasm and big ideas to each, yet none turned into a job offer. She believed it was because, when interviewing for a Jewish legacy institution, one has to "reserve judgment, keep your mouth shut a bit longer then you may want to and honor what's been done," she said. This approach is not Aliza's nature. She has been trained her whole life to speak up and speak out – and she wasn't about to conform to suit the comfort of particular organizations.

Or maybe Aliza's lack of success was because she is a strong *female* leader. As of 2017, only 16 of the 50 organizations who provide the top salaries for their executives are led by women, and no woman lands anywhere near the top 10, as noted in *The Forward's* annual review of top professionals in the Jewish community. There are certainly many factors to consider, but might there be in part an implicit bias towards excluding women from the top job?

There is a lesson here. Mayyim Hayyim and OneTable are both start-ups, where Aliza has been quite successful. Yet, she may have needed to be seen as part of the in-group of legacy institution executives in order to have been selected. *Leading Places to Work*, in their 2018 survey, found that "women feel less psychologically safe – less comfortable expressing themselves and being themselves – then men." It might have been out of place for those on the executive search committees to meet a female who is so comfortably outspoken.

If this is even partially true, it means that we are sending regressive messages to our employees and potential new hires: that to be welcomed, one has to be of a certain type, in this case an outspoken person of a specific gender. Otherwise one may be excluded from the leadership role.

Eventually, Aliza was invited to meet with two large family foundations who were eager to launch a new effort to inspire tens of thousands of young adults to engage in Shabbat. Aliza went into this interview with a different sense of clarity and optimism than she had for the previous opportunities. The opportunity spoke to her, and she spoke up, true to her nature. She was sought after for who she was and felt valued as a result.

 It is fitting that Aliza would gravitate toward, and ultimately lead, an organization in which creating greater access to Jewish ritual is at the core of the organization's mission and vision. She feels suited to help others connect to Jewish ritual on their own terms. Like Jon in Blessing #5, Aliza feels like she is "paying it forward" and seeing the fruits of her labor when she sees emerging adults inspired by a Jewish experience such as an engaging and innovative Shabbat dinner – just as she was inspired when given a chance to lead at Hillel at Wash U. That's the niche she sees herself filling: promoting inclusion. Truly, her and OneTable's larger goal is to help people feel as included as possible.

Taylor discusses the role that strong experiences have in promoting a feeling of belonging to the in-group and thus being more motivated and valued to support the group and notes how this feeling connects to the workplace as well. If one's "social identity is connected to their work, they become more engaged and supportive of that work." (Taylor, *Theory of Intergroup Relations*, 1994). It is clear, though, that Jewish community professionals like Aliza are motivated not only when connected to a mission, but also connected to a group.

How might we create a workplace culture in which everyone feels not only a sense of belonging but truly and completely part of the in-group As an executive, Aliza works daily to address this question, and her experience provides a road map to consider implementing.

It Starts with Whom we Hire

Part of creating a culture of motivation, value and Oneness is to hire top talent. Mort Mandel discusses a similar hiring philosophy in his book *It's All About Who*. He talks about hiring only the "A"s, who have the intellectual firepower and passion to excel at this work." Hiring A's who fully buy in to the philosophy of team culture worked for Mandel and his brothers, who went on to become billionaires and among the most important philanthropists in the Jewish community.

Hiring for OneTable, Aliza also looks for what she calls "wicked smart" talent, as well as those who are excited, energized, and bring joy to the work, who can bring their skill sets to bear, and who don't need to be asked to be creative and resourceful. They, as Aliza put it, "just are." At OneTable, Aliza's team is primarily those in the Millennial and older Gen Z generations similar to those who attend Shabbat dinners and share similar value systems to promote inclusion. "Getting the right people on the bus," as former president of General Electric Jack Welch has put it, is half the puzzle to creating a fully inclusive, and therefore fully valued and blessed, workforce.

Making Collective Success Transparent

Aliza likes positive reinforcement and knowing right away whether the team is producing successful results, and thus makes these results transparent, frequently celebrating their successes. Nearly every week, the entire OneTable team will recognize how many Shabbat dinners they made happen in the prior week and how many are scheduled for the week ahead. It is both fun and exciting for her team to view the measurable evidence to the impact of their work. This also helps to tell a compelling story to current and future OneTable stakeholders. This collective success promotes an in-group feeling and also aligns with seeing the fruits of our labor, we discussed in the previous blessing. When Aliza and her team sees the videos, photos, and social media posts of OneTable Shabbat Dinner participants enjoying themselves and engaging with others, it fills her and her team with joy and purpose. She'll hear her staff scream from across the hall, "ooh this is a good one!" which Aliza can sense is bringing her staff joy, which Aliza then feels. The in-group collective success can be contagious, especially when everyone feels included.

Creating a Culture of "Showing Up"

Aliza wants her staff to know that the organization values when employees bring their whole authentic selves to work. This fuels her and her staff's motivations even further. Aliza notes the challenges of each person sharing their full selves including their personal triumphs, challenges, and vulnerabilities, to a growing staff of over 30 professionals. The OneTable workforce is also dispersed across the country and connecting frequently over zoom, which now feels normal to many more us during COVID-19. Yet, Aliza has a requirement that each person "shows up" and speaks for two minutes at each check-in. She finds this practice helpful because, by sharing with the OneTable professional community, professionals become invested in each other, which again promotes a collaborative, caring, in-group feeling among the entire team. It also helps Aliza better get to know and be in tune with her team. Aliza recognizes that how she spends her weekends, especially as a mom of three, is very different from how her staff of young Millennials and Gen Z individuals spend theirs. These team gatherings allow for an in-group feeling to become cemented. They care for her and she cares about them.

An Abundance Mindset

Creating a strong team and in-group culture can help foster a belief that anything is possible and that the sky is the limit, and that if we build a spirit of partnership, we can create more for everyone. This is the foundational thinking of the *abundance mindset*, which contrasts to scarcity thinking, referring to individuals who feel that the pie of resources in an organization always has to be cut up and distributed and that the current resources are finite. A culture in which there isn't a collective mentality of success, rather a "I win therefore you lose," mentality, often are settled into a scarcity mindset.

Introducing the abundance mindset here for the purposes of motivating and blessing staff by making them feel included is important. If one department within an organization receives more frequent guidance from mentorship or more grant funds, or the "most talented" staff, or the most active lay leaders, then the other departments may feel like they are losing out, as these resources are looked at as finite or scarce. They feel ostracized, othered, and deflated.

People who think this away do not consider that collaboration using these resources could create results in which the whole is greater than the sum of its parts. Aliza, along with many of the Jewish community professionals we meet in this book, find that too many people in our community practice scarcity thinking and are frustrated and de-motivated because they don't believe in the scarcity model at all. They are turned off by the us versus them mentality that is created when people feel they have to fight over pieces of the pie, which hurts our community's ability to reach its full potential.

Aliza practices abundant thinking – looking at strategies to enlarge the pie without having to cut it up in a zero-sum game. For example, when Aliza works with her lay partners, they give themselves permission to experiment, innovate, and iterate without thinking that taking this time and taking these risks may lead to long planning processes or a loss of support. She is, rather, energized by these generative conversations which make her feel that there is no limit to what she along with her lay and professional team together can achieve. When Aliza has completed various leadership assessments, the results typically indicate that Aliza is a persuader, as opposed to an analyzer. She knows that the extreme analyzer who tries to do it all on their own never has enough data to feel confident enough to move forward – thus, often, nothing happens. She has observed organizations crawl through an 18-month program planning process, worried about the limits of finite resources, and then finally conduct a pilot program, only for the funder to decide not to fund the idea fully due to a lack of data on the program. This process exhausts Aliza. Dreaming big, collaborating, being open to all the possibilities, and thinking of innovations and partnerships leads to action, and action fuels Aliza and her fellow Jewish professionals.

Delegate and Practice Tzimtzum

Aliza sees herself as a pretty big delegator and wants to work with people who are resourceful. She shared with me her reflection of a recent OneTable gathering, where her sole role was to speak to the crowd. She had little direct planning in the event specifics and her role was not until the very end. She thoroughly enjoyed just speaking and connecting with the attendees and proud of her staff who led the charge. She appreciates the importance of giving her staff the autonomy to lead and take ownership of the work and developing their own sense of competence and confidence – with Aliza only having to set vision and delegate to them.

Often our staff may feel excluded from the mission or the team because they aren't involved in the decision-making process or feel that their work isn't meaningful or deep, as suggested in Blessing #4. This can come from the executive making the big decisions, steering major program events, or directing policy discussions. Aliza saw her lack of a direct role in this gathering as practicing *tzimtzum*, a Jewish value that loosely translates to an act of humility. In this case, Aliza is practicing *tzimtzum* by letting others lead. In a way, her *tzimtzum* helps others on her team feel part of the in-group because they got to lead.

This blessing is encouraging us to embrace partnership, collaboration, and abundance thinking whenever possible, not only as a business model and a way of scaling success but also as a powerful motivator for staff to do their best work feeling part of a collective in-group team. The best feeling for Jewish community professionals like

Aliza is when they can partner with anyone. She encourages organizations throughout the Jewish world to see each other as collaborators, not competitors, to identify shared goals and how we can harness each other's strengths and resources to achieve great things.

Aliza likens the relationships we have both within our organizations and between them like a marriage. We must make and re-affirm an ongoing commitment to each other to support the causes we care about. We must work to speak the same language. We must use the language of "we," and "us vs. the problem," not "you vs. me" or "us vs. them." We must have no patience either for an exclusive divided Judaism in which some players feel in and others feel out, which perpetuates a mentality of us vs. them. No one, especially in the Jewish community, should ever feel left out – especially our Jewish community professionals.

As the Mayyim Hayyim executive, Aliza worked in close partnership with the founding board chair, Anita Diamant. Aliza felt that she and Anita were true complements of each other, in attitude and expertise. These types of partnership must by studied and then implemented elsewhere – and celebrated! There is no room for adversarial relationships. They are not productive and such toxic cultures may be incredibly de-motivating our Jewish community professionals.

Aliza and I also spoke a lot about power – whether it be the executive who has the power over their staff or the board's power over an executive. Those in power must be advised to stop, reflect and acknowledge the power and imbalance that is present in our working relationships with staff. It is important for the person with more power in any situation to practice appreciative inquiry, curiosity, and humility. Encountering a staff or collaborator whether they have more or less power in a relationship, one must ask:

• What does this person know that I don't?

• What relationships does this person have that I do not?

• What can I learn from this person that can help me grow and better understand?

How we honor each other and see each other as partners, recognizing each other's power and trying to compensate for any imbalance will foster healthy relationships and enable us to overcome challenges, which will only motivate us to work more together. Aliza is hopeful that if we show value by fostering collaboration, we can accomplish more shared successes while increasing the morale and motivations of our staff. We will also have a better time doing the work we do.

QUESTIONS FOR REFLECTION

1. Which of our policies are working, intentionally or otherwise, to bring people together? Do any of our policies push other people out or have them feel othered?

2. How can we practice the abundance mindset in our workplaces and among our staff? How can we focus more on the partnership and policies that can promote inclusion and lead to a whole greater than the sum of its parts?

3. How might we have a conversation with all stakeholders in our organization about power: who has it and how we can be aware of it so we can effectively collaborate, speak our minds and share ideas freely?

cut the BS

Blessing Summary — Jewish community professionals today seek to work in cultures that are efficient, transparent, and fair. If we cut out the inefficiencies, lack of transparency, and unfairness in our organizations, our work places will work better for our Jewish community professionals, who will then feel more motivated and valued, citing the acclaimed work of the Good Jobs Strategy and Dr. Zeynep Ton as our guide.

BS, which I will define here as nonsense or half-truths, exists in every relationship, organization and community, Jewish and otherwise. On the whole, people say they do not like BS, but they often believe it. Cited in *Smithsonian Magazine*: "In a 2015 paper, Gord Pennycook at the University of Waterloo found that some people with a heightened response bias are more disposed to accept corresponding ideas and pseudo-facts they come across. He also found they have lower responses in a part of the frontal lobe called the anterior cingulate cortex, which includes the brain's built-in bullshit detector. For some people, this region simply doesn't sound the alarm in the presence of bullshit."

BS, however unhelpful or unpleasant, is inevitable and prevalent because many of us simply aren't alarmed by it. BS is also necessary. Like our bodies, when our organizations and communal systems use nutrients like people, building, systems, or materials to produce our products and services, we also produce waste. These are the inefficiencies of working with people and systems. Since BS literally and metaphorically smells, it distracts from the work we want to do. When BS makes a mess, we have to clean it up, which can often feel like an additional waste of time, energy, and resources.

The best organizations, however, find ways to reduce or eliminate waste, which leads many of our Jewish community professionals, including our next narrative, Graham Hoffman, to feel the most valued and blessed. Jewish community professionals are most attracted to working for the organizations that prioritize cutting the BS.

I began my career working in Human Resources (HR) for two non-profit organizations. In both places, my colleagues and I would joke that HR was the "restroom" of the organization (we used more colorful language). It was never our goal to be perceived this way: we aspired to be a strategic partner with leadership and labor, a resource that could advance our mission and not only clean up problems, and a place akin to Disneyland for staff who would see HR as their home to address their issues and make them feel like a million bucks when they walked into our offices.

Yet it is more likely that in most of our organizations there are few people who want to visit HR. Rather, they see the HR office as a necessary trip to report an employee relations issue, address a medical or pension benefits issue, or solve some other problem. When they do visit, they want the experience to be clean, easy, and useful (like any desired restroom experience).

One could suggest that the systems we put in place in our Jewish organizations are too like the restrooms we all need to visit at points throughout the day. Our functions take systems that produce energy in the form of programs and services, that generate revenue, and that meet our mission. We also produce waste: red tape, employee conflicts, team or staff challenges, how we properly or improperly support our staff, or projects that commence but doesn't get done. This waste, bureaucracy, or inefficiency must be minimized or used to our advantage. We can either create landfills that build up in the organization's work culture, or we can recycle, reuse, and reduce to create a healthier and more sustainable work experience for all involved.

None of us, I imagine, actually value BS. I have had countless conversations with colleagues, students, and peers who get frustrated when there is a lack of transparency, a lack of fairness, or a lack of smart processes in our organizations. When we combine this reality with low pay or lack of a healthy work-life integration, even a strong mission or a strong manager is no longer enough for a Jewish community professional to remain in their position. This blessing provides a narrative that suggests working toward a virtuous cycle in our organizations that will help us reduce the BS which will strengthen our Jewish community professionals' motivations and feeling that they are valued.

A quick processor, thoughtful and empathetic, and with a keen, strategic, and imaginative mind, Graham Hoffman is a Jewish community professional who, in my view, any organization would be wildly fortunate to have leading their team. Graham is currently the CEO of the Jewish Federation of Southern Arizona and Jewish Community Foundation of Southern Arizona. Graham detests when operations do not work the way they should, let alone reach their optimum potential. If we want to motivate, value and retain superstars like Graham, we need to work on cutting the BS.

Graham's parents divorced when he was relatively young. Graham's dad re-married a person of another faith while Graham's mom and her new partner took steps to become *ba'al tshuvah* in his early adolescence. *Ba'al Tshuvah* literally means "master of return," and refers to formerly liberal or secular Jews who choose Orthodoxy – ultra Orthodoxy in this case. Given the two very different roads Graham lived and observed, he ultimately committed himself to a life of Jewish pluralism, coupled with a strong desire to take ownership of his own Jewish experience, defining for himself what that was going to mean.

Graham attended pluralistic institutions, including his community Jewish day school, Jewish summer camp and BBYO, which shaped his knowledge of and engagement with Jewish life. Despite these generally joyful experiences, Graham had no inclination to become a Jewish community professional in part because he was, and still is today, critical of Jewish organizations who are "stuck in a fixed pie mentality" as Graham put it, reflective of the scarcity mindset introduced in the last blessing.

Graham grew frustrated when leadership saw resources as fixed and limited; that to add one new program or staff person, organizations would have to give up another. Graham didn't want to be on the consuming end of that equation. His initial plan was to work in the for-profit world after university and accumulate enough wealth to become a Jewish philanthropist. His first professional job was at Accenture as a business consultant.

Graham's first impressions and his initial career decision should give us pause. There is great talent out there that thinks Jewish organizations are not worth even considering despite the good work we do. We might then assume that we have a reputation among some, fair or not, of not utilizing resources well.

#1. A KEY BS WE MAY BE COMMITTING — ACCEPTING MEDIOCRITY

Fair assumption or not, this is the perception, and Graham is blunt about his feelings. He is deeply disappointed when what we do is seen as *below excellence*. This may be a high bar, yet he is adamant that we need to have very high standards for what we do and deliver. When people like Graham don't see these high standards, they can turn away from wanting to join our workforce. For example, Graham sees organizations keep people on staff despite their mediocre performance because they have seniority, or because of politics, or due to an acceptance of mediocrity.

Graham acknowledges that we don't want to automatically fire those who have been with us for a long time or if they are well-liked by many in the organization just because their performance starts to dip. Most are good, well-intentioned people, and their work may not always be excellent or even satisfactory, but it is also not poor. Yet there are trade-offs when we lead and manage this way: we lose productivity, revenue, and meeting our mission when our staff are inadequate. Never mind that when inadequate staff remain on the team, it frustrates high-performers who feel irked when they are treated the same way with the same cost of living increases as those not giving one hundred percent effort and delivering impressive results. We need to help all staff fulfill their full potential, but if there are staff that just do not perform well, treating them the same as those who perform at a high level can have negative consequences that may otherwise be overlooked.

Graham isn't alone. In writing about the importance of leadership and culture in the workplace, *Forbes* cites research from Dylan Minor and Michael Housman, who found that: "When leaders refuse to do anything about a (toxic or mediocre) employee, it places a large tax on organizational morale, team engagement and productivity." Further, "These (toxic or mediocre) employees degrade and demotivate the best performers and overall morale more than any other contributing factor. Their impact can also degrade the intangible factors of trust and faith an employee has in their leadership."

Toxic employees are not just the bullies, rabble rousers, or the harassers that may be causing trouble and impeding a healthy work culture. Toxic employees can also be the mediocre ones who say through their actions, "I can do just enough" or, "I have the right connections here to get by without losing my job; heck, I may even get promoted." This a real, albeit slightly cleaned up quote I heard from an employee once. Like Graham, I and many of our peers have witnessed the *culture of mediocrity* of many of our organizations first hand. If we, however, managed all of our staff with the blessings outlined in this book, perhaps their performance would be raised well above mediocre. This is the preferable option, and there is a roadmap for this using the approach of *The Good Jobs Strategy*, outlined a bit later in this Blessing.

There is something to be said for an organization that rewards loyal people and can show that their employees have very long tenures, which can create long-term trust. And yet, these organizations may state that they have limited resources and can't hire new or nurture emerging talent while holding on to staff who may be mediocre. Rewarding mediocrity with continued employment, which is exacerbated when organizations do not have a robust employee performance review process or one that isn't tied to compensation or promotions, sends a message to those newer high-performing staff who want to see reward for results rather than for seniority or connections. These high performers might just leave, which some would call a wasted opportunity, nonsense or, BS. All the while, mediocre employees stick around, continuing to produce mediocre work, dragging others down, and hurting the prospects for the organization to excel, grow, and expand. This is also BS.

We might do better to measure who is a high performer and who isn't. We must start with writing and administering clear job descriptions, laying-out core competencies that promote excellence and results, which can be followed with administering a clear, fair, and measurable performance review process and promoting transparency when implementing performance improvement plans when staff are not performing at acceptable levels.

We also have to reimagine what acceptable deliverables are in Jewish organizations. Professionals can make mistakes as a result of a learning curve or because they took a risk. These are good failures that we can learn from, as we discussed in Blessing #4. Employees can also make consistent errors or have a very slow work pace that is unexplainable and do not help advance the organization, and to accept this reality as "part of what happens here" can only move the organization backward.

A Remedy to Mediocrity — Investing in Good Jobs and Operational Excellence

The exceptional work of Dr. Zeynep Ton, her book *The Good Jobs Strategy*, and current leadership of *The Good Jobs Institute* at MIT have revolutionized how the retail industry thinks about work, crafting jobs, and reducing waste and mediocrity in its companies. Ton has a simple formula for reducing BS in our organizations. She demonstrates that high-performing retail organizations not only invest in their staff, they also invest in their operational processes which includes employees sharing information with each other and with management across the organization, promoting transparency, and creating a culture where empowerment and promoting creative solutions is a virtue.

As a result, these organizations are able to reduce inefficiencies, retain staff, make more money, be more productive, and better fulfill our missions. Put another way, by reducing the operational inefficiencies that occur in most organizations —

inefficiencies in our process, lack of transparency leading to conflict, a culture of micromanagement and frustration — we reduce time wasted in either living with or fixing the mistakes made by these inefficiencies and focus more on innovative thinking, collaboration, and honoring one's staff, which leads to meeting our mission and stronger revenue. We can see this in Ton's vicious vs. virtuous of cycle in retail organizations.

RETAIL'S VICIOUS AND VIRTUOUS CYCLES

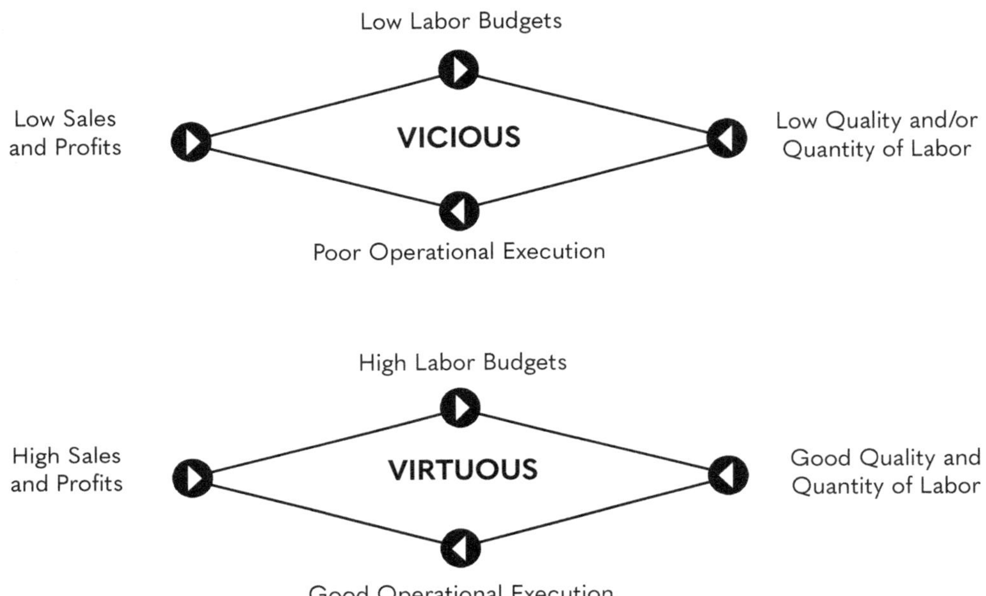

The best side-by-side example in Ton's *Good Jobs Strategy* compares the operations of two leading retailers, Walmart and Costco. Ton reveals that, historically, there have been frequent errors in Walmart's enormous operation. Workers often mislabel prices on items. Employees frequently arrive late or are absent for their shifts in part due to poor scheduling by managers. Workers are often not sufficiently trained and thus miss assignments or commit errors when completing tasks. Walmart has managed to grow tremendously despite these operational missteps in part because of their wide selection of products at low prices. They also devote tremendous resources to acquiring and analyzing-data: knowing who is buying what shows the needs and wants of their customer, but not necessarily their staff.

Many of our Jewish institutions might be like Walmart, enormous operations that can grow due to our high volume and ample resources either through philanthropy, membership, or fee-for-service that compensates for our errors and inefficiencies.

We can still end up profitable or reasonably healthy financially and demonstrating that we achieve our mission. Folks will still keep coming to Walmart, or the large JCC, congregation, or Federation, even if they are sometimes disappointed and the experience isn't always fantastic. These places mostly stay in business though during COVID-19 even our largest organizations may be struggling, and many can *struggle to thrive* also in part because this waste and inefficiencies hold them back. We have to spend time and resources fixing errors, apologizing to consumers, hiring and training new staff more frequently. Reducing or eliminating these inefficiencies could eliminate this BS, that de-motivates staff such as Graham. Operating with structural and human resource inefficiencies means accepting mediocrity as the norm, and that disincentivizes Jewish community professionals.

Costco establishes excellence as the norm. Though a significantly smaller company than its much larger competitor, Costco has excelled in operational efficiencies where Walmart has fallen short, including:

- Costco only offers certain brands of certain products, which allows workers to keep track of less inventory managing, ordering, and stocking.

- They train their staff to collaborate and be transparent about their work, encouraging them to share mistakes or challenges and seek feedback.

- They pay their staff well above market rate and train them extensively to reduce mistakes, encouraging employees to point out how work and systems can function better, empowering them to seek creative solutions to operational problems.

- The institution as a whole, in partnership with employees at all levels, is constantly and vigilantly studying its operational processes and learning how to improve.

As a result, Costco realizes higher individual profits per store and experiences lower employee turnover than Walmart, 4% annual turnover according to 2015 data to Walmart's 15%. Costco's approach to operational excellence and valuing their human resources both in pay and inviting their contributions to the work essentially help Costco cut the BS and allow for a much healthier and vibrant organization to work for, keeping their staff happy and retained.

My 8-year old daughter Noah and 5-year-old son Asher and I shop at Costco approximately twice a month (before COVID-19 at least!). It is delightful. Products are easy to find, there are free food samples, again, before COVID, and most important the staff are helpful and always seem to be enjoying themselves while at work. The employee who reviews our receipts before we leave always draws a smiley face on the back before returning it to my children, who smile in return. Their employee name tags show when they started at Costco, marketing to consumers their long-tenures on staff, often upwards of 5, 10, 15, sometimes 20 years of service.

Costco employees don't deal with the BS that Walmart employees, and thus their consumers, keep returning, because Costco blesses their workforce by investing in their staff, and reducing the BS that often drives them away. They practice excellent abundance model thinking and follow a virtuous cycle of management and leadership.

One might argue that the increased initial costs that arise from investing in staff and operational excellence amounts to increases in overhead costs. We have been trained in the non-profit world to think of overhead as a bad thing. Naomi Korb-Weiss, a management consultant who works with many Jewish organizations has written extensively on our misunderstanding of overhead in Jewish non-profits. She wrote in her 2013 piece in Ejewishphilanthropy.com to encourage non-profits to make impact and not focus on overhead, "It's time to look at organizational overhead differently – to view it as central to our cause as well as a tool for growth." As she explains, overhead has become an evil word to many Jewish funders who expect as much of their money as possible to go to program or direct service, and this is leading to inefficiencies.

Investing in talent and operational excellence, and not settling for mediocrity, contributes directly to program if looked through a different lens. By spending time and resources to understand processes and how we can make them better – and encouraging staff to speak when they see inefficiencies and rewarding them for doing so – we can drive more programs and services that will lead to raising revenue, productivity, and meeting mission. This is a critical component of both Ton's virtuous cycle as noted above, and it also aligns with our success schematic in Blessing #2. Reducing inefficiencies is a direct outcome of training, compensating, and investing in staff so our organizations can then achieve their mission through an abundance model of thinking. Mediocrity is vicious, excellence is virtuous. We can adopt this cycle easily for the Jewish non-profit sector, as seen below:

DR. ZEYNEP TON'S VIRTUOUS CYCLE: ADAPTED FOR THE JEWISH NON-PROFIT SECTOR

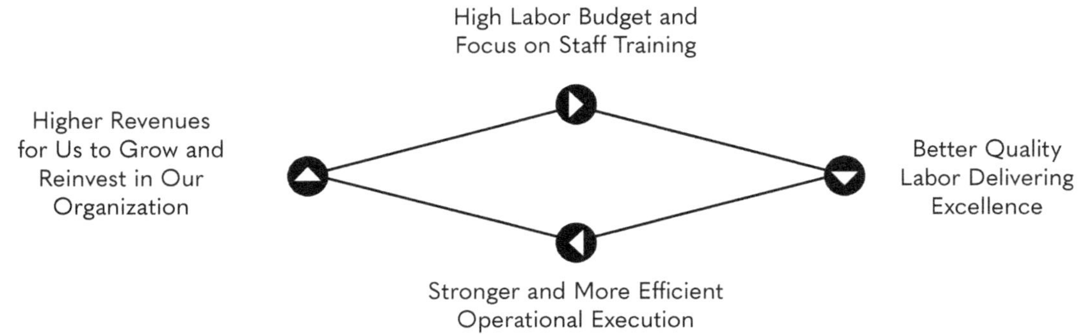

#2. THE BS WE ARE COMMITTING, ARBITRARILY FIGHTING OVER "LIMITED" RESOURCES

Graham is also concerned with the politics and bureaucracy miring our landscape that make it difficult to accomplish our goals. For example, organizations have to fight very hard for resources that Graham considers a "no brainer," such overhead costs or more necessary staffing, which should be easier to fund in a community where there is so much wealth. As David Cygeilman in Blessing #1, shared with me, "we have unlimited money in the Jewish community," yet to the organizations who operate with this funding it often feels we are competing against each other for a limited pool of funds. This promotes unhealthy competition, leading to exclusion, and reduces opportunities to collaborate, foster relationships and come together. We would miss out on taking advantage of the motivational effects of which we spoke of in Blessings #3 and #6.

This waste is also a result of the Jewish philanthropic landscape and funders' relationship to grantees. Significant reporting, measurement, and accountability demanded by funders to their grantees has been driving much of the philanthropic process. Graham acknowledges that stakeholders, foundations, federations, and individual givers deserve to know that their investments have been wisely made, that there is progress, and that we are achieving desired results.

At the same time, organizations consume a great deal of resources trying to deliver on these requirements, including time and money that instead could be spent on program that directly fulfills the mission. This too is an inefficiency, creating waste rather than value for the grantee organization and therefore the funder. Every stakeholder should want to reduce the duration and cumbersome funding process requirements.

In recent years the Jim Joseph Foundation's (JJF) reporting process has changed from a thick report with many specific budgetary and narrative requirements to a leaner report with a process that instead includes quarterly conversations with program officers, inviting partnership and an opportunity for dialogue and transparency. They have streamlined their reporting process, for example, to be a reflective exercise. They want to work with the grantee, thinking and learning, with less of a focus on results and direct deliverables, helping the organization grow and improve – a great model that creates efficiency, transparency, collaboration, and trust.

Fortunately, Jewish organizations already offer a motivation that many corporate jobs do not: personal meaning and fulfillment. After a short while at Accenture, Graham realized that he was able to make good money, yet the work just wasn't meaningful to him. Graham recognized that if he was going to measure his success in terms of salary, either for the company or for himself, it would never be enough. He would always be striving for more – even from the altruistic perspective of wanting to be a better philanthropist. He recognized that the accompanying life choices with constantly striving for more compensation were not consistent with who he wanted to be.

He also recognized that, however the resources of the Jewish community were or weren't being used, without outstanding people those resources would not reach their full potential. Graham thus decided to dedicate his professional life to working at institutions in which he could feel both connected to the mission and be extremely passionate about the work.

#3 CUTTING THE BS - HIGHLIGHTING WHAT MAKES JEWISH ORGANIZATIONS GREAT

Eventually choosing to work for Hillel International, Graham was wildly impressed by the quality of the Hillel staff, the depth of the work content, and the specific work they wanted him to take on. Interestingly, one piece of BS we can cut is our perception that our organizations are not great places to work, when they are in many ways, as *the Leading Places to Work* studies have revealed. The recent Forbes piece "Using Culture to Attract Top Talent," suggested that we ask:

1. What does your company stand for?

2. How does it do things differently than your competitors? and

3. What do you expect from your employees?

If we can present crisp and compelling answers to these questions to teens and college students just starting to consider their career path -- not just what we do and how we do it – they may be more inclined give us a fair look at the beginning of their career explorations.

Graham spent 10 years at Hillel International in part because he saw the answer to these questions. He knew Hillel yearned excellence. He knew the high yet attainable expectations set of him. He knew they were setting a standard different from other Jewish organizations. As a Senior Associate in the Campus Strategic Services division, Graham acted essentially as an internal consulting firm for local Hillel organizations around the country, helping each enhance their internal operations. Perhaps not surprisingly, Graham's job was to help cut the BS out of their operational systems – reduce inefficiencies so local Hillel on campus run more smoothly, to everyone's benefit. Graham saw first-hand in Hillel the benefits of a virtuous cycle and striving for operational and program excellence rather than tolerating mediocrity.

Graham eventually left Hillel for AIPAC (the American Israel Public Affairs Committee), where he was serving as the Deputy Director of Development for nearly five years at the time of our 2017 interview. Graham lauds his time at AIPAC. It was an efficient operation. He knew exactly what he was supposed to do and what success in his job would look like. With his team, Graham supported, led, and advanced the fundraising work of nine regional and satellite offices around the country, designing and delivering fundraising materials and content, sharing AIPAC's story, and soliciting support. Graham's work with high-level donors and with the AIPAC endowment was interesting, enjoyable and, in his words, was highly fulfilling. It fed his creative drive just like curating ELI Talks fed Miriam's in Blessing #4, and it fueled his love for fostering relationships with donors and partners just as relationships fueled Ezra at Federation as discussed in Blessing #3. His AIPAC role was the first time he was fundraising as a full-time endeavor and, like Alyson in Blessing #2, Graham was encouraged to approach his work in a way that spoke to his talents and interests, creating the job around him, which helped change his preconceived notions about fundraising work and made him feel valued as his talents could do produce multiple successful results for the organization. The foundation for all of this was transparency and clarity in his work, and a collaborative team that didn't accept mediocrity and strove for excellence, improving its operational excellence in the process, cutting the BS, and further allowing Graham to feel motivated and valued in his work.

Interestingly, before working at AIPAC, Graham largely saw fundraising as someone in need, asking for money on behalf of a needy organization. Yet, at AIPAC, and now in his role as the CEO of the Jewish Federation and Jewish Community Foundation of Southern Arizona, Graham has a much different understanding of fundraising. He sees it as affording caring and well-meaning stakeholders with the opportunity to invest philanthropic resources in making a meaningful difference in the world. His time at AIPAC especially helped him see the big picture of what organizations are trying to achieve for the larger community and his role in that puzzle.

When the mission is clear, the operational process is working for the staff and not against them, and the job-content fits with the interests and passions of the candidate, one has the makings of a more perfect job situation for Jewish community professionals today, and would make them feel truly blessed. By cutting the BS, professionals like Graham thrive.

#4. SHARING THE WHY OF OUR WORK CAN ALSO REDUCE BS

Graham needs to have a passion for what the organization is committed to doing and achieving, and he needs to see how his work is tangibly and meaningfully helping to achieve its mission. This has been true for Graham, both at Hillel and AIPAC and now thus far in his work in Tucson.

It is an inefficiency or waste when Jewish community professionals perceive their work as "busy work." A simple remedy to preventing this BS is to share the why of our work and be sure everyone in the organization does work that directly supports and is aligned with this why. Each manager, on a regular basis, should consider auditing each of their staff's work tasks. We should ask, "is this work really necessary?" and "Can we accomplish what we are trying to do here more efficiently?"

After such review, we should remove work that is deemed not necessary. In addition, real important work can seem "busy" when we don't understand the rationale behind what we are doing. Simon Sinek, in his widely viewed TED TALK "How Great Leaders Inspire Action," advises companies to consider the WHY of their work and use this narrative as a selling point to consumers. He says famously, "people don't buy what you make, they buy who you are." People buy form Apple whose why is to "Think Different" and are engaged in the culture (and trust) of the company, and thus have bought not just computers but phones, watches, music, and more.

So too, managers can be clear with our employees about the WHY of their work both so they can understand the big picture, which we will talk more about in the next blessing, and so their work has meaning, which will motivate them. By not doing so, there can be misunderstanding, which can create confused or unhappy employees, precipitating high turnover and conflict. We can avoid BS when we make transparent the WHY. We can start by writing clear descriptions that articulate work expectations and connect them to the compelling organizational mission. We can facilitate staff meetings and gatherings with the organizational mission statement at the top of every agenda and connect our discussions with it closely in mind. By making the work more relevant, important, and mission-centric — articulating the WHY — the WHAT becomes more natural, fun, and compelling.

#5. CUTTING THE BS MEANS BEING REAL ABOUT COMPENSATION

For Graham, cutting the BS out of organizations includes being real with our Jewish community professionals about compensation. He has observed the role compensation can play in Jewish community professionals' overall job satisfaction. First, Graham pointed out to me that, in addition to salary, he experiences additional "compensation" at work, to use the term liberally but still authentically. He feels self-actualized at work, in part when BS is not in the picture, and the quality of life he experiences from having meaning, passion, and inspiration in what he is doing on a day-to-day basis improves.

Put another way, cutting the BS allows Jewish community professionals to feel more compensated because they feel their time is being honored. They feel invested when asked for input about how the organization can be more operationally excellent and when their employers care about the experiences they are having. While this isn't necessarily an excuse not to raise salaries, it is an important point that investing in the employee experience can start with investing in operational excellence, cutting the BS, and improving efficiencies as Ton suggests in her virtuous cycle. This will all help in retaining the talent that helps our organizations thrive.

Part of the BS is the lack of transparency around setting compensation. The 2018 Leading Places to Work Survey found that only 38% Jewish professionals understand how compensation is set at their organizations. Only 41% feel that they are fairly compensated for the work they do, and 37% believe their total compensation is fair relative to similar roles at other organizations. These negative feelings lead to high turnover.

For those who remain, it may be fair to argue that they have become institutionalized, tolerating the ensuing mediocrity when accustomed to lower levels of compensation or compensation that is set without transparency. These statistics should be alarming for anyone in a position of leadership in Jewish organizations. Ton's 2018 Harvard Business Review article sums it up brilliantly: "(clearly set) higher wages can turn mediocre jobs into good ones and average employees into high performers." We should heed her message and act.

To be sure, job candidates have their own responsibility to actively negotiate their salaries. At the same time, organizations can make initial salary offers intentionally above the market rate, demonstrating that they value the candidate from the start and want them to stay and thrive.

One of the approaches Graham has taken in his career is that he never takes a new job without a respectable compensation increase. Graham also believes that every Jewish organization should offer outstanding health insurance, an incredible benefit he considers when considering whether to make a move. Graham realized how good he had it at AIPAC, which also provided a significant retirement match. Strong compensation can come in many forms, and organizations must make this explicit.

#6. CUTTING THE BS MEANS REDUCING WASTED TIME, INCLUDING MEANINGLESS MEETINGS

Graham is constantly completing a number of tasks simultaneously, with quick bursts of productivity. He has both the ability to participate in multiple items simultaneously OR deeply focus at the exclusion of everything around him. He strives to only engage in meetings that are working meetings in which colleagues come together to make decisions, move projects forward, or solve problems. He tries to avoid the "Death by Meeting" that Patrick Lencioni coined in his book of the same name, in which little work moves forward and participants feels that time is wasted.

Meetings are another example of BS in our work culture, especially meetings that don't need to happen, meetings with no agenda, or meetings where team members do not feel heard or appreciated. Mamie Kanfer Stewart and her organization MEETEOR, advocate for streamlining meetings, making them more efficient and including every voice. I most appreciate the following tips:

1. Have an agenda with a specific goal to achieve,

2. Use a protocol that allows all voices to be heard and respected,

3. Time each section and have a time keeper to keep you true to your plan, and

4. Be careful whom you invite, and do not require folks to be present who really don't need to be there.

Implementing these four steps immediately will raise engagement by team members, make them feel heard, make time together more productive and enriching, and, of course, eliminate the BS.

LOW ON BS → HIGH ON VALUE

While strong compensation is critical, Graham also points to professional development and the opportunity for growth, both examples of investing in staff and pursuing operational excellence that is the opposite of BS. To be at a place where he feels invested not just by a supervisor but the organization itself is, in his words, "tremendous." He encourages organizations to engage in career mapping for their staff. An operational excellence approach includes not only hiring for current needs but also looking ahead. If we hire talent with the idea that they can grow in the organization and chart a path for them, they'll be much more motivated to work hard now, knowing where this could lead.

A year into his new role in Tucson, Graham is thrilled to be able to address some of the challenges he sees to the big picture of the Jewish future at a local level. He also knows the responsibility of the CEO is to take charge in cutting the BS and encourage operational efficiencies and staff investment, bringing Ton's virtuous cycle to life.

Jewish community professionals like Graham have big ideas, strong values, and intense opinions. If we are able to demonstrate to staff members like Graham that we commit to removing the inefficiencies and avoidable problems in our organizations, we will be on a better track to properly blessing our workforce to the long-term benefit of our organizations and community.

QUESTIONS FOR REFLECTION

1. Are our organizations smart with its resources? If so, how do we best promote this to our teens and young adults having these incredible Jewish experiences? If not, how can we fix this and what is the P.R. we need to deliver to our future talent that we indeed are becoming more efficient so they'll want to work for us?

2. How might we have discussions with staff, presenting Ton's Virtuous Cycle (vs. Vicious Cycle) and pose the question: "How can we be more operationally excellent?" How might we have staff propose solutions and let them own the task of designing and implementing them?

3. Think about our meetings – are they effective or just another example of wasted time (or nonsense or BS) in your organization? How might we try to implement the 4 strategies Mamie Kanfer Stewart proposes?

empower them to see the big picture

Blessing Summary — Jewish community professionals don't only want to perform their given task or project; they want to be a part of the big picture discussions that shape our future. Inviting Jewish community professionals at all organizational levels to join leadership "on the balcony" will strengthen their interests in the mission and add to their feeling that they are valued by leadership.

During my time at JTS, first-year graduate students studying to earn a Master's Degree in Jewish Education met every Wednesday morning for a *mifgash*, (encounter) facilitated by the school's Rabbi-in-Residence at the time, Rabbi Jonathan Lipnick. It is a non-credit but still mandatory seminar and an opportunity for students to reflect outside of class on what they are learning in their courses, to share their challenges, to explore their aspirations as educators, and to gain additional learning that will benefit their career beyond the course curriculum.

I had the pleasure of teaching a session each year entitled, "Navigating the Jewish Educational Landscape." During the hour, I attempted to provide students a tour of the categories of Jewish organizations: religious movements, community organizations (Federation, JCCs, Hillel), institutes of higher education, social justice groups, Israel education and advocacy organizations, and so on. More importantly, we discussed how these organizations fit and work together.

None of our organizations work in a vacuum. When I led this session, our graduate students leaned in as they recognized the importance of appreciating "the big picture" of our Jewish organizational eco-system. Rabbi Laura Baum, our next portrait, is both motivated to participate and feels valued when she is part of a big-picture conversation. Laura exemplifies the Jewish community professional who is motivated when working on the balcony of Jewish life.

Laura happens to be the only ordained rabbi among the thirteen Jewish community professionals I interviewed for this project. Laura has worked mostly outside the pulpit in community organizations and sees her "flock" as the Jewish community *b'gadol*, or at large. Laura explored the idea of becoming a rabbi when she shadowed a rabbi in New Jersey while completing an externship program during her undergraduate studies at Yale. Laura had many conversations with him about what it would mean to be rabbi. It is worth pointing out again the influence of a mentor to help guide talent towards the Jewish non-profit sector and being an initial source of valuing one's commitment to this work.

The rabbi offered Laura a job teaching and performing various pastoral and administrative duties for the congregation. Before she accepted, Laura went to the rabbi she grew up with at her home congregation to share her interest in becoming a rabbi, as well as this job offer. Not expecting it, Laura's childhood rabbi offered her a similar job. Thus, Laura decided to head home, and worked at her home congregation for 2 years. She was called a Rabbinic Intern though she wasn't in Rabbinical School yet, teaching in the early childhood program, religious school, and teen program. This formative experience solidified for Laura that she wanted to be a Jewish community professional for her career.

After two years working at her home congregation, Laura enrolled at Hebrew Union College-Jewish Institute of Religion, studying in Israel for one year and Cincinnati, Ohio for the final 4 years of the program. During her final two years, Laura completed a Rabbinic internship at an independent (not affiliated with a specific movement of Judaism) congregation, which hired her upon Laura's ordination. This particular congregation had both in person and online-only engagement. In the mid-2000's, the "virtual synagogue," was still avant-garde for the Jewish community at the time (what a different place we are in with online worship at the end of 2020!). This gave Laura the opportunity to be in both the traditional congregational environment and the Jewish start-up world simultaneously, and, because it was virtual, engaging congregants located throughout the country, she was forced to take a big picture, or balcony, look at what the larger constituency's needs and challenges were.

About the Balcony

Ronald Heifetz and Marty Linsky of Harvard write in their leadership manifesto *Leadership on the Line* that "achieving a balcony perspective means taking yourself out of the dance, in your mind, even if only for a moment. The only way you can gain both a clearer view of reality and some perspective on the bigger picture is by distancing yourself from the fray. Otherwise, you are likely to misperceive the situation and make the wrong diagnosis, leading you to misguided decisions about whether and how to intervene" (Heifetz and Linsky, *Leadership on the Line*).

Heifetz and Linsky present their balcony idea in the context of introducing the concept of adaptive leadership which, in part, advises leaders not to look for technical solutions to larger and more complex problems often connected to culture. How we change the way we manage our people, for example, is an adaptive problem or challenge. While there may be technical approaches, such as writing clearer job descriptions or raising salaries that can help us better value our employees, the adaptive approach changes the culture in which we manage and nurture our talent. We must change people's belief systems around effective management and the fundamental role of managers when it comes to viewing and supporting their workforce. This involves change, which includes a feeling of loss among many when the status quo, which may be just fine for many people in our field, starts to shift. This is what makes adaptive leadership so difficult.

Yet adaptive leadership is the approach that can most often yield the best long-term results, and to best approach an adaptive problem, we must get on the balcony to gain multiple perspectives on this issue. This book, for example, is an opportunity for all of us to get on that balcony and notice the realities Jewish community professionals are facing from different vantage points.

Getting on the balcony is a huge motivator for Laura, who has found herself drawn towards positions that allow her to figure out problems and solutions. Perhaps veering off a more traditional path, during her last semester at HUC, Laura started business school to earn her MBA. She wanted to be sure she had the skills to be a stellar Jewish community professional leader and manager at a Jewish organization. With a rabbinic degree and MBA in hand, she moved to Boston and, at the time of this interview in fall 2017, Laura had been working for approximately three years at the Combined Jewish Philanthropies or CJP, the official name of the Jewish Federation of Boston, Massachusetts.

Laura never expected to work for a Federation. She was, in fact, recruited, because she was as told by her eventual boss when she was interviewing for the position that she is, "someone who thinks outside the box and pushes boundaries. She's not someone who would just keep doing the same thing for its own sake but would bring new thinking that would make the organization and the Jewish community better." She was hired to challenge CJP, ask hard questions, think differently – to deeply understand what CJP does and "take them to the next level." Laura called this the best professional pick up line she could have heard. She was sold, in part, because she was to play a key role in strategizing the course of CJP's support of Jewish education and engagement throughout Boston. She was hired to be a big player, charged with looking at the big picture and helping to develop the large-scale strategies to transform Jewish education and make change. Laura relished this challenge.

Big Picture Professionals Love to Think, Act, Evaluate, and Think Some More

Laura's role at CJP required critical thinking and observation about Jewish community, Jewish engagement, and Jewish learning across an entire city. She focused on an entire eco-system and the Jewish life-cycle thinking about the Jewish educational handoffs within a child's Jewish educational journey from early childhood to Jewish day school or part-time religious school to becoming a bar-mitzvah to teen experiences and beyond, and how organizations or less-structured groups come together to create a menu of options for Jewish Boston. Laura found taking this 30,000 ft view fascinating. The results of this examination were to make recommendations and take-action to improve Jewish community.

Laura's team also completed a strategic planning process that studied current and new models of Jewish engagement. This gave Laura even more great questions to think about, including: How do we bring people in to Jewish community? How do we engage them more in Jewish life? How do we engage them more in CJP? How do we give them voice? And, how do we deepen their engagement once they are connected? Laura was in a position to allocate significant resources and thus in a position to make what are often challenging decisions on what areas of Jewish education to invest in and determining funding levels. As Laura put it, "it's a big and fun part of the job to be able to grapple with really big questions."

The opportunity to work from the balcony gives Jewish community professionals like Laura context to effectively approach the work and make critical decisions. Laura feels in the loop on the big discussions, referencing both the collaborative spirit in CJP that she experienced. To Laura, participating in the big picture conversation allows the processes of the organization to be transparent and clear for her, which helps reduce the frustrations Jewish community professionals can often feel when they are not, as we discussed in our last blessing. This is clear from the Leading Places to Work Survey in 2018, which stated that only 53% of Jewish community professionals "believe there is open and honest two-way communication" between employees and leadership in Jewish organizations, which is 12% below the US Benchmark. This includes having a deeper sense of what is happening within an organization. When staff feel heard and are privy to the big picture, they, as we see with Laura, feel motivated and valued which, as we have been arguing all along, is great for business.

Unlike previous blessings, there is no equation, flow chart, or cycle to present that can help us best apply this blessing to our staff and in our work settings as leaders. This process is simple. Get to know each staff member - here is a blessing reminder to schedule those coffee dates - and make a sincere invitation to invite professionals onto the balcony and become involved in big picture conversations within the organization. Most importantly, allow them, like Laura felt at CJP and currently does as now the head of school at Rockwern Academy in Cincinnati, to feel they have input and can be heard.

Getting employees who want to be in the big picture conversation requires several steps, many of which reflect our previously discussed blessings:

Time, Work/Life Balance, and Leave Time

Like so many juggling careers and family-life, there are times that work can feel overwhelming. Laura says it's important to not lose sight of the big picture, even in the busiest moments. As a working mom, Laura especially valued the parental leave that CJP provided when she had her first child.

Thanks in large part to the leadership of Shifra Bronznick and the work of Advancing Women's Professionals, hundreds of Jewish organizations have adopted paid parental leave policies so Jewish community professionals such as Laura, who no larger have to rely on just 12 weeks of unpaid leave with the national Family Medical Leave Act (FMLA) or having to exhaust vacation and sick time in order to be paid while taking care of a newborn. As of 2015 over 100 Jewish organizations adopted paid leave policies, and scores more have followed. The problem of no employee parental paid leave policy, however, remains a reality for a significant number of Jewish organizations today.

Out of Balance Compensation

Laura, like Graham, has skills that could be applied in the corporate sector, perhaps at a higher wage. Also, like Graham, Laura loves the work she does and loves the opportunity each day to make a difference in people's lives. It is important to Laura that Jewish community professionals are compensated appropriately for their work. During her previous role at CJP, she focused on the costs of a family engaging in Jewish life, including Jewish camp, day school, teen Israel trips, synagogue membership, and other experiences. Struggling to afford Jewish education for one's family, for example, prohibits Jewish community professionals from being fully present and able to focus on the big picture.

Thinking Big Picture Means Letting Go of the Status Quo

Maya Bernstein, a thought leader in the Jewish community and most recently an associate for the Jewish social entrepreneurial organization Upstart, has written in *Gleanings*, the e-journal of the William Davidson School at JTS, that effective leadership is "an activity with a clear purpose, and that the work of leadership involves being brutally honest about what is working and what is not." Often those in positions who could exercise leadership avoid the conversations in which we must be brutally honest. As a result, the status quo remains.

Laura expressed to me that in her professional roles, she is not interested in simply maintaining the status quo in Jewish life. She doesn't want to make current programs slightly better and merely tweak on the margins. She is much more interested in what we keep, let go of, and make significantly better, and scanning the big picture of Jewish education to identify the "bright spots" and then devising strategies to scale their success. In other words, while she doesn't feel we need to blow everything up, we cannot keep current practices and policies in place merely for their own sake or because that is the least complicated of routes. This can perpetuate mediocrity instead of striving for and achieving excellence.

Operating with Slack

One of the most difficult challenges for Laura is when her team is understaffed. When she has vacancies, there is more pressure on Laura to advance work projects despite fewer team members. Often, this is due to a lack of resources, not necessarily a lack of talent in the field, which is further demotivating because the talent is out there to support Laura and her team and eliminate this challenge, yet the talent isn't available to Laura and her team when they need it most.

Dr. Zeynep Ton offers a solution one of her principles of operational excellence that addresses the issue of limited resources. She describes the principle as "operating with slack." She has found evidence that, in the retail industry, "model retailers cut waste everywhere they can find it except when it comes to labor. There, they like to err on the side of too much labor – or over staffing deliberately building slack into their staffing." For retail, this means "more labor hours on hand than what it expects the workload to be, which reduces costs by preventing the operational problems that come from understaffing, and so more employees are involved in continuous improvement of operations." (Ton, *The Good Jobs Strategy*).

For Jewish non-profits, we can view limited resources as an inefficiency as we discussed in the previous blessing. Employees who work in environments when there are not enough or just enough employees to get the work done can easily feel overwhelmed, especially when an employee calls in sick, goes on leave, or is tasked with an additional assignment. Those who remain can't actually do the work or do it well, which can lead to inefficiencies, mistakes, waste, and employee frustration. Ton suggests that we hire more resources than we actually need. Thus, when there are unexpected vacancies, we still have plenty of resources to operate effectively, without creating undue stress on professionals like Laura. Even during a pandemic, when resources are lean, we can still apply operating with slack by cross-training staff in various different skills – ensuring there are "back-ups" for given positions and a nimbleness among the workforce.

This is another adaptive challenge for Jewish organizations. As we discussed in the last chapter, overhead, which often includes staffing, has historically not been as valued by individual donors or foundations as it should be, and therefore organizations only receive the grant or donor funds or membership dues necessary to operate, which often means without sufficient slack. This stresses our employees and have less operational excellence. We are now back to the vicious cycle.

This, again, is why we need to practice going on to the balcony, just where Laura likes to be. Between our interview until the publication of this book, Laura has completed her first year as the head of school at Rockwern Academy in Cincinnati, returning to Ohio both for family reasons and because, as a head of school, she too can focus on the big picture of an entire community, collaborate with multiple departments, and lead with her values of staff investment and growth.

Laura recognizes each day that she has the opportunity to make a lasting difference in people's lives. She can be the voice that proclaims that the Jewish community is evolving and changing and that the communal organizations must be responsive and pro-active to these changes. She is motivated by not operating towards the status quo. It's exciting for her to think of herself at the leading edge of Jewish history – predicting about what trends are next and how to respond.

QUESTIONS FOR REFLECTION

1. How might we invite our teams to examine their work from 30,000 ft (the balcony)? Might we start be asking them for their input and perspective on big picture issues to help them each understand the big picture goals and challenges of their work?

2. Examine your team and organizational chart. Are you operating with enough slack? How might we add to or re-organize our staff to ensure there are ample individuals to complete the various jobs that need to be done in order to achieve operational excellence and efficiency even when a team member may be absent?

3. How might we invite your team into the field (in person or virtually) where they can connect with Jewish community professionals in other sub-sectors of the Jewish professional field to learn about their work and see if it connects to our team's interests curiosities? Making these connections could further realize each team member's potential, and be an added motivator to retaining them in our sector long term.

bringing their whole integrated selves to work

Blessing Summary — Jewish community professionals have personal and professional identities that often feel naturally blended together. We can invite Jewish community professionals to bring these personal attributes, interests, and vulnerabilities into their work content and work space. In doing so, they'll be more motivated and feel more valued if they are able to bring their whole integrated selves to work.

While at JTS, my colleague Cheryl Magen and I would often advise graduate students that there is an important rule when it comes to positions in Jewish community professional life: "part time means full time, and full time means all the time." Whether due to leadership's expectations or our constant connection with technology, there is a sense that we are always on, especially when Jewish community professionals reach positions of middle management or senior leadership. This may feel even more true now working remotely during a pandemic.

The "all the time," reality of Jewish life is concerning given our talent's need for work/life balance, which we will re-visit again in Blessing #15. To infer in this rule that Jewish community professionals never truly have the rest they need to reflect and recharge is problematic and counter to what Judaism teaches us. We must honor the message of the fourth commandment, found first in the book of Exodus and again in

Deuteronomy, requiring us to keep Shabbat and make it a holy time from the rest of the week. For those of us who have both kept Shabbat in a meaningfully way whether *halachically* (by the precepts of Jewish law) or otherwise, we have experienced how Shabbat allows us to relax and recuperate so we are then ready for the new week. When we work through the Sabbath and do not have the time to rest and recharge, we can remain tired and depleted, which is an unhealthy practice and will lead to professional burnout. To that end, it is critical that we make some adjustments to our "all the time" culture.

One such adjustment can be to help our Jewish community professionals inherently and healthily blend their professional work and personal interests. We can consider how we as managers and leaders can model and encourage our staff to bring their whole integrated selves to work. Our culture trains us to spend so much time either present at, performing, or thinking about work, it would suit us well as managers and leaders to craft the work experience to allow an entire individual to shine, feel seen, heard, visible, and self-actualized. This is what motivates Becky Voorwinde, the Executive Director of the Bronfman Fellowship.

Becky works to bring her whole self to work each day. It helps her harness the energy she needs as a busy and passionate executive director who seeks to both deliver results to the organization and nurture her own personal well-being while at work. She feels fortunate to be in a position in which she feels she can be authentically herself, just like she is at home or in other situations. She ensures that she makes time for her in all spaces of her life, be it work, family, or time outside these two buckets, to maintain motivation and to thrive, and she works with her organizational leadership to maintain this working system and ensure it works for the culture and goals of the organization. As we go through Becky's narrative, we will identify the strategies that we each could employ with our staff to feel encouraged to bring their whole integrated selves to work, thus further motivating and blessing them.

Let us first, though, understand this notion of what bringing one's whole integrated self to work means. For this we turn to Mike Robbins, in his recently published book, who talks about what the title phrase means to him:

> *"Bringing our whole selves to work means showing up authentically, leading with humility, and remembering that we're all vulnerable, imperfect human beings doing the best we can. It's also about having the courage to take risks, speak up, ask for help, connect with others in a genuine way, and allow us to be truly seen. It's not always easy for us to show up this way, especially at work. And it takes commitment, intention, and courage for leaders and organizations to create environments that are conducive to this type of authenticity and humanity." (Robbins, Bring Your Whole Selves to Work).*

I highlight authenticity, humility, and being vulnerable as the responsibility managers and leaders to create the environments necessary for our employees to feel comfortable to show up to work. To that end, I present a series of questions we have to ask ourselves as workers ourselves, and then as managers responsible for our employees' workplace experiences:

- **Authenticity:** Do we present ourselves at work in the ways that we actually are in other parts of our lives?

- **Humility:** Do we listen intently to our colleagues before we speak? Do we allow ourselves to share our mistakes and missteps? Do we openly admit that we were wrong? Do we allow our staff (rather than ourselves) to take the credit?

- **Vulnerability:** Do we share our fears and our concerns with others, including when we fall short on a project or don't always have the knowledge to move forward? Do we allow ourselves to hear openly critical feedback and be okay with accepting and reflecting on it instead of refuting or disregarding it? Do we allow others to share openly their vulnerabilities in a safe and inviting space at work?

Once we address these questions for ourselves, we can broach them with our staff, discovering whether our teams really feel comfortable to be authentic, humble, and vulnerable in the work place. It may be that they feel the culture hasn't allowed or invited them to be their full authentic and integrated selves.

I'd like to offer one of Robbins' equations as the next in our series of schematics to our how we can bless our workforce, and then add to it. For his principle, Be Authentic, Robbins suggests that "honesty minus self-righteousness plus vulnerability equals authenticity." (Robbins, *Bring Your Whole Selves to Work*).

When leadership is authentic by being honest, eliminating any expression of self-righteousness or self-importance, and adding the display of our own vulnerabilities, we become more authentic and we model this for our staff, which fuels their motivations and feeling of value, or, in another virtuous cycle form:

BRINGING OUR WHOLE INTEGRATED SELF TO THE WORK VIRTUOUS CYCLE

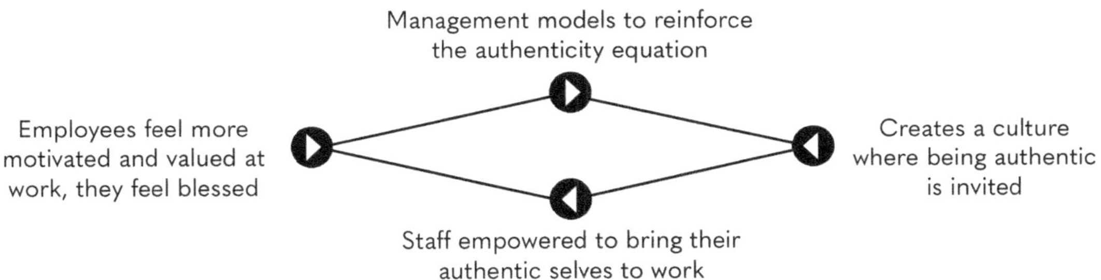

What also strikes me about Robbins' reflections is the notion of visibility, that employees desire to be fully seen and heard in the workplace. Our workforce functions at their best if our workers feel that their entire selves are present to those around them and, perhaps most importantly, to themselves. He defines appreciation as "acknowledging a person's inherent value." Often this can be accomplished through crafting a role that fits with the person's talents, interests, values and attributes.

Speaking personally, I certainly have felt appreciated in this way. During my time song leading at Jewish camp I often took the opportunity to perform the original songs I had written when not at camp, including them along with the Jewish and English folk songs I was required to song lead. When I would sing my own tunes, especially when they were well received, I often felt like I was approaching a form of professional heaven and Flow we discussed in Blessing #4. I was still fulfilling the goals of my job and was able to bring a deeper, fuller sense of me while doing so. In addition, the campers and fellow staff got to see this part of me. This was deeply meaningful and part of the reason I returned as the camp song leader for five wonderful summers. To Robbins' point, my full authentic self was literally being seen and heard. I was able to mix the part of my heart that desired to show my Jewish self, musical self, teacher self, creative self, and social-community self all into one integrated whole. I felt motivated to perform at my best, validated and valued each time my director or peers honored me for who I was and what I brought to camp.

This wasn't just about sharing my original songs. I was in a role and managed in such a way that I could take care of me in the process. I felt the autonomy that we talked about in Blessing #1, whether being granted an hour off to go for a run to clear my head and center myself before leading Friday evening services or empowered to set the vision for the camp's Jewish and musical experiences. I was granted both the time to care for myself and invited to bring my own ideas and self to my work.

Ironically, the notion of bringing our whole selves to work seems to run counter to the way many of us have been taught to think about our time and space in the world. We think work time is for work and that we are in service to someone or something else. As a result of this thinking, we view our personal goals and interests as existing outside of work only, and that work time encroaches on personal time. For many of us who have busy work roles and family lives, finding the space for "me time" can be frustrating. We can be demotivated at work and at home if we don't get sufficient me time.

Becky's narrative highlights how we can encourage employees to bring a bit of that "me time" to work. Becky's integrated self-approach has been evident to her for as long as he can remember and has been heavily influenced by her love for and connection to Judaism and Jewish life. She received a Jewish day school education until eighth grade and shuffled between Jewish experiences of Modern Orthodox Jewish life with her father and Conservative Judaism with her mother. She had exposure to many different homes and Jewish communities in her childhood and adolescence, feeling at home in many of them. While some of Becky's peers rolled their eyes during Jewish experiences, she loved them.

For Becky, integrating her Jewish self with the rest of her life has been an authentic act for her because she was modeled this from a young age by family, teachers, and mentors alike. When Becky was in second grade, her Judaic Studies teacher, Tzvi, would write the name of a student in the class who asked a phenomenal question, and that name would stay up there until another phenomenal question was asked – sometimes for the entire school year. Becky recalls asking a question (she doesn't recall what the question was and wishes she remembered!) that got her name on that board. It was a special accomplishment for Becky. This experience taught her about the value of questions, and that being in dialogue is core to Jewish practice and tradition. She hasn't forgotten this in any aspect of her life today, including the workplace.

In seventh grade, Becky began attending Camp Ramah in New England. She recalls experiencing, in her words, "wonderful and enriching Jewish experiential learning." She continued at Ramah for many more years as a camper and then staff summers thereafter, first as a counselor and then as *Rosh Edah* (unit head), which she describes as the most exhausting and challenging position thus far in her life which she found powerful and all encompassing. She was living out her Jewish self in her work self while fostering the relationships that kept her engaged and with a feeling of belonging, teaching her the value of bringing one's authentic self and integrating it into one's work.

Becky learned how to bring her whole integrated self to work at summer camp. Camp is often a setting in which campers and staff are encouraged to discover and practice being their full and multiple aspects of themselves. In a way, we can think of this particular blessing as bringing the best of summer camp, and similar immersive experiences, to the workplace. Summer camp is a type of place that allows individuals to become self-actualized, which psychologist Abraham Maslow considered the top level in his hierarchy of needs. Peter Scales, a noted researcher, writes on the American Camping Association (ACA) website:

> *The biggest plus of camp is that camps help young people discover and explore their talents, interests, and values. Most schools don't satisfy all these needs. Kids who have had these kinds of (camp) experiences end up being healthier and have less problems which concern us all.*

Jewish community work can also help our employees discover and explore their talents, interests, and values if we allow such an authentic culture to thrive. When we do, we will benefit greatly as staff members become more passionate in their workplaces, which extends to their work and engaging with their constituencies.

With Becky's early formative experiences and their power in mind, we can better appreciate what this phrase, bringing our whole integrated selves to work, means to her. To be an integrated human being for Becky is "when one's work, values, and all of one's interactions can mesh in one holistic experience, and when one does not have to push part of oneself aside to fit into a specific area of one's life experience." Put another way, home/family Becky, work Becky, Jewish Becky, creative Becky, and business Becky, can all be the same Becky, and all can exist, be present, and be visible and vulnerable in each setting of her life. She was able to experience this for the first time in second grade and again at summer camp, and she aspires to continue experiencing this in her work today leading the Bronfman Fellowship.

Bringing her whole integrated self to work wasn't always easy for Becky, and it remains a daily challenge. During college, like many of us may have felt, Becky felt a bit lost - searching for this ideal state. She majored in American Studies with a focus on American Jewish History and Literature, an acceptable major if her career dream remained becoming an academic. After she met her now husband Michael during her study abroad program, Becky's plans and aspirations began to change, and she soon found herself in a work life for several years in consulting, both for corporate and non-profit organizations outside the Jewish organizational world, followed by roles in the area of corporate responsibility, most recently for a large accounting firm.

Becky found the accounting firm a wonderful place for learning and professional growth. Yet, her major and ongoing challenge was that there seemed to be a very specific way a worker was supposed to be in the work place. It was not a culture that allowed for much individuality. Perhaps obviously, there was also little room to integrate her Jewish self into her work. This contrasted with her former work experiences in Jewish contexts in which she thrived. At Camp Ramah, on the contrary, she was able to bring her whole integrated self to her work experiences while at the corporate accounting firm, her Jewish self and personal self largely had to remain dormant.

Between her time and Camp Ramah and the accounting firm was her participation as a senior in high school with the Bronfman Fellowship, a leadership development program for graduating high school students in Israel and North America with experiences throughout the year in both Israel and the United States. This was a golden opportunity for Becky as a teen to foster deep relationships with peers and teachers from multiple cultures, and to broaden her horizons and her understanding of what she could accomplish.

It was fortuitous then, if not *b'shert* (meant to be), that, while at the firm, just at the time she was feeling frustrated that parts of herself were invisible at work, Becky received a call from the board president of the Bronfman Fellowship asking her to apply to be their director of alumni engagement. At the time, it wasn't clear for Becky that this was going to be the right move. Though she wasn't able to bring her full authentic and integrated self to work at the accounting firm, she was performing exceptionally well and steadily rising up the corporate ladder. It wasn't perfect, but she was content. She actually recalls deleting the email from the alumni board president and even suggested to someone else that they should apply. Thankfully though, the board president was persistent. He knew something that Becky didn't yet realize. Becky's husband Michael knew it too, taking one look at the job and saying exuberantly to Becky, "It's got your name written all over it, totally you, on every level; put your hat in the ring and see where it goes."

It has been well over a decade since that inflection point, and Becky has now risen to the position of executive director. The Bronfman Fellowship has allowed Becky to be her integrated self in part because her own fellowship experience was her first pluralistic experience. Previous to the fellowship she was in purely denominational or movement-oriented experiences: Modern Orthodox synagogue, a Conservative day school, and a Conservative Jewish summer camp. Finding Jewish life outside of a movement was very freeing and helped her discover what mattered to her Jewishly outside of an institutional framework.

In addition, Becky and Michael, who is a person of another faith, were seeking to find a Jewish community in sync with their values of pluralism and openness to all families (Becky and Michael have personally chosen to raise their children exclusively Jewish). As a program alumna, Becky initially sought out the Bronfman Fellowship when her family returned to New York – to fill in this gap that her previous professional role was lacking. She became a volunteer, advisor, and member of the alumni board even though she didn't initially see a professional future there.

Examining Becky's work experiences more deeply, let us consider tactical strategies to bring this Blessing to life for each of our staff:

Allow our Employees to Make Their Work in Their Own Image

At Bronfman, Becky doesn't have to fit in to the mold like she did at the accounting firm; she can make her work in her own image – sharing and living her values at work, designing her hours to fit her family, incorporating what loves into what she does. This reminds me of the Jewish value of b'tzelem Elohim, that we are all made in the image of the divine. We all have something in our full selves that we can offer to the people and organizations we are a part of: our traditions, ethnicities, interests, talents, family, and curiosities. Every bit of all of us is divine. Let us invite our staff figure out how their job goals fit into their personal attributes, Jewishly and otherwise. This exploration can start during those coffee dates. This is certainly a corollary to Blessing #4, allowing them feed their creative drive.

Mitigate Work Conflicts with Transparency, and Promote Kindness at Work

As the top executive, Becky has to navigate issues of strategic sustainability, fundraising and visioning for the organization and how it fits with budget constraints, so that the funders understand how the numbers fit the story and goals of the organization. Throughout this work, Becky recognizes that sometimes feelings are hurt. As a result, Becky works to manage complaints whether from her board or her staff. She doesn't avoid these conflicts. She approaches them head on with conversations that are transparent and with kindness. Her approach validates her staff's concerns, leaves them feeling seen and heard and, even if they disagree with her decisions, they know the why behind them. They still feel valued and thus encouraged to continue to bring their full selves to work.

Choosing Our Work

To a considerable degree, Becky chooses the things she wants to do. As the executive she, of course, has considerable latitude of how she wants to spend her time relative to her staff, though she is intentional about trying to provide autonomy for her staff as well. Becky, like her staff, has to complete tasks she doesn't always love to do. Yet she works to balance these less-desirable tasks with those she relishes. For example, Becky wants to be wrapped in the work content that gives her energy, which includes meeting with applicants to the fellowship. She recognizes that this is time consuming and doesn't have to be part of her role, yet it gives her what she needs to do the overall job well. This, too, is part of Becky bringing her whole integrated self to her work, crafting the position around her own talents and interests while still recognizing and completing, as Stephen Covey puts it in his book, *The 7 Habits of Highly Effective People*, the "jobs (that need to be) to be done."

Offering Balance, and Focusing on Results

We see that both the executives and other management staff profiled in this book are often pulled in multiple directions. The number of decisions Becky has to make in a day or week can often feel exhausting. Becky recognizes that one of her personal challenges is that, if a small decision is in front of her, she'll fully engage with it even if she should be delegating or giving this small decision less time, which can lead to feeling that her whole job is overwhelming. However difficult, she thus works to ensure balance between being supportive and overseeing quality control with her staff while also not micromanaging. She encourages this with her staff well, encouraging them to practice balance and focusing on the larger results of one's work rather than giving minor tasks too much time and priority.

Further, we must allow our staff to take care of their home life business when necessary, even during work hours, as long as they are not abusing this flexibility and unavailable during essential times. Regardless of whether they have families at home or not, Jewish community professionals will feel more present and fully themselves at work if they know they don't have to shut their home life off, as long as at the end of the day or week, they get their work done.

Improper Compensation Can Only Get in the Way

When Becky moved to Bronfman, there was no reduction in compensation although Bronfman offered a less generous benefits package. As a seasoned professional, Becky knew what to ask for in negotiation, including a strong paid parental leave. She had the knowledge and confidence to negotiate, allowing her compensation needs to align, not be a deterrent, to making the job change into the Jewish world. To advocate for her compensation package also allowed her to bring her whole integrated self to work. As we've discussed throughout this book, Jewish community professionals are not motivated primarily by the money, yet the compensation package does represent how the organization values them, and a generous package allows compensation not to get in the way of employees embracing what they truly value in the role: working for an inspiring mission, fostering relationships, being creative, and so on, including Becky being able to bring her whole integrated self to her work.

Becky's salary has grown significantly in light of her new responsibilities. She feels well compensated despite having very little expendable or discretionary income. She lives in Park Slope , Brooklyn, with a full-time nanny and, at the time of our interview, was paying for preschool for her two children. These are choices, she recognizes. She also views the compensation for her staff as a constant challenge, noting that if it isn't where it needs to be, our professionals can become stressed over their lives. We don't want them to have to ask, "how can I pay for what I need?" rather, "how can I bring my whole self to work in order to do my best work?" The latter question is the conversation we want each of our professionals to have each day. Becky tries to set compensation levels for staff so they are thinking about this second question rather than the first.

Allowing our Professionals 20% Time For a Passion Project

Google is known for its 20% time rule, allowing employees to use up to 20% of their work time to devote to a passion project of their choice. It is what helped them create now core products such as Gmail and Google Maps. Inc.com has highlighted that the 20%-time rule spawns many positive benefits that lead toward strengthening employee motivations and retention, including a feeling of empowerment, driving to innovate, both of which strengthens corporate culture. This is another strategy to help employees bring their full and integrated selves to work. Becky, for example, loves thinking about and implementing educational theory. She shared with me that it is hard working in an environment where most of the educators are rabbis and professors, so she looks at her value added as bringing the social-emotional aspect, thinking about the diversity of ideas and texts the Bronfman Fellowship can offer to their participants, and then helping bring the best out of the educators she hires. Researching texts isn't part of her executive director role, but it isn't not part of her role either. It sparks her curiosity and interest, which strengthens the experience both of her work life and of the fellowship.

Much of this *Bless Our Workforce* book project has been researched, written, and edited as a 20% work time project. Writing a book about how we bless our workforce wasn't explicitly in my job description when I was the managing director of the Leadership Commons at JTS. That said, it is a project that I am passionate about that will also support Jewish leadership development, which runs to the core purpose of my work, including supporting talent in the JCC Movement in my role with JCC Association. Working on this book has helped helps me do the core part of my role better and with more energy, as I bring more of my own personal interests and integrated self to work.

An X-Factor in Truly Being Seen — Gender Bias in the Jewish Workplace

Becky has personally experienced sexism in the Jewish world. As a younger woman, she recalls that sexist attitudes only amplified as she became more senior in her work. For example, she has often felt pigeonholed as a good administrator and not a holder of wisdom because she is a woman. She has often been reminded that she used to be the co-executive director, partnered with a younger male Rabbi who was seen as the vision and wisdom behind the venture, whereas Becky may have been seen as the *numbers* woman, keeping it altogether in the background.

Becky and her co-director were true partners, yet Becky observed that folks nearly always assumed that he was the more important one in leadership. When he decided to move on, the questions that were asked of Becky were, in her heart, downright hurtful: "Who could possibly replace him?" and "How can you possibly replace him?" They were looking past her and it was hard to maintain her confidence and bring her integrated self to work for a period of time. She had to overcome the many assumptions that a female non-clergy member could take over a role she was already flourishing in but was assumed to be insufficient to fill.

On a subtler level, Becky often notices that she and other women are interrupted or spoken down to frequently in the workplace. She also finds that, while any executive has to deal with participants or lay leaders who complain, these individuals more quickly and more frequently share complaints with her than with male counterparts. She's open, available, and perhaps less physically intimidating than most men, which leads people to have less of a filter with her. While there is certainly a benefit to her being perceived as open and welcoming, she senses a sexist element: she can be the relational leader but not the visionary or scholarly leader that she is just as qualified to be. To be perceived in such a way simply because of one's gender directly challenges the feeling that one can bring their whole integrated unique and authentic self to work. It is thus incumbent upon us to view all of our actions, including when we support and partner with our colleagues, through a gender lens. Our intention may not be to act through bias we must act with *kavanah*, intention, examining our actions so we steer free of bias, further allowing our employees to be the full authentic and integrated selves at work, without consequence.

Becky is still figuring out what the optimal professional role is for her. She has loved her current role and yet knows it may not last forever. She wonders, for her and all of us, how we keep being able to bring our whole integrated selves to work when variables change?

A wonderful exercise to suggest to our employees: ask them to list the passions, curiosities and interests that light them up and have them share with each other and leadership Have them share their interests that may not have been evident until now. Employees should also share with us what they need and where they hope to add value. We first must listen and try, as best we can, to align the context of the jobs that need to be done to who our talent are in all aspects of their being.

We can reflect on valuing our Jewish community professionals through the lens of both personal responsibility and a collective care, focusing on what each individual can give in the ways they can and want to. When we take care of each other and claim responsibility for ourselves and each other at work, we can move forward with generating and implementing big ideas that can move Jewish life forward. When our operations reflect this framework, Becky quite simply calls this, "the best." She knows this approach works: she receives and reviews staff feedback that reveals how supported they feel having Becky as their mentor. That drives Becky further, nourishing her whole self, as it resonates with how she wants to be seen.

Looking way into the future, Becky hopes her legacy will be as someone who did well for others because she got to be 100% Becky in what she did and enables others to be 100% themselves in all they did at work. She also hopes she is recalled as someone who made a significant impact in people's lives. As Becky's sees someone else's emerging gifts come to light, she aims to help them grow, expose, and amplify their strengths so that person can reach their full potential and be their full integrated authentic selves to whatever places and passions they pursue. This mission drives Becky 100%. It's part of her *neshama*, her soul, and it is what she wants to do both in her personal life and her professional life for the rest of her life — hence her gratitude for being able to integrate it.

QUESTIONS FOR REFLECTION

1. How might we model authenticity, humility, and vulnerability in the work place for our staff?

2. Consider how we can help our staff thrive and bring their whole integrated selves to work by:
   a) reviewing compensation practices and discussing them with your professionals
   b) structuring jobs to maximize relationship-building in a manner that speaks to the professional, and
   c) empowering and allowing professionals to explore and examine their own ideas (i.e. a 20% passion project)?

3. How might we better operate through a non-biased gender or racial lens so employees can bring their whole selves to work without consequence?

it is not about them

Blessing Summary — By exploring the *middot* (values) we find in the Jewish practices of mindfulness and *Mussar*, specifically *anavah* (humility) and *kavod* (honor), as well as the use of the love languages to serve and inspire others, Jewish community professionals can become more motivated and valued in their work as they focus their efforts on those around them rather than their own wants.

In the 19th Century Rabbi Yisrael Salanter began what we know today as the *Mussar* Movement. Though I had been actively involved in Jewish life for close to 35 years and have heard the term *Mussar* previously, I didn't have much familiarity with it until I engaged in six months of deep learning with three of my professional colleagues and our *Mussar* facilitator, Rabbi David Jaffe, over zoom once every few weeks. We examined in depth key *middot* (Jewish values) that included *seder* (order), *chesed* (loving kindness), *savlanut* (patience) and *anavah* (humility) through text, narrative, and personal reflections. One text David taught us was from Rabbi Abraham Isaac Hakohen Kook when studying *anavah*:

הענוה משלימה את הרצון, ובזה
היא הכלי היותר טוב לקבל כל ברכה

Anavah (Humility) completes, or makes whole, Ratzon (Will).
It is for this reason that Anavah is the best vessel for receiving all blessing.

This text guides us to the power of *anavah*, our humility. To help our staff prioritize other's needs over our own can also make us whole and feel blessed. Rachel Felber, the director of Camp Wise, the Jewish overnight summer camp program of the Mandel JCC of Cleveland, Ohio, embodies *anavah* in her Jewish community professional work every day, leading hundreds of staff members and campers, and liaising with parents, board members, and other stakeholders each summer. She shared that she feels most valued when it is "not about me, but about my people."

To be humble is not purely to be altruistic. As we can learn from negotiation and conflict resolution books such as *Getting To Yes and Difficult Conversations*, to act with humility gives us the opportunity to listen more, better understand situations, and better foster relationships. Ultimately, acting with *anavah* often helps us achieve what we wanted from a situation in the first place, and getting what we want can help us feel more motivated and blessed at work too. We can see how *anavah* works as a motivational tool in the *anavah* schematic below.

THE ANAVAH SCHEMATIC

If we encourage ourselves and our staff to act with humility, which includes encouraging them to listen with empathy to those around them, both our staff and ourselves will better understand and appreciate those around us. With humility and empathy at play, we will be in a better position both to resolve conflicts and inspire others through our actions. This will also enable us to better achieve the goals we initially set out to achieve both for our organizations and in working with our staff. As a result, both ourselves and our staff will feel content and, of course, more valued and blessed. We will see this schematic play out in Rachel's narrative.

Rachel's young life and professional career has mostly been within Jewish Community Centers (JCCs). She often jokes that she is the ultimate poster child for the JCC Movement. She was a graduate of a JCC pre-school, attended JCC camp, received a graduate scholarship from JCC Association, and has worked for multiple JCCs. She also attended a Jewish day school until 3rd grade. She was the little kid who often asked her parents, "Why don't we light candles on Friday night?" At some point during her childhood, it become clear in Rachel's core that a close connection to both the cultural and ritual aspects of Judaism were always going to be important to her. In fact, Rachel recalls that when she was preparing for her Bat Mitzvah, she asked the Rabbi, "Can I do more for my service?" Unlike most of her peers in the congregation who completed only the minimum requirements, Rachel wanted to do as much as she was allowed and given opportunity to learn more prayers and then lead them. She was tenacious about learning and her own personal growth.

Yet her humility, her *anavah*, perhaps disguised at first as fear, was also ever present. Rachel is not a huge fan of being in the front of the crowd, which can be challenging as a camp director. She wants, instead, to learn and excel as the person behind the scenes making the magic happen for those around her.

Rachel feels motivated when the spotlight is not on her, in part because she identifies as an introvert. In the book *Quiet*, Susan Cain discusses how society often intentionally or subconsciously values leaders who display qualities of extroverts more than introverts. We seem to be attracted to charisma regardless of what's behind it. One of the ways we can better get to know and then better apply the success schematic from Blessing #2 and our learning here is to understand each of our staff's extroverted and introverted attributes, and allow each to thrive in a manner that best fits them. Rachel likes to hang back, have one-on-one conversations rather than speak in front of the group, and let others on her staff shine in the spotlight that they relish.

Rachel attended both at Camp Wise at and Camp Beber in Wisconsin, both of which were foundational in setting Rachel's career path. She also had a transformative experience in BBYO, getting comfortable in her own skin and giving her just enough confidence to lead a camp activity one summer. As she became confident with her peers both in a Jewish space and in positions of leadership, she was able to transfer that feeling back to her summer job.

After college Rachel worked at Kent State University Hillel as a JCSC (Jewish Campus Service Corps fellow), a program quite popular in the early and mid 2000's among entry-level Jewish community professionals. She would have coffee with dozens of Jewish college students, and while she found pretty quickly that she wasn't interested in working with college kids on campus, the experience did further her interest in working in a space where she could access her interest in helping others find their own paths and thrive. She decided to pursue a Master of Science and Social Administration, at Case Western Reserve University. In the summers during grad school, she returned to Jewish camp and began to notice the moments when, as a bunk counselor, campers were so excited to see her and have her with them. Feeling valued by those she was serving and seeing the fruits of her labor, as we discussed in Blessing #5 have been pivotal for her motivations. She began thinking that she could make a career out of working at Jewish Camp.

Rachel's *anavah* is rooted in her deep knowledge and history of camp and sharing its enduring legacy with her staff. For example, in 2017, when Camp Wise celebrated 110 years of operation, she told her staff about the "crop corps.," campers at Camp Wise during World War II. During the camp day, the crop corps. worked the crop fields of Northeast Ohio to support the war effort. It was the camp's way of engaging the campers in what was happening in society. At the end of the 2017 summer, Rachel brought in one of the former crop corps. campers, now in her nineties, along with her niece, who was also an alumna of Camp Wise. At that moment, one of Rachel's staff members gave Rachel a look that caught her attention. She later went up to Rachel and shared how she remembered when Rachel discussed the crop corps. earlier in the summer and never thought they would meet someone who had experienced it. This staff member lit up with pride, joy, and excitement feeling that she was a part of this on-going and inspiring camp story. Rachel didn't have to be in the spotlight for her to feel valued. Rather, she facilitated a narrative that allowed others to shine, and when she saw her staff light up, Rachel lit up, motivated by the fact that, for Rachel, it's all about her staff and the campers they serve, not about her. This example speaks to the anavah, the humility, Rachel practices as a camp director and utilizes to motivate her staff and make them feel most valued, motivating herself in the process.

Much of the practice of *Mussar* helps us take the spotlight off ourselves. Unsurprisingly, Rachel and many of her camp director colleagues are motivated by these *Mussar middot* in order to get through summers that, however joyful and rewarding, are stressful, exhausting, and complicated, and this was the case well before COVID-19 upended summer camp even further. Rachel is motivated by practicing patience, or *savlanut*, organization, and trust, or *emet*, in her staff, who secure the livelihood of hundreds of campers for the summer.

Above them all for Rachel is *anavah*, which helps her remember that, when bombarded by the stresses, or de-motivators, her focus should be on her people. Rachel recognizes that certain situations – a family that can't afford camp, a child who needs more resources than camp can provide — are "de-motivating in the moment," and it is a challenge to get past these deflating moments. Yet "it is what it is" is not an acceptable answer for Rachel and is, in her mind, not humble at all; it's just giving up. Thus, her *anavah* motivates Rachel to engage in substantive conversations that can lead to real change.

Rachel also realized going into this job that she'd have little work/life balance, but this doesn't de-motivate her. Rather, Rachel creates strategies to overcome moments of frustration. Camp directors often use the Broadway terminology about "going dark." Just like there are no Broadway shows on Mondays, again before and hopefully again over COVID-19, (when they "go dark"), camp directors often go dark, or shut themselves off, from the rest of their lives in the summer, and Rachel recognizes that they also are very much dark throughout the year as well. Camp life can feel very insular and all-consuming even when camp isn't officially in session. Thus, Rachel understands when she needs to be humble and that her work is also not about her, it's about her people. When she puts the focus on others, her own challenges either become less important or she is further motivated to make change so she can further benefit those she serves and supports.

How might we encourage others to practice humility as a way to motivate them? One strategy might be in the lesson of Blessing #2 that, if we create positions around the needs and interests of the talent, then Jewish community professionals can devote less of the mental energy to home responsibilities while at work and thus better able to practice both humility and gratitude for their work lives. Or we can apply the lessons from Blessing #5 and create positions in which folks easily and regularly observe the fruits of their labor, as camp directors can easily see when they attend a camp meal or look out of their office window. They are humbled by what they can then accomplish, further feeding this motivation.

When I asked Rachel about her legacy, she brought it back to her people: her staff. Every summer she speaks to her staff about what they want their legacies to be as they prepare for their jobs and then connect with their campers. Rachel hopes she inspires her staff by sharing with her the hope that people see her as someone who is caring for this community of staff in the spirit of the success schematic from Blessing #2, happy staff → happy campers → happy camp, which she and I both learned under our former camp director Jodi Sperling.

Rachel recognizes that if she follows this strategy and properly invests in and supports the staff, campers and parents will likely feel comfortable and that they belong. Ultimately, if every person who works with Rachel has a similar narrative, then Rachel knows she has done the job well, and she doesn't need to be on stage or in the newspaper to feel the blessing that stems from her quiet yet powerful efforts.

Rachel speaks about camp in a way that I'll suggest here we should speak about all of our organizations. She truly believes that while camp is a business and they sell "weeks" or "sessions" that include activities from boating to drama, a camp summer is often deemed successful when it engages campers and staff alike in community building and bonding. In this sense, camp is selling the opportunity to belong and forge deep, meaningful relationships.

As we learned in Blessing #3 with Ezra, Jewish community professionals may have entered into this field because of interest in the work, yet they remain here because of the people with whom they build relationships. For those of us who regularly attend conferences that engage Jewish community professional, we see people thrilled to reconnect with friends and colleagues from past work experiences, former collaborations, or even from their own youth attending Jewish camp, youth groups, and Israel trips. Reuniting with close friends is certainly a major retention tool for camp staff and Jewish community professionals alike.

Rachel too hopes that people think of camp and her leadership this way: "At Camp Wise, I got this amazing experience and skill, and I met and built friendships with amazing people. During that time the director was Rachel Felber; therefore I appreciate and give her credit for her leadership and the way she ran camp." More simply, she hopes that, looking back, people will say, "the summers when Rachel was director were awesome!" Feeling part of the Jewish professional community can achieve the same results, fueling motivations and a deep feeling of being valued.

As in each interview, Rachel and I talked about how compensation impacts her motivations. Rachel feels she is paid fairly as a camp director, though when she was a full time assistant director or program director, she felt underpaid. Part of this may be her location. Cleveland, with a lower cost of living than the northeast or west coast, may have lower salaries than assistant or associate directors in other regions. Rachel has a master's degree and close to 15 years professional experience. Yet in her positions prior to camp director, either in Austin, TX or in Ohio, her salaries were nowhere near even $50,000 annually. For the number of hours she worked, she feels this salary was not acceptable. As we've seen in previous blessings, salary isn't a prime motivator, but when an employee feels undercompensated, the other strategies we can employ won't be as impactful, and we risk losing this talent from the Jewish community professional pipeline.

Even for the Jewish community professionals who live the mantra that it is about my people and not myself and find their place of value in the professional practice of *anavah*, a low salary can stymie the passion and joy that one would otherwise naturally feel. As we have observed in all our portraits, it's not about making the big bucks; it's about fairness. We must review how we compensate all positions, not just in leadership, so we can minimize, if not eliminate, the variable of unfair pay diluting talent's natural overflow of passion and commitment.

Rachel recognizes that she did not go into this field to become a millionaire. Yet, she expected to, sooner rather than later, pay off her student loans. She is nowhere near able to do that and probably won't be for many years to come. Now that Rachel is in the director's chair, she feels camp is doing a better job of more fairly compensating her other full-time staff, though she wishes she could do even more especially for her support and maintenance staff, who aren't yet making a wage that Rachel is proud of.

As a female director, Rachel considered questions around gender as well and mused whether her compensation was comparable not only to other camp directors of similar sized camps or in cities with a similar cost of living but whether her male counterparts make more. Rachel has never felt "gendered" in her jobs. Yet, she admits that it is hard to be a woman no matter where one is working. She feels that her voice as a woman is heard differently from a man's. She isn't sure if she'd be compensated differently if she were a man with a similar career trajectory, and it's hard to compare herself to other female camp directors of her age as females remain a small overall percentage of Jewish camp directors. Rachel hopes that, if camp continues to grow under Rachel's leadership, her salary can grow accordingly. She also wonders whether her introversion and her tendency towards humility impacts her getting more compensation or being treated more like a leader, as if she were to be less humble and more extraverted, she might make more money. However, Rachel recognizes and has shared that this would push her completely out of her comfort zone and likely much less happy at work.

STRATEGIES TO MOTIVATE THE HUMBLE

Considering Rachel's narrative, there are several actions and techniques we can follow to motivate those fueled when they make work not about others, and practice *anavah*.

Raise Up the Positive Experiences

If many Jewish community professionals are motivated by stepping back and helping others shine, we must take the opportunities to point out when their actions do just that. Rachel puts herself in positions to observe the experiences of her campers and staff in their many moments of joy at camp, which helps her feel valued. That feeling becomes more tangible when she opens up enrollment numbers for the next year and sees both the high retention rates of current families and the strong interest and sign-ups from new families. Those numbers reinforce the power of the work "we all do," she says.

Motivated by Data

Those who are motivated by *anavah* and are introverts may, like Rachel, not need or want to be publicly cheered on by the crowd. Yet, they may still want to know that their work provides value, even on paper. For Rachel, when enrollment numbers go up and the business is going well, her value chamber is filled. She doesn't need folks to come up to her and say "good job" all the time. For her, seeing the value and feeling that reinforcement is simply seeing the results of the work she is doing, akin to Blessing #5.

Use of the Love Languages

There are many ways we can show our appreciation for others' work, taking from the languages of love that those in personal relationships use to express their gratitude and affection for each other. They are: 1) receiving gifts, 2) spending quality time with each other, 3) words of affirmation, 4) acts of service or devotion, and 5) physical touch (which may be less applicable or appropriate for work relationships and during COVID-19!). Regardless of whether a professional is motivated by practicing *anavah*, people need to be shown their value in different ways. For Rachel, it is receiving the gift of seeing the result of her team's work, and her staff being inspired and growing each summer. That's the love language that works for her. All Jewish community professionals deserve to have some expression of their value, whether from the CEO, their direct supervisor, peers, or other stakeholders. A regular expression of meaningful recognition can go a long way toward a Jewish community professional feeling valued and thus being retained.

FROM ANAVAH TO KAVOD

In the world of work, and in the Jewish sector in particular, running a camp is different than nearly every other job . It's hard to compare to, say, a development associate at a Jewish Federation. However, for both roles, the end goals, including strengthening the Jewish future and engaging more individuals in Jewish life, may still be the same. In other words, at the end of the day we are all in service to the Jewish community. If Rachel were a director of an overnight camp outside of the Jewish community, she knows she wouldn't feel nearly as much passion for the work, and it is the passion particularly for Jewish community that needs to be harnessed, cherished, and utilized so our talent doesn't leave in spite of their incredible passion to serve Jewish community. We need to lead and be motivated by our own *anavah* to be in service to our staff, because we know that if we do otherwise, our professionals may leave the field entirely.

Understanding Rachel's leadership and self-motivation through *anavah* also allows her to feel another *mussar middah, kavod*. She feels honored and respected for the work that she does and validated by those around her. If we, as those who supervise and support Jewish community professionals, can make our work not about us but about supporting and valuing them, then they can spend their energy feeling honored modeling this humility approach, fully enhancing the experiences of their staff and constituents so the Jewish work and program space feels truly like a "home of happiness," the Camp Wise slogan. The life of a camp director, and all Jewish community professionals, can be stressful, but if we focus on the strategies that fit their needs, we can come closer to meeting the needs of the entire operation.

QUESTIONS FOR REFLECTION

1. How might we start a study of the *mussar middot* with our staff as part of staff getting to know each other and themselves? One might start with the book *Everyday Holiness* by Alan Morinis and build discussions from there.

2. How might the practice of humility, or *anavah*, allow us and our teams set a culture around a set of healthy work values and practices?

3. How might we appropriately adopt one or a few of the love languages in the way we can frame valuing our professionals? Perhaps we can ask our professionals which love language (or professional relationship language) speaks most to them. This is a simple step to help managers understand how to best support, motivate and value their staff.

make it all about them

Blessing Summary — This blessing discusses several strategies, including the emotional bank account and the strategies of validation, applying them to how we manage and support Jewish community professionals so they feel respected and honored.

"All I Want is A Little Respect!" the comedian Rodney Dangerfield used to famously say and Aretha Franklin use to sing. But what happens when Jewish community professionals feel a lack of respect or validation for their work and efforts from their leaders, supervisor, or those they serve? This is not a universal issue, many of our professionals do feel respected and recognized, many of whom we have already encountered in this book. Yet, if we are to be serious about strengthening the pipeline for the future and managing our staff in the spirit of adhering to the Jewish values of *kavod* (honor) and *hakarat ha-tov* (gratitude or literally translated to "noticing the good"), we must do our best to ensure everyone in our workforce feels validated.

So where do we start? One strategy is the *emotional bank account*. Popularized by Stephen Covey, the emotional bank account works like a regular bank. One can make deposits or withdrawals. A deposit can be a thank you, a "you did a great job," or any validation that signifies the importance of someone else's role and their accomplishments. Deposits make us feel that we matter and that others care. Of course, deposits have a transactional value as well. Our wealth with the other person rises, accumulates, and earns interest.

Therefore, when we need something — a favor, a "no worries" from the person after we apologize for a mistake, assistance with a project, or a request to purchase cookies for our daughter's troop — they are willing, hopefully more than willing, to oblige. When we engage in these requests, we are making a withdrawal. The more deposits we as their manager have in their emotional bank account, the more willing the individual will be ok with a withdrawal. Depending on the nature of the withdrawal, as some deposits and withdrawals may weigh more than others, Covey suggests that we need at least 5 emotional deposits in one's account before we make a withdrawal in order to keep the relationship strong and avoid resentment. As a transactional action, this makes sense, and in a transformational relationship it does too. Our stock in their eyes won't go down because we have made so many sincere deposits.

Such is the case when we ask withdrawals from our Jewish community professionals, especially those already in jobs that involve several sacrifices, including lower pay, non-traditional hours, or other difficult circumstances.

Marc Fein is one of those talented and inspirational individuals — deeply connected to serving and inspiring the next generation and feeling privileged to do this work. Yet there have been times when he has felt a lack of meaningful validation for his work. We will examine his narrative through the lens of the emotional bank account and the idea that we can bless our workforce if we indeed make it all about them.

Marc and I began our discussion debating whether it was a total accident or *b'shert* (meant to be) that Marc ended up in the professional roles he has been in thus far: primarily part-time or full-time youth director roles for Jewish teen youth groups. He has achieved success and been most comfortable in the Modern Orthodox space that he grew up and continues to practice within, steadily rising up the professional ladder with the National Conference of Jewish Youth (NCSY), the Modern Orthodox youth group movement. His initial thought was that his career path was an accident, but as we reflected together, he concluded that these roles suit and fulfill him, and he is becoming more OK with this career path being *b'shert*.

We dug a bit deeper and understood that Marc became a Jewish youth leader because it filled up his emotional bank account. Marc's first career inflection point came as he entered Yeshiva University (YU) in New York for undergraduate studies and discovered a program called, Torah Tours, which brought undergraduates at YU to various Jewish communities across the USA to spread the joy, spirit, and knowledge of Jewish holidays. As a part of this program, Marc was sent to Schenectady, NY, an aging Jewish community. When Marc arrived, the community did not have a significant focus or priority to engage its teens.

Two of the teens in Schenectady invited Marc to an NCSY *Shabbaton*, or a weekend retreat, shortly after he arrived. He had heard about NCSY *Shabbatonim* from a couple of his friends who were advisers and was intrigued. He attended and, within hours he was "hooked." He loved the *ruach* (spirit) of the teens and the commitment of the other staff attending. In observing the staff, Marc saw himself in such a role. He saw the potential to positively influence these youth who were not so much younger than he was. He wanted more.

This particular NCSY region has a motto that Marc found compelling: "big enough to be a region, small enough to be a family." Marc appreciated the group's familial culture that included a sense of acceptance and an invitation to express oneself, something Marc sorely needed. He also observed that there was little else engaging Jewish teens in upstate New York at the time and believes without NCSY, these teens may not have had a meaningful connection to Judaism.

We can see some of these variables starting to fill his emotional bank account. Marc is inspired by the work, finds meaning and connection to the culture, and feels accepted by the community. We may not always recognize what is around a young professional that can add emotional deposits to their bank, which is important for managers to know as we seek to make withdrawals. It is also a good blessing reminder to make those coffee dates with our staff so we can better understand the aspects of their work that acts as deposits, adding to their emotional banks.

Another inflection point and a subsequent emotional deposit was his own guidance from mentoring. Upon graduating from YU, Marc stayed on campus to serve as a Presidential Fellow. Marc worked directly for the YU President, Richard Joel, for one year, followed by another year working as President Joel's speechwriter. He felt lucky that a mentor and colleague suggested he apply to work in the President's office. He was also pleased to find a route that helped him hone his education and facilitation skills.

Participating in this fellowship was Marc's entre into the professional Jewish world. Marc admitted that it wasn't the path he envisioned for himself. In fact, like his peers, his family suggested he become a lawyer or businessman. Prior to these inflection points, Marc had never dreamed of a specific career path; rather, he had assumed that there was a preordained path. His previous college internships, after all, were working for both lawyer or for a hedge fund, where deposits into his emotional bank were a rare occurrence. His experiences both with NCSY and in the YU President's office illuminated an emerging path to become a Jewish community professional by, in part, filling up his emotional bank.

It is important to point out the outsized role mentoring, in this case a peer mentor, can have in helping identify and guide talent into our field by making significant deposits into our professionals' emotional banks. Marc's mentor made 3 significant deposits, advising in words or in actions the following statements:

- Marc, I think you will be good at this.

- Marc, I can tell you enjoy this work, and here is a way to do this more.

- Marc, I will be with you on this journey.

All of these specific deposits connect to this larger idea of validation: Marc had a feeling when he entered the NCSY space, and this mentor, seeing alignment between the staff role at NCSY and the 2-year Presidential Fellowship at YU, *validated* Marc's inklings through acknowledging his talents, guiding his passions, and ensuring that he wouldn't be alone. As we will re-visit in Blessing #14, mentors can play an all important role in validating one's work and passions, and adding deposits to a Jewish community professional's emotional bank.

Marc has had a working relationship with NCSY ever since, both seeking out and being approached with opportunities to move up from advisor, to chapter advisor, to associate regional director, to regional director, to director of several NCSY summer programs. As of the time of our 2017 interview, Marc was in charge of running summer programs for public school students who travel to Poland and Israel. Marc's commitment with NCSY has been part time, which is in itself a withdrawal he accepts from NCSY, as he'd rather make enough money to be full time in the job.

As is the case for other Jewish youth professionals who work part time, Marc needs to have "side hustles." In many respects he enjoys the side work immensely, and it helps him grow professionally. He, for example, has facilitated for an Israeli Tech Company called FreshBiz, which makes board games that teach entrepreneurial and collaborative thinking. Marc also teaches about mental health, anxiety and depression at schools and synagogues, and he has a strong reputation as a dynamic public speaker and educator. He also has just started as a professional coach, working with his first clients.

As Marc receives emotional deposits from the content of his work, the culture he is a part of and the relationships he builds, he is also constantly being asked to accept withdrawals, many of which are not explicit asks but built in to his role, including working part time, having side hustles, and not earning a salary that matches his value. Perhaps it is the nature of the job of youth group worker, or perhaps we are undervaluing the critical importance of this work.

When teaching budgeting or financial management to students, I say that budgets are often a reflection of our values, not just how much revenue we can earn and the various expenses that must be paid, but also what we most care about and the value we put on them. We may value expenses only to the degree that they generate revenue. For example, youth group conventions and programs don't necessarily generate a whole lot of revenue, and thus it may be difficult to substantiate larger more "living wage" full time salaries for Jewish youth professionals.

Yet we also live in a time when the focus of Jewish life is that we must engage the next generation, or the future Judaism may not thrive. It is perhaps ironic then that we might fail to properly honor the direct service professionals who engage with this next generation, compensating and validating them just enough to get by but not enough to truly thrive. These are with "withdrawals" each time they received their paycheck and every time our supervisor does not say "well done," it can burn our professionals out. Luckily, there are ways to bring emotional deposits into the bank even if the increased pay isn't always available. We need to embark on a strategy of validation.

We can learn how to employ such a strategy by going deeper into Marc's story:

Building

Marc loves building. He created the TJJ summer program to Poland and Israel from scratch and, after four years in, continued to expand, increasing enrollment nearly 50% from 2017 to 2018. He relishes the opportunity to grow capacity and therefore have stronger overall impact, so he doesn't have to turn away teens from this transformational experience. He loves the iterative process and bringing a vision to a successful reality. A mentor of mine has often called this skill being able to "put long legs on big ideas."

Interfacing

Marc also loves interfacing with youth and teens at critical moments in their lives. Marc has realized personally how inflection points experienced during this age have a tremendous impact on one's personal trajectory. Marc takes pride and great care to be influential in these teens' lives during these points, pointing out their skills and insights and developing these further through trips and other Jewish experiences. Marc sees in this an opportunity to be of use, or "tov" aligning with our discussion in Blessing #4.

Good People

Marc also loves being surrounded by good people. Most of the people Marc meets through work are "good passionate people who want to do the right thing, stand for something and want to build a better world." He noted that in Jewish community professional work there is a golden opportunity to create positions surrounded by good people, who set a foundation for autonomy, competence, purpose, and belonging. This in itself can lead to validation.

Marc is also hugely motivated when the validation is not only built in but is a direct action, whether he is sought out for a new challenging opportunity, given some personal attention, or, of course, awarded more generous and fair compensation. Marc appreciates when employers or peers alike take the time to honor what Marc uniquely brings to the table.

Accessing Their Knowledge and Challenging Them

When we as employers want to learn from our professionals, challenge them, and help them grow, we make a simple statement: "We see you, we care about you, and we aim to validate your contributions to fulfilling our mission." This statement says a great deal to Marc. It only furthers Marc's desire to do well for his leadership.

Considering the emotional deposit strategy and that building, interfacing, good people, accessing their knowledge, and providing challenging work are effective and meaningful emotional deposits, we can incorporate all of these when aiming to strengthen our professional's motivations and ensure they feel valued. We see this in our next schematic, the **validation equation**:

THE VALIDATION EQUATION

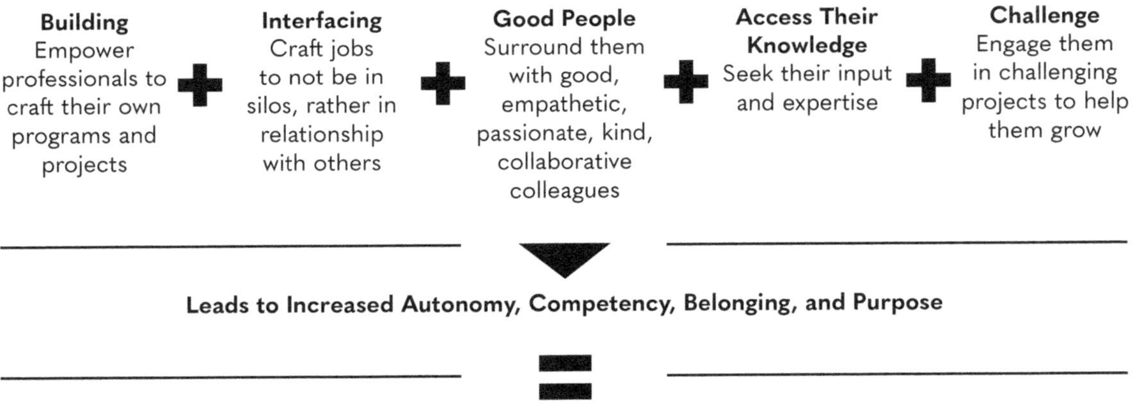

We can see here that the building blocks of validation lead to the very internal motivations Deci cites and that we introduced in Blessing #1. We see this in Marc, who feels that sense of autonomy, competence, belonging, and purpose in his work as a result.

Again, Covey advises us that healthy relationships consist of those in which the individuals receives at least five emotional deposits per every withdrawal. That is, our Jewish community professionals will be prepared to sacrifice if they have already been repeatedly honored or validated. One may think that this is an unmanageable ratio, yet considering how much we do ask of our Jewish community professionals, it may be imperative. As for these withdrawals, we make many of them.

Unclear Professional Direction

The first withdrawal may not feel like one to the employer or manager, yet as a result of Marc needing multiple jobs to get by, he admits that his various roles do not always help in burnishing a clear professional brand. He receives feedback that he is "too much of a hodgepodge" and is frequently asked, "what's your lane?" It is possible Marc missed out on work because a potential future employer doesn't exactly "get" what Marc does. When Jewish community professionals have unclear job descriptions or are required for financial reasons to take on multiple jobs, it can confuse both their branding and career trajectory. We can turn this withdrawal into an emotional deposit by crafting job descriptions in partnership with the Jewish community professional with clear goals and functions, reasonable expectations, align with the employee's skill sets and interests, and properly challenge them to grow.

Toxic Colleagues

Marc believes that the Jewish youth space is intended to be pure and free from divisiveness and disrespect. Yet, Marc also knows we operate in the real world and that in any organization there are individuals who are actively or passive-aggressively disruptive, otherwise toxic. Nevertheless, when he comes across such individuals in our field, possibly motivated and fueled by an inflated ego or exclusively self-interested, Marc feels flattened. A difficult colleague in any form can often rip out the joy from an otherwise positive and motivating work experience.

Who we hire determines so much of who a company is and the culture the organization aims to set, as we learn from Mort Mandel in his book *It's All About Who*. Again, this withdrawal can be flipped into a deposit, following our validation equation of surrounding our Jewish community professionals by good people and ensuring all of our hires meet a moral and ethical standard of kindness, collaboration, and care to others.

Lack of Balance

Marc finds any kind of work/life balance or integration in the Jewish youth space consistently challenging. Unlike Becky in Blessing #9 who, as an executive, has found ways to integrate her multiple selves into her work, Marc requires the opposite. For example, Marc chooses not to be on the board of any Jewish organization because Jewish is his entire life . He admits that he finds the 24 hours a day, 7 days a week, 365 days a year nature of his Jewish personal and professional life suffocating at times. He desires a bit more balance outside of the Jewish space rather than doubling down with more Jewish spaces in his life.

This is most apparent, ironically, when Marc directs or staffs *Shabbatonim*. Due to this work requirement, no matter how enjoyable it is, Marc finds that he did not have a Shabbat, or day of rest, on his own; Shabbat is often his busiest work time from Marc and, though Marc is part time, because he must side hustle, he doesn't often have the compensatory weekday off that full time clergy or educators, who incidentally also make livable salaries, often do.

Jewish community professionals who experience the field the same way as Marc would be fortunate if they could work with their employers to find ways to earn more time off, either through greater flexibility in one's full time job or more compensation so part-timers do not have to side hustle. When these aren't viable options, we can look again to the validation equation and explicitly implement elements that can add more emotional deposits to the bank and help offset some of these withdrawals.

I Just Can't Get No Respect

Perhaps the most potent withdrawal is when Marc feels least valued when his work by feeling plainly disrespected or ignored. Marc, as a Jewish youth worker, often receives the same comments, including: "so when are you getting a real job?" as if to say his work programming, teaching, and coaching teens is just "play" time and Marc hadn't yet grown up to adult work yet. The overall lower pay for youth workers contributes to this feeling. In addition, when Marc does his work well and no one in a position of power seems to notice or care it simply just hurts. As we discussed in our previous blessing, even Jewish community professionals who thrive on *anavah*, a sense of feeling motivated through humility and helping others shine, still need some regular validation or recognition. For any of us, when it feels like there is zero effort to recognize one's efforts and accomplishments, this withdrawal may become too difficult to offset.

Interestingly, now that Marc is ten years into his career and more established in his work, he receives these deflating comments less. Yet, in those first critical years post-college to be constantly questioned about his work was extremely disheartening. This is likely also to permeate other sectors of the Jewish community professional space, especially those who work through spaces known to many still as informal Jewish education, outside of the traditional educator role in a day school or synagogue classroom.

For the Jewish community professionals who nod their heads when reading Marc's narrative, there is an ongoing sense that these withdrawals, which aren't one-time transactions but compounded daily, affect a professional's long-term career trajectory. The trajectory is already far from consistent or easily mapped, especially for those who don't want to stray too far from direct service. At best, Marc often feels the deposits equal the withdrawals, which means the balance of his emotional bank is often around zero. Thus, despite the advantages, Marc can feel drained.

To that end, there are additional strategies that can add deposits to a Jewish community professional's emotional bank account and that we could consider adding to an already busy validation equation!

Coaching

There are students that Marc feels got away from him. He wonders if he had handled a certain conversation with one teen differently, for example, whether he would have been able to better support and nurture this particular individual. Marc is probably his own worst critic, and it is possible he actually did do well by these teens and that his legacy is stronger than he thinks. Yet, to be able to talk through these concerns with a professional coach would help raise the balance of his emotional bank. As we have seen throughout this book, the support, guidance, and championing from coaches or mentors can fuel our professional's motivations and drive.

Validation and Transparent Compensation

Marc's actual salary is far less a direct motivator and far more an opportunity for recognition and validation. Marc feels this tension between his payment and the importance of this work to the point that he's happy to help no matter what the compensation, even if it is zero. He'll gladly give up thirty to sixty minutes of his time for a phone call to guide a person, program or organization, though he then feels a bit uneasy that he just "gave the away the store." He recognizes that he doesn't work for a fancy consulting firm and can't just say, "for $500 you can have my time for an hour." Marc has always believed in the importance of Jewish youth work, so how could he charge to help someone out? He doesn't want to let money get in the way of work happening.

To that point, perhaps we could do a better job of linking validation to compensation if the field was more transparent about setting compensation levels and linking validation with compensation. Marc notes our inability to talk transparently about each other's compensation, which probably speaks to how, when we feel less validated, we struggle to know and advocate for our worth. Marc shared that he received a 25% raise to direct the NCSY summer program in part because he asked others in similar positions in the Jewish world what they made and then brought this information to NCSY. Marc's boss was receptive to a raise and easily agreed to Marc's ask. Marc quickly points out, though, that he would never expect that independently his boss would have gone to Marc and suggested a raise.

For our purposes here, we can consider validating our Jewish community professionals by saying, "you are doing great; in recognition, here is a nice bump." It would have been HUGE for Marc's motivation, as they independently would have validated and recognized his efforts. Again, it is not about the raise; it is about what the raise stands for. Marc understands that we must be advocates for ourselves to get what we want, but that approach can leave employers missing the opportunity to capitalize on the raise they don't mind giving but never offer, which would catapult employees like Marc whose motivations would soar. *What an emotional deposit this would be!*

Validation When Feeling Visible

Marc knows what he is doing is sophisticated and important. Yet, if Marc isn't verbally or financially recognized by leadership, he begins to wonder whether they even know what he is doing or how he is adding value to the organization's mission. I imagine Marc is not alone. If we are to show it is all about our staff, we must ensure that they see that we see the value and contributions both our actions and our words, using the validation equation set forth earlier as our guide.

Feeling Valued, Creating Value

At the end of each summer, Marc and his staff conduct a thank you ritual. The staff creates a song and dance routine, and they describe their experience in their own language and with their own *ruach* (spirit). Marc observes his students "getting" what he hoped they would learn about community, Jewish life, and life skills and then sharing this with each other. Marc knows at that moment that his hard work was worthwhile. Marc at this moment feels both like Jon in Blessing #5 and Rachel in our previous blessing, when the fruits of his labor are apparent and when he is making it all about his staff and teens and not himself. It is the moment when Marc really feels like he matters to others and yes, when he does feel most validated, respected, and valued. This feeling puts a ton of deposits in his emotional bank.

Marc thrives on this affirmation. He has a whole file for himself filled with letters of parents who thank him for their teen's experiences, or from the teens themselves to remind him of his value – it's everything to Marc. Marc also feels valued when he gets asked to contribute to projects or teach or be a part of what he feels is important and special. He felt a little thrill when I approached him to be profiled for this book, another example to him that he is visible, and that what he has to say and what he contributes has value.

Marc has a recurring dream of standing at the pitcher's mound at Yankee Stadium filled to capacity; out in the crowd are all of the teens he has worked with, along with his former supervisors, and Marc receives a standing ovation followed with each person sharing one of the following statements:

- "You made me feel like I mattered, and I know I mattered because I interacted with you."

- "You supported me and helped me reach my full potential in life."

- "You helped me thrive Jewishly, personally, and professionally. Thank you."

This speaks to the core of the work that Marc does and his completely reasonable desire for the respect and validation that fuels him. It's not just Jewish knowledge or building a positive Jewish identity that Marc aims to impart. Rather, it is working to ensure those we serves feel that what each brought to this world is valuable and worth pursuing. In some respects, that is all the validation and respect that he needs.

QUESTIONS FOR REFLECTION

1. How might we begin to remove the pieces of the work culture and surroundings for our professionals that lead to unnecessary withdrawals from their emotional bank?

2. How might we create systems that naturally and regularly add in deposits to the emotional bank?

3. How might we instill the rituals that allow for meaningful validation, respect, honor of one's work and an affirmation of the values they perceive they are bringing to the work?

champion the relentless pursuit

Blessing Summary — Many of our Jewish community professionals have a dream to create something new, and all they want is to have this dream fulfilled. The best thing we can do for these superstars is provide them with the resources and confidence to make their dreams a reality. We can help place their passion at their foreground so we can help them, in the paraphrased words of Theodore Herzl, "will it, so it is no dream."

Theodore Herzl was a young man in Europe with a dream for his people, to start a new nation in its old dwelling place. He had a vision that seemed virtually impossible to accomplish. How do a people who have been treated as inferior by their "home" countries for close to two millennia rise up to both establish and grow a nation of their own?

Constraints didn't hold Herzl back. He said, "If you will it, it is no dream." Today we look upon the 72-year-old state of Israel, with all of its accomplishments and wonder, along with its imperfections and shortcomings, as the greatest Jewish start-up project of all time, one continuously fed by the unending entrepreneurial spirit of Herzl and those who followed him.

Certainly Herzl wasn't alone in his relentless pursuit. In short order he gained followers and partners, forming the first World Zionist Congress in Europe in the 1890's. Yet one could argue that without his vision and unquenchable thirst to see his dream and the dream of his people fulfilled, Israel might not exist today. It should give us pause as we consider the gifts, advancements, and institutions we have as a result of remarkable and relentless entrepreneurship.

This blessing asks us to consider how we can best champion the Jewish community professionals who are in the midst of a relentless pursuit that, if properly nurtured, can see dreams for the Jewish world come true. While many of our previous narratives embody such a spirit, there is perhaps no one whom I have met who exemplifies this relentless pursuit more than Carine Warsawski. She is one of those remarkable individuals who can teach us that perhaps the most important thing we can do as managers and leaders, especially for those with this kind of vision and spirit, is to figure out how we can best feed their spirit, support their vision, and then get the heck out of the way so their vision comes to life, benefiting us all.

Carine is a Jewish community professional because her heart beats in service to her dream. Her talents and drive are beyond impressive, and there is no doubt that she would be paid a lot more if she were an innovation consultant. Yet she has chosen to dedicate her prime working years to a vision and idea that fuels her soul twenty-four hours a day, seven days a week even though, as of yet, it is not filling up her financial bank account.

Her journey can help us reflect and advise how we motivate, value, and support the hundreds Jewish community entrepreneurs, as well as, intrapreneur (those who innovate and create within organizations), types in our field.

Upstart, the organization that helps generate and support Jewish entrepreneurs has supported over 3000 people in their innovative projects over the past 20 years, launching hundreds of new 501©3 not-for-profit organizations and scores of additional innovative products within our legacy institutions Measuring in the thousands of professionals involved in these ventures, Jewish community professional entrepreneurs are no small subset of our Jewish workforce. If we seek to capture their innovative spirit to help the Jewish world generate the new ideas, technologies, and organizations we need in order to be relevant during the 21st Century, we must take care to focus on what makes this type of Jewish community professional tick.

Similar to many of our other professionals portraits, Carine fell into her role by mistake. Again, we have another exceptional talent who almost didn't find her way to our field, which reminds us to compellingly make a case for a career in Jewish life as early on as we can, seeking to invite talent that have been sparked by a Jewish experience into our field.

Carine's Jewish life growing up was, in her words, "ok, but not all that inspiring." This is until she spent a year during high school traveling in Israel. Carine had been to Jewish summer camp much of her young life; her Mom is Israeli and her Dad is Peruvian-Jewish, so there was always a strong connection to both diaspora Jewry and Israel in her home. Yet it was that year in Israel, on the North American Federation of Temple Youth (NFTY) Educational Israel Experience (EIE) that changed it all for Carine. Her exposure to and resulting love for Israel subconsciously began crafting her path toward both a career in, and the desire to shake up, Jewish life.

It was, in fact, a particularly emotional and eventful year abroad. Carine was in Israel during the second intifada that had begun in September 2000 and continued through 2002. Most potent, she was in Jerusalem during the terrorist attacks of September 11th, 2001. These events changed Carine who wanted to show her now unwavering commitment to Israel and the Jewish people. Carine decided not to go home after her junior year abroad experience. This was the first time, Carine reflected to me, that she stood up for something she truly believed in. The way Carine put it, "you don't show your solidarity with a check." Her fiery passion for what she cares about is very clear.

As noted in the online site Entrepreneur.com, part of identifying the type of person who has a relentless pursuit, a dream, or the spirit of an entrepreneur is simply to ask them the following:

• "what do you truly believe in?"

• "what would you show solidarity to or stand up for?"

• "what actions have you taken or would you take to show this?"

Just as we seek to best understand our employees, their self-reflection will enable them to better understand themselves. We can best value and motivate them by getting to know what they truly believe in and would stand up for. This, by the way, is a perfect time to remind you once again to make those coffee dates with each of your staff. Asking them these three questions during your conversation could reveal the extent to which they have their own relentless pursuits.

Carine's time in Israel began a life-long struggle to determine "how much Israel" she would want in her life at any given time. She wondered at the time and still occasionally does today, "could she do anything outside of work around Israel that would truly make her happy?" She thus engaged in several subsequent participatory and staff experiences to help her answer her own questions. Carine kept going for the big adventure experiences. She participated in several summer experiences with the company Outward Board across the continent. She returned to staff NFTY in Israel programs. She was on staff at URJ Camp Eisner and completed a semester abroad at Hebrew University in Jerusalem. She was beginning to accumulate multiple touch points to Israel, all while planting the seeds of her future entrepreneurial pursuits.

When Carine graduated from Bates College, she had a defining experience that explains her career in the Jewish sector. Carine wanted to explore the adventure experience a bit further, so she staffed an Outward Bound trip to Norway. It was totally different from anything she had ever done. She was in Norway for a month with twelve teens, and it was explicitly a secular program. They went hiking in the Norwegian fjords and whitewater rafting in the spectacular rivers in the countryside. Yet, for Carine, something was missing. Unlike all of her prior experiences, it was just a trip. It was a whole a lot of fun and the terrain was beautiful, but it was just another trip. It was not feeding any of her passions.

Carine realized what was missing: ideology and connection to tradition. She and her teens were taking pictures of the land, but they were not connecting with it; they just moved on. She contrasted this with her Birthright experience in Israel. When they connected to the land in Israel, it was so core to the purpose and hope of these experiences. It was a tough realization yet at the same time freeing and informative for Carine to acknowledge that she didn't feel the same elsewhere.

IDENTIFYING ONE'S PASSION AND PLACING IT AT THE CENTER

Part of fueling an entrepreneurial (or intrapreneurial) spirit is to identify and understand what a prospective Jewish community professional is passionate about and invested in, and then place these passions at the center of their work. We might think that our professionals are working on projects in their "Israel" when they actually feel they are in their "Norway." That is, the work may be interesting, but the content, environment, or context of the work may not be fueling their passion. It could also be the reverse. A professional may desire to work in or around "Israel" (literally or metaphorically) but the content of their work may be less desirable, and they would prefer, say, curriculum writing or fundraising rather than programming or staff learning experiences. Accumulating this data by deeply getting to know our professionals can help manager and employee together set the stage for each professional to move forward pursuing their dreams in direct correlation to their core. The answer, again, starts but getting to know each of our professionals at their core, and let them reflect on these passions with you.

Upon returning from Outward Bound, Carine called the Union for Reform Judaism (URJ) and said, "thank you." She wanted to make visible her gratitude to URJ for what she saw was the intentional and well-built curriculum. Perhaps it was fate that Carine placed that call of gratitude, as the URJ immediately offered Carine a full-time job in New York. There, she developed marketing materials and a message to attract new participants to URJ Israel travel programs. This planted yet another seed into what would eventually become Carine's current passion.

After 3 years at URJ, Carine was offered a position working for a competitor, Authentic Israel, to do a similar job, where she was able to double her salary move to Washington, D.C. She worked for Authentic Israel 4 years, providing trip experiences to Birthright, BBYO and other client organizations, until, then, as budding entrepreneurs often do, got itchy, and wanted something new and in a position in which she could grow.

Without hesitation, she called up Anne Lanski, Executive Director of the I-Center for Israel Education, whose mission is to be the "national hub and catalyst for building, shaping, and supporting the field of Israel education." Carine developed a mentor-mentee relationship with Anne and told her, "I need a fellowship." Carine knew that her next trip was to a graduate school program to help get her to her next step, but she didn't know which program and didn't have the funding to pay for it. Carine called upon her mentor to help figure this next step out.

Anne quickly responded and said, "You have to go to business school, and you have to be a Wexner Graduate Fellow." Carine was taken aback. As she reflected to me, "I had never said M, B, and A in that order in my life, and I had never heard of the Wexner Foundation."

She applied and got in to both, intentionally seeking out a degree program that wasn't exclusive to or even primarily serving the Jewish world. Carine had a vision to learn from the wisdom and experience outside the Jewish sector and then bring that wisdom back in to our field. Her emerging vision was to integrate the best of for-profit and non-profit Jewish and Israel travel programs… and then create her own.

Enrolled in Business school at Boston University, Carine became further enthused by entrepreneurship and innovation. While in school she planned and directed two "I-Track Programs, (I for Israel)" which brought seventy of her peers, mostly people of other faiths, to Israel, with Carine independently fundraising. Her initial motivation was simply to have fun with an interesting project. Yet she didn't anticipate how much impact this trip could have not just for the Jewish individuals participating but also for the people of all faiths who relished the trip experience.

Their reactions were the final seed needed for Carine's entrepreneurial spirit to take root and begin to grow. Carine, now with the skill sets, network, and motivation completed her MBA with an internship at Start-Up Nation Central in Tel-Aviv. While at Start-Up Nation, Carine worked with multinational agencies and businesses, partnering with Israeli start-ups. Through this experience, she decided to start her own business. Her dream became crystal clear: create Jewish Camp for Adulthood experiences and call her organization Trybal Gatherings. She graduated with her MBA and started her business in May 2016.

As we reflect on Carine's journey up until this point, it is worth pointing out what we should be looking for when identifying and then nurturing the Jewish community professionals among us with the relentless pursuit who thrive on innovation and willing a dream to reality. A simple guide is outlined in the *Harvard Business Review* article from 2013 by Tomas Chamorro-Premuzic, who describes in detail the five characteristics of the innovator. These include:

- An opportunistic mindset

- Formal education or training

- Proactivity and a high degree of persistence

- A healthy dose of prudence

- Social capital

Charmorro-Premuzic sees an **opportunistic mindset** as someone who can identify a gap in a marketplace and are pre-wired for novelty. Carine's experiences along with her natural talents allowed her to identify a market gap which she's described as "meaningful and life-changing Jewish immersive experiences for young adults." She is building from what she has experienced with people of all faiths and in varied contexts to create a new product . This is in part why understanding the narratives of all of our staff are so important. We may not yet realize the market gaps our staff may be noticing.

Charmorro-Premuzic also stresses that only those with **formal education or training** can identify the "noise from the signals," which is understanding which information is relevant to bring an idea to life. Carine's move to earn her MBA and a Wexner Fellowship, as well as her training internship at Start-Up Central, has helped focus her mind and her innovative lens, strengthening her ability to make smart decisions and decipher which inputs in her life will help her and which will not. The more our staff are invited to participate in professional development or meaningful training, the more they may be become wired to identify "noise from the signals," (signals being the core ideas worthy of remembering versus the unimportant noise around them) and relentlessly pursue an innovative idea.

Carine has sacrificed much of her personal life for the pursuit of her dream, which has come with a series of setbacks even in her short time leading this effort. Interestingly, her setbacks have only fueled her fire more. I encourage all of us to watch Carine's ELI Talk given at Upstart's Collaboratory conference in May 2018, where she talks in her CollabraSTORY about her power of NO to fuel her. If you were to look up **persistence**, especially in the face of adversity, the third of Charmorro-Permuzic's characteristics of the innovator, I wouldn't be surprised if Carine's picture was front and center.

Charmorro-Premuzic describes the fourth characteristic, **prudence**, as organized, cautious and risk-averse, which we may at first glance not attribute to the characteristics of an innovator. One might think of the creative type as one with a messy desk, a free-wheeling risk taker who attempts all ideas without much thought. Carine recognizes the risk she has taken to start her own organization, so she has started this game slowly and worked diligently for an entire year before launching her first retreat experience, then preparing for another entire year before expanding to an additional experience per year. To Charmorro-Premuzic, risk isn't taking action willy-nilly but ensuring care and organization at each step. Carine is an example of taking a BIG risk in small, carefully-organized steps.

Finally, there is **social capital**, which we can define here as mastering the use of one's network, and as Charmorro-Premuzic puts it, "mobilizing resources and building strong alliances, both internally and externally" to realize one's vision. Throughout the early phases of her career, Carine has amassed an exceptionally impressive network, one that only expanded through her participation in the Wexner Graduate Fellowship, her MBA program and the Upstart community. She is strategically making the most of each network contact to attract grant funding, corporate sponsors, camp sites, marketing, and programming. This may be her dream, yet she is creating an entire village to make the dream come true. In doing so, she is connecting to one of the ten principles of networking from Curtis Ogden, switching our mindset from what Ogden terms "You're the Leader" to "We're the Leaders." Carine is trying to not make Trybal Gathering's identity one and the same with her but allowing everyone involved to own the experience.

Charmorro-Premuzic expands on the five characteristics by stressing the importance of something that Carine has in spades: "Even when people possess these five characteristics, true innovation is unlikely to occur in the absence of a meaningful mission or clear long-term vision. Indeed, vision is where entrepreneurship meets leadership: regardless of how creative, opportunistic, or proactive you are, the ability to propel others toward innovation is a critical feature of successful innovation. (Charmorro-Premuzic, 2013)." As we consider how to harness these five characteristics to best identify and retain talented Jewish community professionals, we must recognize that part of our role is to give our professionals ample opportunity to craft a vision of their own.

With these characteristics and Carine's journey thus far in our minds, we can scan our workforce for these five characteristics and identify what bubbles to the surface. There are likely extraordinary ideas and incredibly talented individuals within our organizations. Once we make it a priority to get to know our staff deeply and encourage each of them to share their bold ideas, we must support and nurture them by giving them what they need to thrive. This starts with the lessons of Blessing #1: creating an environment of autonomy, the resources and training they need to feel competent in their work and to pursue their passion, and a community for which they can network to grow and feel a sense of belonging.

HOW ELSE CAN WE MOTIVATE THOSE WITH A RELENTLESS PURSUIT?

Expose Innovators to Different Environments and Inspirations

As an innovator, one of Carine's deepest motivations comes from the challenge to best infuse the exceptional practices she has been exposed to outside the Jewish world into Trybal Gatherings. As Carine's journey reveals, being exposed to different experiences can be an enormous motivating factor. Another is to ask our staff, as Carine frequently asks of herself, to push the envelope by noting what each of us is inspired by and then motivating our staff to translate that to something impactful in their work.

Provide Unlimited Agency

Whether we are the funder or the manager, we must give our Jewish community professionals with an entrepreneurial spirit unlimited agency and ample time for creativity. Carine loves that no one has ever done what she is doing now in the Jewish context, but to get this far she needed a lot of time to prepare before launching. Being the prudent innovator, she spent 12 months refining her vision and planning before her first retreat. She felt freedom in the fact that no one, at least no professional, was around to tell her NO. She was in charge. She got to make the calls.

Although the Jewish community professionals who work for us cannot call all the shots, we can create an environment in which they have ample time to pursue passion projects, such as the 20% time projects we discussed in Blessing #9 or simply providing sufficient time to complete a project. Sometimes a time-bound goal is helpful and other times it may be a deterrent to greatness.

The Innovator as Client

Carine is also motivated to pursue Trybal Gatherings because she loves serving her own age group, which has been part of her job in all of her professional roles. She has evolved with her peer group, planning programs for and getting feedback from them. When she sees them engaged in a Jewish experience that she brought to life, it is beyond validating and motivating for Carine. Thus, a subset of her dream is to create programs that age with her as she, the innovator, feels personally impacted by her own work, and thus, in a way, she is her own client.

Allowing One's Creation to Inspire Others to Take the Own Leaps

Carine is also motivated and feels valued when she sees people have taken from what she has given them through a Trybal Gatherings retreat. Carine shared with me that a former participant on one of the trips Carine staffed recently decided to go to medical school in Israel because Carine took her there during a trip. There was also the case in which one of her former Trybal Gatherings campers decided to sign up for a OneTable Shabbat dinner experience in Los Angeles after an amazing time at Trybal. The former camper didn't know anyone in Los Angeles, and OneTable seemed to have the same vibe as the Jewish camp experience Carine directed, so she decided to give OneTable a try. For Carine, this gives her a feeling of "YES! – that is what I hope you would do!" Her most recent example was two people who participated in a recent Trybal Gatherings experience and subsequently started dating, and one asked the other out using a gift which was a painting of the Trybal logo. Carine was beyond touched.

Although these experiences touch on many of the blessings in this book, and they all overlap to some degree, there is also something unique here: Carine's vision. Her vision, her dream, wasn't just the Trybal Gatherings experiences. That is simply the program that helps the dream come true. Her dream is creating impact for others through these retreat experiences. Herzl's dream was not merely a state of Israel, but what a formal homeland would mean to the Jewish people of future generations. Carine's dream isn't simply camp. It is providing her campers an entry point into further participation in Jewish and healthy adult life. According to initial testimonials and participant evaluations Carine shared with me, many who have experienced Trybal Gatherings now take more risks then they used to, and they are building new healthy relationships, and feel they are living life to the fullest. Carine's vision is coming true, which only feeds the vision more. When Herzl got the world Zionist Congress together, or when he was able to help Jews set up the first communities in Palestine, he didn't stop – and had he seen the day in 1948 when Israel became a state, he wouldn't have stopped – because a vision fulfilled is not a vision completed.

Encouraging Them to Keep Going

It is thus incumbent upon us as supporters of professionals with this *ruach*, this spirit, to help them continue once they have reached a milestone, to encourage them to keep going, iterating, experimenting and growing, because that is what their spirit desires and will only positively impact our Jewish community further. Carine believes that these motivations must be intrinsic. Work like this is one that no one is going to push us to do. Rather, the person with the dream has to dig deep.

I sometimes felt this way as I wrote this book, which no one has told me to write; it is a passion project that I have been dreaming about. My dean at JTS gave me the tools, autonomy, 20% time, and sense of value so I could be in a position to commence project even as now it comes to fruition over a year after moving on to a new organization, knowing that this volume will (hopefully) benefit and be of value to the stakeholders of Jewish community professional life. A supportive and nurturing community around Jewish community professionals can only help this intrinsic motivation expand.

Removing the Rosh Katans

It is also critical to remove the barriers that can demotivate Jewish community professionals with a relentless pursuit. For example, Carine hates those individuals she refers to as a *Rosh Katan* (literally "small head" but figuratively "small mind"). These people go out of their way focus on themselves and not the collective, often to the frustration of others around them. We must remove these people from the path of our relentless pursuers are on.

Carine, and I imagine nearly all of us, would rather work with individuals we could describe as a *Rosh Gadol*, (a "great" – or wise, kind – head). These are people who give themselves up for others, who help and who are selfless about their ideas and time, and who aren't consumed by their own vanity. These are the individuals who are best suited to inspire the Jewish community professionals around us and help those with a dream and will to make it a reality get there.

Recognizing and Nurturing the Ambition and Perseverance

Carine is more than just proactive and persistent; she is ambitious. She doesn't desire work/life balance or integration. She's been deconditioned to expect any type of balance, given both the organizations that she has worked with and the drive inside of her. Neither she nor I are sure if that is a good thing, but, given her 24/6 approach (she does give herself a Shabbat) to Trybal Gatherings, she seems to be ok with this.

In an early pivot for Trybal Gatherings, Carine lost part of her funding and was in danger of not being able to run the six programs she was responsible for. Carine was "a little freaked out," as she put it. Yet she did not panic. Rather, she calmly made a plan to scale back, chose which programs to run, and began heeding advice from the many smart people in her network, using her social capital. Most told her just to run one program, but Carine was adamant about running at least two. Those around her pressed her to have her "proof of concept" and get it done, and that it had to be run really well so this dream could be sustained and expanded.

She was in crisis mode. She didn't have any funding, yet characteristic of a true innovator, she was persistent. She cold called donors to raise money. She realized her personal and professional reputation was on the line and that if she didn't run any of these programs, Trybal Gatherings would be sunk. She knew it was time to put up or shut up and had no choice but to make these two programs happen. Many people had doubted her success, so she had to ensure that these two retreats were "grand slams."

This particular challenge was an enormous motivator for Carine. She had been told NO by so many people. Folks told her to cut her losses even though her first gatherings already had press releases and promotional materials out; to not run them simply would have been a disaster, and Carine would not let that happen. Carine reflects that she never had to work as hard in her life to make those initial gatherings happen. On the precipice of failure, Carine was fueled with her desire to succeed. Nothing drove her more, in part because so many people told her she wasn't going to be able to do it.

The funding challenge that came Carine's way was also fueled by a challenge by a prominent Jewish leader. As Carine explained to me, there was someone high up in the Jewish world who had said to a colleague, "if Carine can pull (this initial gathering) off, then she is a true entrepreneur!" Carine heard that and thought, "Oh my G-d, if this person said this, then I am going to make sure that this happens!" Having her ambition and perseverance recognized in this way was a huge motivator. She wanted to know that she did it despite all the NOs and obstacles in her way. This is her ultimate motivation and what she hopes is a part of her legacy. Carine delivered two exceptional retreats, which has helped Trybal expand to an organization with multiple staff and three 4-day Jewish adult camp experiences in 2019, with retreats to resume again post COVID-19.

Poor Compensation Again, De-Motivates, Even the Entrepreneur

Carine dislikes disproportionate compensation. Aligned with our other portraits, when Carine is compensated appropriately, it isn't a motivator per say — she has a ton of intrinsic motivation and endless optimism — but it is certainly a demotivator when she isn't paid well. As we've seen before, money is not the motivator, but a lack of healthy compensation, even for the entrepreneur, can create stress, feeling a lack of value, and, in the worst-case scenarios, failure for all of us to have our best innovative ideas and projects ever come close to fruition.

Yet where the story differs from our previous narratives then for Carine and Jewish community professionals with a relentless pursuit who want to see her entrepreneurial dream come true, is her desire to sacrifice her own financial well-being for her dream. She had dipped into her savings so she wouldn't need to take a salary for at least the first two years of this venture. Sometimes she questions herself if she wants to take this difficult path anymore. In her mid-thirties at the time of this publication, she wants to buy a house, which she actually has the down payment for but she can't get a loan because she hadn't yet demonstrated sufficient income.

While there are serious financial frustrations with her current position, there are also many moments of optimism. When at scale, Trybal Gatherings can hopefully model Carine's values around compensation.

Carine also notes her personal situation; at the time of this publication, she is single, with no kids and no debt, except for a debt of gratitude to the Wexner Foundation for covering graduate school tuition and providing a living stipend for several years. Put another way, she has no liabilities other than her own well-being as she pursues her dream. More often, Jewish community professionals have student debt, mortgages, families, or other liabilities that often make it difficult for them to take the risks that Carine is undertaking to will her dreams to reality.

One can say that this makes it all easier for Carine, though pursuing this dream may also mean sacrificing her family and social goals in the process. Perhaps this is just the life of an entrepreneur. My hope is that this blessing and the strategies it has identified for us can help us more generously support our entrepreneurial Jewish community professionals so their dreams can be more easily fulfilled and our Jewish community can appreciate and feel the impact.

What else can we do to motivate and strengthen the work of these innovative Jewish professionals? Here are a few more strategies to consider as we reflect on Carine's journey:

Allow Them to Dream, Even During the Off-Times

Carine has an extremely strong work ethic, which she acknowledges is probably a detriment to her social life. She loves getting up in the morning and tackling the challenges ahead of her. She often gets her best ideas when she is "not trying," often referred to as shower moments. She then keeps working on the idea, refining them sometimes until 4:00 a.m.

Encourage Them To Exercise Self-Control

Carine also realizes every day that it takes a lot of motivation to work alone and from home. Carine describes herself as a "flaming extrovert," yet she can be laser focused and "dialed in" while working. Carine also has great self-control, and if she knows she is supposed to work from 9am-6pm every day, she does it, without fail.

Looking Outside to Strengthen the Inside

To harness her creativity and strengthen her work ethic, Carine spends significant time outside the bubble of the Jewish world, around other creative people. As we discussed earlier in this blessing, this is a practice that we should encourage all of our Jewish community innovators to do. Let us give them the time and compensation to spend time outside the bubble. Those of us fortunate enough to receive a graduate or field-professional fellowship often receive additional funds or time to pursue professional development or new learning experiences. This on its own furthers one's motivations but can also spark new ideas and innovations that can benefit Jewish life. For the vast majority of Jewish community professionals who are not part of these fellowships, organizations themselves can prioritize such time for staff so they can grow, innovate, and dream.

Most of Carine's creative ideas come from practices from outside Jewish community, often from hanging out in secular spaces with friends and colleagues of all faiths, observing interesting programs and then considering how she can bring them to the Jewish world. That's when her best ideas come and, during those shower moments, is when she synthesizes her secular experiences with Jewish community.

Placing Constraints to Strengthen Creativity

There is a phrase that Carine learned long ago when she was working in Israel: "constraints increase creativity." This is Carine's mantra. Sometimes Carine will give herself thought exercises: "what would I do if I had to subtract one element of my product and still deliver it?" This mode of creative thought is part of the S.I.T. model, or Systematic Inventive Thinking, whose slogan is "don't do innovation, innovate in what you do."

The SIT model is core to the innovator's practice. When translating programs from outside the Jewish world into our field, it is inevitable that practices such as subtraction, addition, or other SIT models occur. Carine also generates and keeps an IDEA LIST on her phone that she's been maintaining for close to a decade. She now has hundreds of ideas that she keeps adding to and referring back to, some of which she will eventually pursue and execute either within or in addition to Trybal Gatherings.

To review, additional ways we can best motivate and strengthen the work of these innovative Jewish community professionals is by:

• Giving them time to dream

• Allow them to control their own work ethic and destiny

• Allow them time to explore ideas from outside our world

• Place creative constraints to help them imagine and foster creative innovative thinking

Ultimately, Carine strongly believes that an entrepreneur cannot survive motivated solely by external accolades and recognition. The motivation most be internal and with no chance for it to go to empty, and this intrinsic motivation must be nurtured and celebrated.

Lastly, though the motivation must come from inside, there is power providing the entrepreneur direct feedback and recognition. Direct, specific feedback can feel amazing to Carine even if it isn't always glowing. It is data that Carine can then connect back to the work, amplifying what's working and adjusting what may not be. Perhaps the times when Carine feels the most valued though are in the post-camp thank you notes. One read, "I was in a dark place, then you brought me to camp, and now I feel light." Some of those letters brought tears to Carine's eyes, especially when she didn't even ask for that positive feedback. This organic validation is tremendously motivation, and can be model for us managers and leaders, encouraging those around us and ourselves to write these unsolicited notes of appreciation.

Carine is willing it, and Trybal Gatherings is no longer a dream. So many of our Jewish community professionals today, like Carine, not only have dreams, but they have the courage to pursue them. It is up to us to amplify what we are doing well and adjusting what we are not, for these Jewish community professionals to help make their dreams reality, benefiting our entire community.

1. How might we scan our staff for the characteristics of an innovator, identifying those who have a big dream or idea they could pursue as part of or as a corollary to their work? How might we then apply the learning from this blessing to help these Jewish community professionals pursue their dreams?

2. How might we place fair constraints, through the SIT Model or other means, on people's work in order to maximize creativity and innovation?

3. Given Carine's experiences how might we encourage unsolicited direct feedback to strengthen internal motivation and feelings of validation in our employees' work?

what success can look like

Blessing Summary — A narrative in which we notice many of the blessings we have discussed working in concert with one another. This narrative is instructive for how we can intentionally apply the blessings of this book to create healthy and inviting environments from the beginning of one's Jewish community professional experiences that can help motivate and bless our Jewish community professionals for the long-term.

The 12 Jewish community professionals we have gotten to know thus far and the big idea of how to best motivate, value, and bless our workforce are all from individuals 10-20 years into their careers. They have each experienced highs and lows and continue to evolve, each a work in progress.

Our last portrait is significantly earlier in his career path, having graduated from the University of Kansas in 2016. Thus far, all seems to be going well for Evan Traylor. Many of the blessings we have introduced throughout this volume are present in Evan's journey, keeping him motivated and blessed to be in our workforce. Thus, Evan is an emerging success story from our newest generation of Jewish community professionals. Examining a bit of his journey can help us uncover how to be intentionally successful with motivating and blessing upcoming talent. I place in **bold** areas in which Evan's journey were impacted by our noted blessings.

Evan's journey begins in Oklahoma City where he was frequently engaged with vibrant and exciting Jewish life experiences. He was active in his Reform congregation and spent summers at the Union for Reform Judaism's Greene Family Camp. In high school he got involved in NFTY (North American Federation of Temple Youth), and by his senior year was elected as NFTY's North American President. He also had the opportunity to spend time at URJ Camp Kutz, a teen leadership camp in Warwick, NY which closed after the 2019 Summer. During these childhood and adolescent experiences, Evan recalled being surrounded by passionate and engaging young Jewish adults. From a young age, Evan thought it would be "really cool" to be a rabbi or serve a Jewish organization, campus, or camp at a leadership level. Evan was surrounded by **mentors** and peers who modeled the joy and soul-fulfillment that comes from working in Jewish life. He **built meaningful relationships** with them and his co-participants and was **able to see the fruits of their labor** frequently. He would also easily notice them getting fired up when they got to **feed their creative drive** in planning and executing new programs, which got Evan fired up.

Still, Evan had other passions, including policy and politics, which led him to double major in political science and Jewish studies at the University of Kansas. During the spring semester of his junior year, Evan completed an internship in Washington, D.C. working for the central office of the D.C. public schools. He assisted with recruiting, hiring, and training principals and assistant principals for the district,

Similar to Ezra Shanken's journey in Blessing #3, though, something was missing. He went back to URJ Kutz Camp the following summer to teach teens and work closely with fellow counselors, and he felt he was in a space that made a visible and lasting difference. Though politics and policy still called to Evan, he found **the challenge** of serving in Jewish life more compelling. He also felt the social connections and **received the validation** in Jewish spaces that spoke to his core. By his senior year, Evan made the decision to look for a job in Jewish life.

During his college years, Evan kept strong connections to leadership at URJ and they began considering together how Evan could serve them post-graduation. Evan was able to land a unique role as the Presidential Fellow for Millennial engagement, which he described as "everything he was looking for" in his first job. He was able to work with friends with whom he had **built deep relationships**. He was able to work at a place that where **felt belonging and a sense of purpose**. He was also tasked with a **broad big-picture assignment**, engaging colleges students 20's and 30's in Jewish life, which required Evan to look at the big picture of operations for the movement. Further, Evan was fortunate to receive **mentorship** on a bi-weekly basis from the URJ President, Rabbi Rick Jacobs. It would not be hyperbole to say that Evan felt blessed with this set up.

After two years as a Presidential Fellow, Evan continued with the URJ, shifting his work back to the college space as its Associate Director for College Engagement, a position he held at the time of our interview. His **job was created his needs, giving them the flexibility** to move back to D.C. in part to be close to his partner and to feed his continuing passion for politics. He was tasked with building meaningful relationships with college students across the continent as well as with partners and collaborators, including Hillel International. He is encouraged to identify gaps in the services the Reform movement may be missing to best serve the college-age population and encouraged to be innovative and iterative, which **feeds his entrepreneurial spirit**. Evan is given ample space and flexibility to operate and start new initiatives, which was different to his experience, for example, working for DC public schools, where he often observed colleagues "going through the motions." Evan also felt like he can see a path of long-term growth for him at URJ. As he put it to me, "he can paint the picture of when we can do more of this work on a larger scale."

Evan's situation isn't perfect. He acknowledges getting frustrated when he has a creative idea that he is eager to pursue yet has to slow down because of bureaucracy. It is this inefficiency, that frustrates Evan. As he worked for a very big legacy organization, there was the struggle to keep the right people in the loop while still attempting to move forward in a timely manner and being sure he is kept in on the loop as well. This is often complicated further when he collaborates with other legacy institutions that face similar issues.

Certainly, it is difficult to remove all bureaucracy from a job. Processes and systems are often set up for good reason. Yet, Evan, despite all the blessings that have helped him enter and stay happily in the Jewish community professional sector, feels a constant tension between the need to be creative and the reality that most Jewish organizations are not prepared to run at a million miles per hour.

Still, the blessings that surround Evan's Jewish personal and professional journey thus far have far outweighed the frustrations. Given what we have learned throughout the journey of this Bless Our Workforce project, we could make the case that the presence and application of these blessings are largely why Evan became a Jewish community professional and why he sees a long-term vibrant and enjoyable future on this path. In addition, and as we will extrapolate further in our next blessing, the determinative factors for many of the Jewish community professionals we have met have also been true for Evan. Evan was heavily influenced by **mentors and role models** from a young age who showed him the joy working in Jewish community and encouraged him to become professionally involved. Evan is also incredibly connected to the **mission** of the Reform Movement, having been inspired by it all his life and holding positions in which it is abundantly clear how his work directly serves the cause.

Further, Evan has been given **ample flexibility** in each of his roles, from managing his own time to being granted the move to D.C., demonstrating **trust and autonomy** that allow Evan to thrive.

For Evan compensation, work/life balance, and DEIJ (diversity, equity, inclusion, and justice), areas of adjustments we will discuss in Blessing #15, are not major issues in his Jewish community professional experience. Evan generally has felt fairly well compensated in his professional roles. He has never viewed the rates to be overly generous, yet has always had enough to pay the rent, buy food, and have at least some income for discretionary expenses. Of course, Evan is still in his 20's and, like many of his peers, has fewer expenses than many of the more senior Jewish community professionals we have encountered. Evan recognizes that over time, for his wage not to be a demotivator, his compensation will need to grow.

What is unique about Evan relative to most of the other professionals we have met is that he is a Jew of color. As has become more prominent in today's discussions around diversity in Jewish life, we now know, thanks to many Jewish organizations including Dimensions and the Jews of Color Field Building Initiative, approximately 20% of Jews in the United States are people of color, and one has to infer that at least a meaningful percentage of Jewish community professionals are also people of color. Growing up in a small Jewish community in Oklahoma City, being a Jew of Color (JOC) wasn't something that Evan felt every time he went to synagogue. However, in high school and college, Evan came to take more ownership in exploring his identities and understanding the unique opportunities and challenges that came with being a JOC.

He recognizes now, though, that while it hadn't been part of his personal narrative, it was now going to be a part of his public one. There was a lot of awakening around Jews of color during the time that Evan was college (2012-2016), and because was already in several leadership roles in the Jewish community, he was primed for the time today in which more JOC and, frankly, more diversity overall would obtain leadership roles in Jewish life.

Despite having his own fair share of experiences with alienation, as that is the reality for many JOC feeling like they don't belong in many Jewish spaces, Evan's experience of staying in the Jewish community demonstrate the importance of creating more inclusive spaces. We can look to Evan's experience as a road map. In the Jewish spaces he grew up in, from Oklahoma to NYC to DC, he always felt **included, part of the oneness**, in the tribe of Jewish community and later in Jewish professional life. Evan felt comfortable working for the URJ because of personal relationships with staff and lay leaders.

Our important lesson here is to be especially intentional that our actions convey that all Jewish community professionals feel belonging in Jewish community spaces, which requires all of us to do a lot of deep listening and learning. We must have these coffee dates with Jewish community professionals of all backgrounds, ethnicities, and races, and continue to make a meaningful and substantive attempt to create and nurture spaces that celebrate all of us and make us feel that we belong.

Evan is just one story among the thousands of younger individuals today who have had meaningful, engaging, and joyful Jewish experiences from a young age and perhaps hundreds, hopefully at least dozens, that have been further inspired to seek a career in Jewish life. As this book is published Evan is enrolled in Rabbinical School at Hebrew Union College – Jewish Institute of Religion. To those not yet inspired but whom we also can attract to our field, we can see Evan's narrative as instructive. We have the power to intentionally make use of the blessings in this book, and create the environments in our organizations in which the strategies and techniques from these blessings are implemented, visible, and vibrant.

amplify our strengths

Blessing Summary — Making use of these blessings and how they can work in concert with one another, we can also examine the practices we are already doing well and amplify them in order to bless our workforce. These include listening, focusing on the mission of our work, providing Jewish community professionals with flexibility, and providing mentorship.

We have just journeyed through twelve blessings, each with big ideas and strategies that we can now try out on our staff. We also have a thirteenth narrative that explores an emerging picture of success, a bright spot, in which we see many of these blessings in action. This produces a large benefit not only for Evan but for the whole field. The individuals, we have encountered bared their hearts and souls, including sharing their many frustrations with their Jewish professional experience. If we *Shema*, or listen, closely, to their stories, we find that there is so much to celebrate about how we already motivate, value and bestow blessing onto our Jewish professionals.

One of these ways includes how we listen, which is core to who we are as Jews. We say the *Shema* every morning and every evening:

שמע ישראל יהוה אלהינו יהוה אחד

Shema Yisrael Ado-shem Elo-keinu Ado-shem Echad.
Hear O Israel The Lord is Our God the Lord is One.

It is our most sacred prayer and perhaps an emblem of our greatest strength. The prayer describes our community as being part of one included whole. In recalling what we learned from Aliza Kline in Blessing #6, we could learn from this text to **amplify** our work to make every member of our team feel included, part of the oneness of our community. Working to achieve such oneness can include a commitment to seek out and forge partnerships under one larger goal and a desire to scale our own successes through working to achieve the successes of others. The *Shema* implies that when we listen, people are and feel heard, included. At least among the people we connected with in this book, it is clear that many supporting and nurturing Jewish community professionals can be pretty good listeners.

AMPLIFYING OUR LISTENING

Each of those profiled has gotten to where they are because there was someone – a mentor, a clergy, a teacher, a supervisor, a colleague– who was paying attention to their talents, dreams, ideas and challenges, and then acted. Morris Squire listened to David before he offered his challenge. Alyson's youth advisor in high school listened and paid attention to her in high school before encouraging her on her path to becoming a Jewish educator. Miriam's clergy team paid attention to her, noticing not just her singing talents but her inner voice of passion, and planted the idea to pursue serving Jewish life. We could note an example of listening and consequential mentorship from nearly each of our blessings.

We say the *Shema*, whether during a prayer service or when we wake up in the morning or go to sleep at night, not only offering a blessing to God, or to whatever your concept of God or a higher being or sacredness may be, but as a reminder to ourselves: when we listen, when we *shema*, we give ourselves the presence of mind to act on these words, which take actions that can benefit those around us, helping steer each of them in the right direction.

Amplifying our listening strength means really listening, asking the deep questions we asked to each of our Jewish community professionals in this book, which can be found in the appendix, to our staff, colleagues, supervisors, and our lay leaders. We have to remind ourselves that, as a Jewish community and as non-for-profit professionals, we are generally pretty good at listening, paying attention, and acting when there is a person searching for direction. We pay attention to those less fortunate in our society, whether in poverty, crisis, persecution, or affected by disaster, and we are often among the first to aid and support. We pay attention to the latest technologies and innovate. We can also pay attention to the human talent around us and then act to **amplify** this practice so we, and they, can feel blessed and steered toward success.

We can focus on what is working within the network and do more of it. We feel less threatened and exposed when we focus on the positive. We are proud of what we do well – and are often enthused when we are charged with doing more of what we love and what we are good at – when we "strengthen our strengths."

Adam Simon, mentioned earlier, talks about this in his ELI Talk about managing talent. In his talk, Simon advises us explicitly to build teams to focus on each team member's respective strengths and, in the performance review processes, work on strengthening each other's best qualities as opposed to trying to improve what professionals may not be able to do as well. Athletes and professional sports teams' practice this. A great pitcher in baseball works on his pitching and doesn't focus much on his hitting. To get even more granular, a Closer, a pitcher who comes in to try to earn the last few outs of a game when their team is winning by a close margin, may only try to focus on perfecting his super-quick fastball, and maybe one curve ball or off-speed pitch, and that's it. He is not bothered by other pitches, hitting, or any other positions and their related skill sets. He focuses on what is working and how to do more of it to become an exemplary.

We as leaders and managers can more deeply listen to our professionals, understand their strengths, and further help them grow in areas where they already are excelling. As a result, we can be equally incredible at how we are already blessing our workforce by doing more of it. By amplifying what we already do well, some of the other problems we encounter may become less of an issue over time. A few issues may even resolve themselves, overcome by the strengths that we have perfected.

AMPLIFYING OUR MISSION

The Leading Edge *Leading Places to Work Surveys* deliver a clear message that Jewish community professionals are highly motivated and inspired by our organizational and communal missions. In fact, recent Leading Edge report in 2018 identifies that 87% of our employees are motivated by mission. Our narratives reinforce this, and many of their motivations directly point to this.

Our employees are *already* inspired by what we are trying to achieve. Much of the workforce on this continent, whether in the corporate sector, government, or other non-profits, are not nearly as inspired by the mission and values of their employer as they are in the Jewish world. According to Inc.com, 60% of Millennials, the generation found to be most motivated by a company mission, are motivated by the mission of their company. We can compare this to the 87% of all Jewish community professionals who are motivated by their mission. This is a gold mine for us, and we need to make the most of it.

Using Marc Fein in Blessing #11 as an example, he was often frustrated by the lack of validation he receives as a youth professional but is incredibly inspired by the mission of NCSY. This is a disconnect with a clear remedy. To limit these types of frustrations we should follow this simple schematic: Listen, Validate and Connect, Honor:

THE HONOR SCHEMATIC

- **Listen to our Jewish** community professional, so they know that we recognize their frustration

- **Validate and Connect** their work by expressing gratitude and congratulations (or even just a thank you) and then connect explicitly to the overall organizational mission that their efforts have helped achieve

- **Honor** by nurturing their own strengths and develop further the skills that have helped them advance the mission so they can accomplish even more

Perhaps, in amplifying our mission strengths, we take the time to make the mission clearer, simpler, and more evidently connected to our professional's work. For them to know why we do the work we do and see it in their work every day has the most powerful effect. A prime example again is with Rachel in Blessing #10, who feels blessed each time she observes her young staff members make the connections between what was occurring during the summer and what Rachel had taught them at the beginning of the summer. Let us make a commitment to **amplify** our Jewish professionals' mission awareness, turning up the motivation.

AMPLIFYING FLEXIBILITY

The more flexible we can allow our Jewish community professionals to be so they can be fully present during their work hours, the more appreciation they have for the supervisors and organizations Jewish professionals support. We can no longer go back to the rigid work hours of the 20th century, especially now after all we are learning during COVID-19. It is no longer the society we live in and, in fact, as our narratives shared plainly with us, job flexibility is already a key reason they feel motivated and valued in their jobs.

Certainly, many of those profiled who have reached senior executive or creative positions have an enormous amount of flexibility, working several days from home even before COVID, such as Rabbi Laura Baum in Blessing #8 , Alyson Bazeley in Blessing #2, and Carine Warsawski in Blessing #12.

We are becoming more comfortable and proficient at promoting flexibility in the Jewish professional space in part because we have to be. It is clear from the individuals we have met over these pages that Jewish community professionals are committed to getting the work done. Yet they are not committed, and actually sometimes frustrated, when they always have to be on someone else's schedule or at their workstation at the same hours on the same days, sometimes to the detriment of doing their job well. Using the language of Blessing #7 and in getting to know Graham Hoffman, we might say that following rules that prohibit us from doing our best work is a form of nonsense, inefficiency, or BS.

Certainly, there are roles that require in person coverage at specific hours, and it is important to have face time among the staff. Fostering collaborations and building relationships within a workforce does require people to build meaningful relationships with each other, as we learned from Ezra Shanken in Blessing #3. We can and should require certain times, whether some are in person and some over video conference, for fostering such interactions.

Yet this shouldn't take away from the need and desire for flexibility among Jewish community professionals today so they can get their jobs done in the manner that speaks to their strengths. Since our professionals are largely motivated by the foundations of internal motivations outlined in Blessing #1 — *autonomy, competence, belonging, and purpose* — to give our professionals as much as flexibility as possible fosters their sense of both autonomy and competence. The purpose is reinforced with the amplifying of our mission discussed just earlier, and the belonging can come from the innovative manner that we foster relationships.

AMPLIFYING OUR MENTORSHIP

There is also significant belonging to be nurtured in the relationships that got us to where we are and continue to guide us, which leads us to the final **amplification** that we have been highlighting all along, the use and practice of **mentors and coaches**. We have encountered repeatedly how Jewish community professionals are challenged, inspired, and nurtured by mentors. When most folks were telling Carine NO to Trybal Gatherings, her mentors from the Wexner Graduate Fellowship were showing support that helped her eventually get to the YES, she's needed. Ezra learned the power of relationships from the mentorship of former head of UJA-Federation of New York Jon

Ruskay. Mentors can be our partners too. Aliza Kline's mentor coached and supported her through the growth of Mayim Chayim, to the point that she was ready to succeed at a new challenge, creating and expanding OneTable. The Jewish community is so darn good at mentorship; we can be more explicit about assigning mentors to our staff, taking more advantage of this strength in order to bless our workforce!

Let me tell you about one of my mentors, Jane Slotin. I call Jane my professional angel. Jane has been an exceptional mentor for me for over 15 years. She **identified** my potential and pointed it out to me while I was a young coordinator, **gave me permission** to be creative and practice leadership, **thought of me** for roles I hadn't yet identified for myself, and gave me **courage and confidence** to tackle new challenges. She then went out of her way to **celebrate** my success so I wouldn't feel alone in celebrating them and that I wouldn't undervalue my own achievements.

When I was in my first role at the 92nd Street Y as a recruiter in the Human Resource Department, I worked with Jane to help her hire new staff, which eventually led to her hiring me part time when I was in graduate school. That was the **identification**. I was then working for Jane as her community service coordinator, planning volunteer events for younger Jews in their 20's and 30's. I was nervous programming my first social events for these volunteer groups. I remember clearly walking into Jane's office one day with my questions and trepidations. Jane simply said back to me, "you are the director of this program, you create and lead this, and I'll simply give you some feedback, but I am not going to answer all of your questions about how to do this." Jane was **giving me permission** to be an autonomous, entrepreneurial, and creative leader.

Many years later, Jane and I had both left the 92nd Street Y but kept in touch. In fact, she made it a point to support me through a somewhat challenging time in my career. She took personal care of seeing me reach my long-term potential, which included returning to the Jewish professional field. It was Jane who identified the program coordinator position at JTS that would eventually change my life and transform my career – and it was a job I might not have noticed, and more likely I wouldn't have even gotten an interview for, if it weren't for Jane **thinking of me**, and promoting me as ideal for this position.

As the years progressed and I advanced in my roles at JTS, I would continually hire Jane as a mentor for my students. As a member of my faculty team, Jane wouldn't hesitate to provide me with constructive feedback. Yet, each comment was always couched with sincere compliments about my work and leadership that, especially coming from a mentor like Jane, gave me the **courage and confidence** to continue to lead and design feeling motivated, positively challenged, and valued, and with an ambition to achieve at levels beyond what I had achieved previously.

Today, although elements of the first four of these steps still come in to play in our conversations, she mainly ensures that I have someone to **celebrate** my successes with. In fact, I make sure that I pay it back and celebrate in her successes as well, and provide feedback and thoughts when appropriate.

I share again here a bit of my own narrative to complement the journeys we have gotten to know in this book in the hopes that most readers will have similar stories of mentors or coaches who have helped them in similar ways. As we look at our supervisors within our field, let us consider how to **amplify the power of mentorship** that already exists in our Jewish community professional environment, notably how we can provide our talent with:

- *Identification* – to ensure Jewish community professionals see what they are capable of and the talents they can nurture in their current or future positions

- *Permission to Lead* – Providing Jewish community professionals a feeling of autonomy and competence, assigning projects and otherwise couching them in a way to give our employees the feeling of a directorship of all or part of our project so they can shine

- *Thinking of our Jewish community professionals first* – Connecting back to our success schematic in Blessing #2 (Happy Staff → Happy Camper → Happy Camp), thinking less of solely what is best for the organization and more about what is best for our staff now and in the long-term, which we have come to learn is actually best for the organization too. You may have a great staff person in a role fit for them, yet they may now or soon be ready for a new great challenge – and as a coach or mentor thinking of them and encouraging them to go for this new challenge.

- *Courage and Confidence* – at all stages of a Jewish community professional's career providing them with the positive and constructive feedback that gives them the courage and confidence to excel and do what they are doing better, capitalizing on their strengths.

- *Celebration* – Acting as the cheerleader, champion and number one fan for each of our Jewish community professionals, so they don't have to be alone in celebrating their successes.

Keeping It Up at 11 Without Blowing the Amp

One of my favorite but also least known songs from The Beatles is "It's All Too Much," written by George Harrison on the *Yellow Submarine* soundtrack. It is a loud psychedelic track with many instruments played at once. I enjoy listening to it, yet it is also very cacophonous and sometimes when the amplifier is turned up too high and all the time it can be overwhelming. That is all to say for us, we have a duty to **amplify** what we are already doing well to best motivate, value and bless our workforce. We are excellent at listening, inspiring others through our organizational missions, providing job flexibility, and as mentors and coaches who can transform careers. A word of caution though, not to turn these practices up willy-nilly like in "It's All Too Much." If we do, Jewish community professionals may feel it to be inauthentic. Therefore, as we begin to play with these ideas in our organizations, we must also consider how to strategically and authentically make our missions more apparent, provide flexibility, and embrace the concepts of mentoring each other within and among our organizations. Let's just be cautious not to turn the amplifiers up too much more than we already are.

adjust our imperfections

Blessing Summary — This blessing highlights 3 areas in which we can collectively make some adjustments to better motivate and value our Jewish community professionals today. This will ultimately lead to stronger organizations tomorrow that can more successfully accomplish their missions to strengthen Jewish life.

This blessing highlights three areas in which we as managers and leaders of Jewish organizations can make some adjustments in how we work with our professionals, based on themes we have visited throughout this book. We take a hard look at compensation, how we can re-imagine work/life balance, and how we can remove gender and other biases in our field. If we, collectively, make at least some of the necessary adjustments, we will better motivate and value our Jewish professionals. This will ultimately lead to stronger organizations tomorrow that can more successfully accomplish their missions.

ADJUSTING OUR COMPENSATION PRACTICES

The Leading Places to Work Studies have revealed that, among a fairly representative sample of Jewish community professionals, 47% feel they are *not* compensated fairly. Why is that? Our narratives have provided for us the following insights:

Lack of Transparency

We lack a culture of transparency around salary rationale. Often there is a lack of sufficient data to understand how different salaries compare. While this is slowly changing, it is still a norm rather than the exception that organizations do not post the salary range when advertising, presumably in order to hold leverage in a forthcoming salary negotiation with the desired candidate. Further, within an organization, folks can only guess, unless they work in Human Resources or in a position of leadership where they become aware of staff salaries, what others make and if their salary or other benefits compares fairly. The only salaries an employee or anyone outside the organization might know publicly are the top 5 organizational salaries that are publicly found on the organizations form 990 tax return, which can be found on guidestar.org, or in *The Forward's* annual survey of the Top 50 earning CEOs in our field.

Lack of Transparency creates a culture of guessing, not of blessing. It creates a culture of confusion, not a culture of fairness and feeling good about one's compensation. Narrative after narrative has made it clear that Jewish community professionals do not need to make a very high salary to feel valued, but they do not want to feel stressed over their compensation, to have their perceived low compensation a demotivator to an otherwise motivating job situation. They also want to be able to know that the organization takes their role seriously and is investing its own resources into their success.

It was unclear, for example, if Marc Fein's employer is taking seriously those serving youth today, or if Rachel, whose camp is a major source of the JCC's revenue, earns a salary that represents her essential role in the sustainability of the entire institution. It certainly is visible when the executive is paid well – David, Ezra, Aliza, and Becky among them – though, interestingly, Aliza and Becky worry if they are being underpaid and undervalued as a result of their gender, which can lower their motivations. Needless to say, a lack of transparency can lead to employees guessing and often perceiving they are being paid less than what they are worth, an enormous demotivating factor.

A Culture of Mediocrity

In Blessing #7, we talked a lot about cutting the BS and the systems that prevent us from doing our best work and that frustrate our Jewish community professionals. One of these systems is the way we look at salaries and at raises. Many of our organizations indicate that they want to be fair to all of their employees. Executives and Boards of Directors often interpret this as either no or all employees getting a raise in a given year as a COLA, or cost of living adjustment increase. Further, everyone should get the same COLA, typically 2-3% per year. Many organizations follow the COLA adjustments the government makes to social security payments, which in 2018 was 2.8% according to the AARP.

Yet for Jewish community professionals who perceive themselves as or are told that they are high performers, this practice can feel very unfair. High performers must be recognized through an increase that isn't the same as the employees whose work is deemed merely satisfactory. For us to implement such a practice in our organizations, we need to have a fair and robust performance review process and consider a hybrid COLA practice coupled with a pay-for-performance model in which employees receive additional salary increases related to their performance, which is more prevalent in industries such as healthcare where there are quantifiable deliverables. In the Jewish sector, deliverables can also be quantifiable as they relate to meeting fundraising goals, achieving high quality programs as measured by attendee surveys or testimonials, or simply exceeding one's job expectations as determined by management in partnership with the professional, with supervisors recommending merit increases to those who have demonstrated exceptional work.

Again, compensation matters, not merely to pay the bills, and certainly not in an effort to get rich, but as a statement of how much the organization values their contributions and how each can feel recognized for their strong performance and dedication to the organization. Though non-profit professionals aren't "in it for the money," to give a blanket uniform increase to everyone also gives this message: "work hard or don't work hard, and you'll get the same reward." This too can de-motivate our staff even though our intent may be the opposite.

Certainly, compensation is more than merely one's annual or hourly salary, and a high performer can receive a myriad of benefits outside of an increase in base salary to feel valued for their work, including intriguing professional development, increased flexibility to do their work, more interesting projects, or access to learn from important leaders in the field, including their own executives. Yet, the paycheck still is an important marker, so we must make a statement that high performance and contributions are properly recognized in their bank accounts as well as elsewhere.

Lack of Abundance Thinking

Naomi Korb-Weiss, formerly the Executive Director of PresenTense, North America, and currently a consultant to many Jewish not-for-profits, wrote a superb piece on ejewishphilanthropy.com several years ago that summed up our obsession with not investing too much in overhead expenses, quoting Dan Palotta. She includes staff salaries in her definition of overhead. The misguided thinking starts with the idea that donors want to have their donations applied directly to the program or the project, not to keeping the lights on or, often, to the people who are making the project come to life.

Similarly, the misguided thinking goes that if we give too much to investing in people, there won't be enough funds for the program or other needed expenses. This is, again, an example of the zero-sum game thinking that is part of a scarcity, rather than an abundance, model of thinking. If programming wins, staff loses. If staff wins then programming doesn't have enough funds to be successful, and that is not what the donors want to see in how their money is invested anyway. It is easy to locate an annual report that proudly demonstrates its 90% program/10% overhead ratio.

Sadly, this can leave Jewish community professionals today feeling that they are underpaid, undervalued, underinvested in, and under-appreciated. We have to remind ourselves of Zeynep Ton's Virtuous Cycle, one that Palotta in his TED Talk aimed at not-for-profit organizations:

DR. ZEYNEP TON'S VIRTUOUS CYCLE: ADAPTED FOR THE JEWISH NON-PROFIT SECTOR

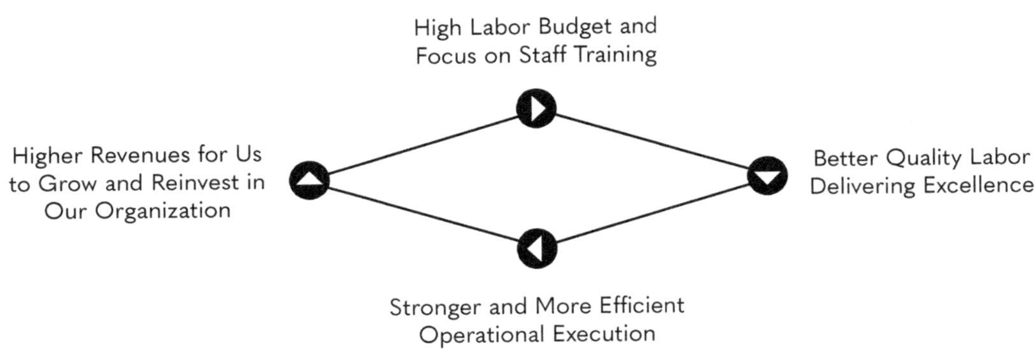

If we have higher labor costs, and we execute our operations well and cut the BS, we will have better operational execution and higher sales and profits. Yes, if we pay our staff MORE then we will make more both in the mission bottom line and the financial bottom line in return!

How to Adjust — Pay Well and Above the Market Rate

If we examine our profiles, those who feel they are paid really well, typically but not exclusively the male executives, feel valued by their pay check and don't worry so much about their compensation. Those that feel they are not still give their one hundred percent, yet they take notice of it, which takes up energy and decreases their feeling of being valued. In the long term, this may impact their performance and precipitate an exit from our field altogether. For example, Marc felt his pay as a youth director was undervalued, which sometimes undermines his passion for this work.

Instead of paying our staff just enough, or doing so without a clear sense of transparency or considering past performance, I would simply reinforce Ton's recommendation to pay them a bit more than enough. If we practice this approach consistently and regularly, in time the culture in our field will shift. We will save funds and resources while experiencing lower turnover, increased efficiency and productivity, and revenue growth. It happened for Costco; it can happen for us.

Yes, this requires up-front investment, and an understanding from donors, patrons, and foundations what is truly the cost of doing our work in a way that will lead to ultimate and sustainable success.

ADJUSTING OUR PRACTICES TO ACHIEVE GENDER EQUITY

We have thirteen narratives in this book, seven women and six men. Seven are now in an executive or #1 position, as both Graham and Laura moved CEO or Head of School roles respectively after my Fall 2017 interview with them. Four of the seven executives are women. I intended to profile a diverse breadth of Jewish community professionals, yet these numbers are not truly representative of our larger field, in which the workforce predominantly is approximately 70% women yet the leadership of our organizations, especially legacy institutions, is approximately 70% men. In *The Forward* survey of CEO salaries in 2017, only two women were in the top 30, and they held positions #29 and #30.

Similarly, according to both Pew and Leading Places to Work, the gender pay gap in the Jewish world merely mirrors global society. Those who identify as women were paid $.79 to every $1 man were paid as of 2019. So, clearly, the gap in leadership roles and pay isn't unique to the Jewish community, but today's Jewish community professionals are still cursed with this reality.

During my time as the Managing Director of the Leadership Commons at the William Davidson School of JTS, the Leadership Commons conducted a research initiative that examined how we and various collaborators could advance women into more leadership positions and reduce the gender pay gap in Jewish Education. Our initial thoughts were to provide more training to women to give them the tools and skills to navigate hiring committees and salary negotiations. We quickly understood, however, that this was the wrong strategy. Thanks to the leadership of two extraordinary academics and project directors, JTS Faculty Dr. Shira Epstein, now Dean of the William Davidson School, and Project Director Dr. Andrea Jacobs, we reexamined our models to ask what we expect of our executives, regardless of gender.

We have an expectation that leadership must always come from the top and must always work 24 hours a day 7 days week (many times working by attending social functions during the Sabbath as well) in order to be "successful." This model also includes posting a laundry list of expectations and functions in the job-descriptions we see on jewishjobs.com or on the websites of executive firms. These jobs are often untenable for anyone committed to be a present parent, a responsibility society still largely places on women.

Our model of negotiating also fails to work properly. We put the onus on the candidate to advocate for themselves for the highest salary possible instead of offering our best offer from the start to their desired candidate which, on its own as a solution, would reduce the gender pay gap. This is coupled with living in a society where it is ok for men to be aggressive, to negotiate and be tough, and still today, women might be called "difficult" when they act identically.

In light of today's societal changes and in reflecting the experiences of the profiles we have just seen, we have ample data to help change the models of leadership with respect to gender. In doing so, all of today's Jewish community professionals could then feel that they are playing on level playing field, and thus be more enthused to be part of a Jewish community who lives up to these values. We can get there by **adjusting** our practices and regularly practicing the following:

- *Returning to Compensation* — Be transparent. Stop negotiating. Set a salary level, not even a range, that is impressive for the role, non-negotiable, and identical regardless of the new hire's gender. Follow the guidance from the Talmud (Bava Metzia 83b) to "raise our worker's wages in order for them to do better work."

- *Re-writing the Job Description* — We must not write job descriptions that look like a laundry list of obligations. Let us be realistic with the job functions and expectations of our executives and all of our employees so they can do better work and have a meaningful life with family or other interests and friends beyond work.

- *Training Hiring Committees* — In the 2019 Gender Equity and Leadership Initiative report released by the Leadership Commons, Epstein and Jacobs advocate for training hiring committees through a gender lens. We need to put our biases out in the open and have someone on our committees say out loud, "are we saying this about this person because of their gender? Let's be honest with ourselves." Further, JTS's Seeds of Innovation program, which provided seed money for JTS alumni to create an innovative project that supports the Jewish community, granted JTS alumnae Dr. Sara Shapiro-Plevan and Rabbi Rebecca Sirbu, funds to launch a hiring committee training program which can train a "gender lens ambassador" on every executive hiring committee – which every organization reading would benefit from participating in.

In considering her legacy, Aliza from Blessing #6 shared with me a frustration she's had for most of her professional life: finding female role models in the Jewish sector who are also executives. Aliza laments that it is not a long list. While she hopes she can be such a role model for others by the end of her career, she hopes she doesn't reach that point without having to find such a role model for herself. She wants to be celebrated within a network of other change makers and other women leaders who helped change the face of what leadership looks like in the Jewish community.

Aliza's concerns resonated with many of our female portraits notably Becky and Carine, as well as several of the male-identifying individuals we profiled. Our field is predominately female, yet the vast majority of executives especially at legacy institutions are male, and this hasn't changed much over the past two generations as more females have entered the work force and obtained graduate degrees. This, sadly, has sent a clear message to females that they, other than occasionally, will not be welcomed and accepted as executives in our field. As we consider the consequence of Blessing #6 when we allow many of our Jewish community professionals to feel "ostracized" or "othered," the current emerging generation of Jewish community professional leadership has, like Aliza, much less patience for this reality.

REINFORCE WORK-LIFE BALANCE

The story of creation in the book of Genesis is a story that gave us the most precious gift of Jewish tradition, Shabbat. On Shabbat we have the space to commit to three actions: *to rest, reflect, and express gratitude*. Shabbat can lead to a happier life because we regain our energy learn from our reflections and feel more appreciative of our lives. Consider our week, or our work, to be like a symphony. In playing a page of sheet music, there are notes and there are rests. The music only works well when the performers rest at the right times, makes the notes they do play clear, ordered, crisp and compelling.

Jewish community professionals must be allowed to have a similar approach. Alyson, for example, has the rest time to be with her family. As a result, she is a stronger Jewish educator, performing with excellence when she is playing the notes of her job. Carine can set her own schedule so she can give herself the time off when she needs it. Those professionals who can have true time off, both during their work and doing their year, are able to rest, reflect, and express gratitude, and play their work notes with gusto.

A new trend in promoting work/life balance is the Sabbatical – which more and more executives are taking, not just clergy. The Jim Joseph Foundation is currently exploring how to support for organizations and employees at multiple levels to take a significant Sabbatical. We can think of the Sabbatical – etymologically related to "Shabbat" – as a way to take time off in order to recharge and feel blessed for what we have and have accomplished.

We already know empirically and anecdotally that today's Jewish community professionals work hard, and they shouldn't feel as if they need to work all the time in order to get the work done. Here are simple steps we can take to help bless our Jewish community professionals in the area of balance:

- Review job descriptions and responsibilities with them – are we asking for too much? Allow the professional to have input into the formation and balance of their own job.

- Review their work hours – do they make sense given the work they need to complete? Perhaps it is possible they can navigate their responsibilities in a modified schedule that works for them and still satisfies the organization.

- Review a staff person's needs - Perhaps a great worker needs time during a weekday for family or different work hours given their current commute time.

- As we explored in Blessing #9, consider with the professional how they can bring more of their personal interests and integrated self to their work. In addition to rest, the professional may find more balance if they find more of their full selves in the workplace.

By being aware of employees' needs, they will already feel a sense of value, motivation, and blessing. This again speaks to our Jewish professionals today simply needing to feel heard, visible, and validated. This shouldn't be the exception in our field; it must standard operating practice.

Make the Adjustments, and Reap the Benefits

Just as amplifying what we do well will help better bless our workforce and help us get out of the vicious cycle and onto the virtuous cycle, so will making the necessary adjustments. The idea of blessing is nothing new in the area of Jewish tradition. To conclude our journey together, let's go back to our original source, the Torah and a story from my own journey that has led to this project to *Bless Our Workforce, Mah Tovu.*

mah tovu

When I was 12, my rabbi assigned me the Torah Portion Balak, from the Book of *Bamidbar* (Numbers), as the portion I would read from and then speak about during the morning I became a Bar Mitzvah. I had not yet studied Balak, the King of the Amalekites, and his quest to destroy the Israelites, who had just escaped from slavery in Egypt. Balak wanted to halt the Israelites' journey and attack the wandering tribes. He figured the best way to do this was to hire a wizard to curse the Israelites as they were dwelling in their makeshift tents.

 This wizard, Balaam, was happy to take the job. After meeting with Balak and assigned to curse the Israelites in their tents, he took his donkey and headed towards the Israelite camp. It is at this point that this donkey turned out to be a pain in Balaam's ass. He veered off track, distracting Balaam from completing his mission.

 Balaam beat the donkey until the donkey began to talk. I paraphrase from the Torah and take a little creative license here. "Why do you beat me?" the donkey asked. In Balaam's frustration, he continued to beat the donkey until the presence of God appeared. Balaam was humbled. God's presence had shifted Balaam's perspective. He was no longer a man on a mission to curse a people. Instead, when he arrived at the Israelite Camp, out came words of blessing, from the Book of Numbers, Chapter 24 Verse 5:

מה טבו אהליך יעקב משכנתך ישראל

Mah Tovu O'Halecha Ya'akov, Miskhenotecha Yisrael.
How Goodly Are Your Tents O'Jacob, your Houses of Israel.

Balaam, sent by Balak because of his power through words to curse the Israelites and thus be beneficial for his Amalekite people, actually performs the opposite directive. Balaam's powerful words bless the Israelites. I often like to think that this blessing was one of the reasons the Israelites made it to the promised land, and that this blessing has helped the Jewish community survive these thousands of years, through triumph and persecution, condemnation and liberation, to a position in the early 21st Century in which, despite our numerous challenges, we thrive both in the state of Israel today and in our many diaspora communities around the globe.

As a budding adolescent in 1994, I read this portion and took the lesson to be about the magic, or power, of words. I recall quoting the parable, "sticks and stones may break my bones, but words will never hurt me," and challenging it, re-stating that "words may actually hurt the most," during my speech, or d'var Torah. I still believe in the power of this lesson today, that the words we say, or we choose not to say, that can either bless or curse.

We, stewards of the Jewish organizational experience are, in many ways, exactly like Balaam, and in a key way the opposite. We are like Balaam in that we have tremendous power when leading our organizations. Our words and deeds matter and have consequences. They can have tremendous benefit and can cause tremendous harm.

Yet what may not be obvious is when our words and deeds unintentionally, without our *kavanah*, curse our workforce, inhibiting our employees from reaching their full potential. As stewards of our organizations this is, of course, the last thing we would want. We want to maximize our investment in our buildings, programs, missions, projects, and especially our people, who bring all of our assets to life and to good use. Yet, if our exploration throughout this book has taught us anything, it is that this isn't always the case.

In fact, this is where we are the direct opposite of Balaam. He was intent on cursing the Israelite people, yet thanks to a talking donkey followed by the presence and persuasion of God, Balaam blesses them with the beautiful words of *Mah Tovu* we continue to chant to this day. Balaam was the beneficiary of a pain in the ass that allowed his point of view to shift, and he began to understand the consequences of his actions, of what was truly important and what truly mattered. For Balaam, that was subservience to God rather than to fulfilling a job given to him by Balak, and a promotion of peace, tranquility, and prosperity rather than war and conflict.

I would bet that anyone reading this is on the side of wanting to bless our workforce, wanting to be a part of the solution, aspiring to deliver the words and deeds to bless each of our employees. We should all seek to provide our talent with the job environment and motivational tools not only to survive in this field despite our systemic deficiencies and challenges, but to thrive, to have a huge smile on their faces and feeling of love in their hearts every day while preforming this work. I applaud you for wanting to gain a deeper sense of how to better bless our workforce.

Going forward, we must commit to ensuring that our *keva*, our actions, align with our *kavanah*, our intentions. Rabbi Jonathan Lipnick, one of my esteemed colleagues while I was at JTS, would often teach our graduate students about prayer, and how to teach prayer. He would talk a lot about aligning our *keva* with our *kavanah*. We fail by not aligning the two when we are participating in our teaching prayer. We teach how to read, or decode, the Hebrew; we teach when to bend and when to bow during the *Amidah* (the standing silent devotion found in the thrice daily religious service), yet we don't always teach the why of our prayers, the intention behind the prayers we recite. What do these words mean? What do we hope comes from wearing *tefillin* (phylacteries), a *tallis* (prayer shawl), and a *kippah* (head covering)? I went to religious school throughout my childhood and adolescence and was a star student, yet I fail to recall having those conversations. This, thankfully, is changing in religious school environments today.

Our talented human resources, like all of humanity, need to be taken care of in order to thrive. When, for example, we compensate according to a scarcity model and try to set standards of compensation and staff investment according to the marketplace, what is that accomplishing? When we set up job structures without clear job descriptions that create a lack of clarity between the manager and the employee, our *keva* does not align with the *kavanah*, of wanting our employees to feel blessed? When we hire without putting on gender or other diverse lenses and thus perpetuate the trends that frustrate and turn away the talent of emerging generations, why? Will this actually set us up for long term success?

I hope that, with these blessings now in our toolbox, we can bring *kavanah* into our words and deeds, amplifying the *kevas* that are already aligning with our intentions. The blessings we act upon will also allow us to adjust the *keva* that is not aligning with our intentions. No matter how much of a pain it may be in the short term, aligning our deeds with our intentions in the long-term, will raise up our talent, our organizations, and community for long-term success.

I humbly proposed the following in my ELI Talk, and it bears repeating here: We as Jews believe in the magic, the wizardry of blessings; we bless the food before we eat, our children before they go to bed and before Shabbat, when there is a rainbow in the sky and when the rain falls. We bless because it allows us to be intentional with our actions, that our actions will follow our words, that we will eat the best food for our bodies, that we will be kind parents to our children, and that we will do well by this earth. How about we go into our organizations, into YOUR organization, tomorrow, the next day, and the next, and say this *Mah Tovu*:

> *How goodly is our talent in our organizations, our workforce in this Jewish community.*

Let us put action to these words. If we meet this call to action, this industry, the Jewish professional sector, will be the greatest place to work because we already have inspiring missions with meaningful work that already provide so much soul-fulfillment, as our narratives prove.

By adding the virtuous cycle of employee investment introduced to us by Dr. Zeynep Ton, and the various blessings we now have in our toolbox, we can be the ideal, if not the envy, of all other industries, attracting and retaining the best and brightest talent who may already have an affinity for serving Jewish community and are inspired by our Jewish organizational missions and results.

I didn't yet realize the power and long-lasting soul-fulfillment of this work when I was sitting in that meeting with the JCC professional while a young counselor at Jewish summer camp. I didn't understand the impact a Jewish community professional could have on the lives of others, the ability to create and manage entire organizations such as Moishe House, OneTable, and Bronfman Fellowships that have engaged and inspired tens of thousands into Jewish experiences filled with love, community, nurturing, celebrating each other's strengths and differences, and valuing the importance of one's learning and professional growth. I had no idea the impact of a Federation, Camp, or Day School director to set policy, innovate new educational practices, help alleviate poverty, and set the next generation on a course towards a more successful and fulfilling life. I had no idea at the sheer creativity and innovation spread throughout our field, those who share and bring to life big bold ideas to the masses, engage in the arts and technologies in our JCCs and youth groups, and help advocate for a better tomorrow. I had no concept of the entrepreneurial and leadership spirit that embodies our thousands of Jewish community professionals and the start-ups, legacy institutions and various projects within which they serve.

Now I do, and now we know more about some of the journeys that have led select folks to join in this collective venture, supporting this one all-important goal: securing a thriving Jewish community for today and tomorrow. We know how special these Jewish community professionals are, their needs, challenges, frustrations, hopes and dreams. We now we have clear concrete strategies to properly motivate, demonstrate value, and bless them.

Now that we are armed with these strategies, we have an obligation to examine our practices, to identify where our actions do not currently align with our intentions and in which we are, however inadvertently, inhibiting our workforce from reaching its full potential. Let us amplify what we are doing well and have the courage to make changes where we need to.

Any positive change will do good: starting a robust and clear performance review process in our organizations or setting clear job descriptions and compensation levels, making our mission more explicit, fostering more partnerships, or adopting any one of these blessings. Start with our golden role: make time to deeply know each of your staff members. Have them really get to know you too, so we can best manage, support, and bless each other in our noble and critically important efforts.

WE ARE THE WIZARDS

We have every ability, and all the magic in our hearts, souls, and collective might, to make the Jewish sector the best place possible to work for each of our Jewish community professionals. We just need to make a promise to ourselves and to each other to align with our *keva* with our *kavanah* to bless our workforce. For the teenager at summer camp first hearing about this field, or the entry-level professional, or the mid-manager, or the executive – and to all of them collectively – I ask, what will you do first to bless your workforce? How will you *Mah Tovu*?

in gratitude

I'd first like to extend to my gratitude to my family, my wife Mara and children Noah Sadie and Asher Russell, who support me in everything I do and love me no matter what. In addition to paying honor to my late Mom in the dedications, I also want to thank my Dad, Dr. Dennis Young, thankfully alive and well, for modeling the importance of thought leadership and sharing one's ideas with the world. I am not sure how you have the stamina and discipline to write so many books. This was a lot more difficult for me then it seems to be for you.

A thank you to Dr. Bill Robinson, Dean of the William Davidson Graduate School of Jewish Education, gave me the autonomy and creative space to begin this book project as part of my work directing our Leadership Commons.

A thank you to the Wexner Foundation. As part of participating in the Wexner Field Fellowship I was able to make use of a book coach, Lee Kravetz, to guide me in the process of developing a book proposal, writing the formal volume and editing. Thank you to Lee, and to Wexner, for helping me bring this book to life and these ideas to the field. Thank you also to my professional editor, Gillian Steinberg, for your detailed review, insights that helped each chapter stay focused, and dramatically improving my writing. Thank you to my friend Kate Stambler Levy for her graphic design expertise, and my best friend Ira Horowitz and Cornershop Creative who helped me develop the *Bless Our Workforce* website.

A thank you to those with whom I have had the pleasure to learn from as my supervisors, Brian Lefkoff, Anthony Giunta, Jodi Sperling, Jane Slotin, Jessica Hickman, Dr. Barry Holtz, Dr. Jeff Kress, Sue Gelsey, and Bill. Thank you for challenging and validating my work and allowing me to focus on the big picture and see the fruits of my own labor so I can grow, be motivated, and feel valued.

Gratitude to Brenda Gevertz, former executive director of JCSA/JPRO Network and to Dan Brown of ejewishphilanthropy for giving me the forum initially to share my ideas on how we can best value our Jewish professionals publishing my initial The $54,000 Strategy: A Bold Solution to Undervaluing our Jewish Professionals piece in the Journal of Jewish Communal Service and on ejewishphilanthropy in the Spring of 2013. I wouldn't have gotten to this point and the completion of this book without both of you opening up the door. A profound thank you to my colleague and friend

Miriam Brosseau, one of our book profiles, who granted me the chance to share the germ of these ideas in my 2016 ELI TALK: Mah Tovu, and to my ELI Talks Coach Bonnie Swencionis for teaching me how to be persuasive, concise, and stay on message.

Of course, thank you to all those who trust me with their stories and partnered with me in this project: David Cygeilman, Alyson Bazeley, Ezra Shanken, Miriam Brosseau, Jon Shapiro, Aliza Kline, Graham Hoffman, Rabbi Laura Baum, Becky Voorwinde, Rachel Felber, Marc Fein, Carine Warsawski, and Evan Traylor. I hope I represented you kindly and accurately, and in a manner that taught all of us better ways to manage our people.

Thank you to Steven Rod, Brian Schreiber, Cindy Goldstein, Rabby Abby Sosland, Scott Brown, and Barb Gelb, for championing this project, your guidance, and your kind words.

Lastly, thank you to all of my family, friends, colleagues, for our respective relationships that have been my rock during the course of the past three years and always. Because of all of you I feel truly blessed every minute of every day.

appendix

I structured each discussion with the same 10 sets of questions:

1. What is your Jewish educator/community professional story? How did you get here?

2. Tell us in detail about your job: what do you seek to achieve in your role and what are your job activities that will help you get to those achievements? Tell me all the parts that are interesting to you.

3. How would you describe the motivators to your work? What drives you? Please be specific and elaborate...

4. How would you describe the de-motivators to your work? What challenges you? What might make you want to turn away or quit? Please be specific and elaborate...

5. Decades from now, what would you want folks at your retirement party to say about you and your professional work? What wouldn't you want them to say? Would this even matter to you now? Is this a source of motivation for you?

6. Tell me about the relationship for you between your compensation and how it impacts your work, your motivation, and your career goals. Please be specific and elaborate. Tell me, if you would, your salary history and current-salary.

7. Tell me about your work ethic. How do you work? What are your strategies to get what you want to get done? What are your strategies to harness your creativity?

8. When you think about the Jewish community – what excites you the most about the possibilities for the future, and what keeps you up at night?

9. At what point do you feel most valued in your work by those around you: those accountable for your work, those you are accountable for, peers, constituents, and all other potential stakeholders and field colleagues you are at all closely or not so closely connected with.

10. Based on our conversation, what do you want to share with me especially considering my purpose and goals for the book above that you haven't already shared?

I encourage you to get to know your staff and colleagues beginning with these ten questions, or at least the first 9 unless you decide to write your own *Bless Our Workforce* book!

resources and works cited

PRE-BLESSING: PREPARING THE CANVAS

- The Pew Study: A Portrait of Jewish Americans:
  https://www.pewforum.org/dataset/a-portrait-of-jewish-americans/

- Leading Edge: *Leading Places to Work Studies*, 2016, 2017, and 2018:
  https://leadingedge.org/lptw/

- Tauber, Sarah. Open Minds, Devoted Hearts: Portraits of Adult Religious Educators
  (Horizons in Religious Education), Horizons in Religious Education, 2015.

BLESSING #1: CHALLENGE OUR TALENT

- Personal Interview with David Cygeilman, August 1st, 2017

- Deci, Edward L. with Flaste, Richard. *Why We Do What We Do: Understanding Self-Motivation*. Penguin Books; Reprint edition (August 1, 1996)

- Ton, Zeynep. The Good Jobs Strategy: How the Smartest Companies Invest in
  Employees to Lower Costs and Boost Profits, Houghton Mifflin Harcourt, 2014.

- Moishe House Website: https://www.moishehouse.org/

BLESSING #2: BUILD THE JOB AROUND THE TALENT

- Personal Interview with Alyson Bazeley, August 8th, 2017

- Charity (Tzedakah): Eight Levels of Charitable Giving
  https://www.jewishvirtuallibrary.org/eight-levels-of-charitable-giving

- Conversations with Jodi Sperling, 2007-2014

- Ogden, Curtis. Thinking Like a Network 2.0, Interaction Institute of Social
  Change, 2017
  http://interactioninstitute.org/thinking-like-a-network-2-0/

- Herring, Avi, Korb-Weiss, Naomi. Rosen-Smolen, Justin, Snyder, Tamar,
  Walfish, Mordecai, Warshenbrot, Ruthie. "The American Jewish Scene /
  Toward Transparency: An Analysis of the 2012 Jewish Communal Professional
  Compensation Survey: ejewishphilanthropy and Journal of Jewish Communal
  Service. April 4th, 2013.
  https://ejewishphilanthropy.com/toward-transparency-an-analysis-of-the-2012-jewish-communal-professional-compensation-survey/

BLESSING #3: FOSTER THE RELATIONSHIPS

- Personal Interview with Ezra Shanken, August 2nd, 2017

- Wertheimer, Jack. *The New American Judaism*. How Jews Practice Their Religion Today, Princeton University Press, August 28th, 2018.

- Wolfson, Ron. *Relational Judaism*: Using the Power of Relationships to Transform the Jewish Community, Jewish Lights Publishing; 1 edition, February 15, 2013.

- Pink, Daniel. Drive: The Surprising Truth About What Motivates Us Riverhead Books, April 5, 201.1

- "Six Factors that Promote Knowledge Worker Productivity." Advanced Workplace Associates and Center for Evidence Based Management https://www.advanced-workplace.com/wp content/uploads/2015/04/6_Factors_Paper.pdf

- "Friendships at Work." *The Harvard Business Review*, https://www.shrm.org/hr-today/trends-and-forecasting/special-reports-and-expert-views/pages/kay-sargent.aspx

- Bolman, Lee & Deal, Terrence. *Reframing Organizations*: Artistry, Choice, and Leadership Jossey-Bass; 5 edition (August 5, 2013)

- Wolfson, Ron. "It's About People, Not Programs." CJ Voices: Kolot Magazine. http://www.cjvoices.org/article/its-about-people-not-programs/

- "A Closer Look at Empathy." https://www.shamayim.org/content/rosh-hashanah-5775-closer-look-empathy

- Higginbottom, Karen. "Why Empathy Matters in the Workspace" Forbes Magazine, May 31, 2018 https://www.forbes.com/sites/karenhigginbottom/2018/05/31/why-empathy-matters-in-the-workplace/#3a7d5dc81130

- "Empathy, group norms and children's ethnic attitudes," Journal of Applied Developmental Psychology Volume 26, Issue 6 November–December 2005,

BLESSING #4: FEED THEIR CREATIVE DRIVE

- Personal Interview with Miriam Brosseau, August 17th, 2017.

- Simon, Adam. "What Makes People Stand Up, Say Heneni, and Lead?" ELI Talk: https://elitalks.org/what-makes-people-stand-say-hineini-and-lead

- Csikszentmihalyi, Mihaly. Finding Flow: *The Psychology of Engagement with Everyday Life*, Basic Books; 1st edition (April 6, 1998)

- The Hero's Journey: an Author's Guide to Plotting, Perfecting your Craft. https://blog.reedsy.com/heros-journey/

- Robbins, Mike. Bring Your Whole Self to Work: How Vulnerability Unlocks Creativity, Connection, and Performance, Hay House Inc. (May 1, 2018).

- Young, Mark. *Mah-Tovu: Treating Your Workforce with Blessings*, Not Curses. ELI Talk: www.elitalks.org/mah-tovu

- Newport, Cal. Deep Work: Rules for Focused Success in a Distracted World, Grand Central Publishing; (January 5, 2016)

- Re-Boot website: http://www.rebooters.net/about-us

- Drucker, Peter. *Management by Objectives* https://www.toolshero.com/management/management-by-objectives-drucker/

- Brosseau, Miriam. "The Revelation will Not Be Televised" JDOV Talk 2013. http://jdov.org/talk/the-revelation-will-not-be-televised/

BLESSING #5: HELP THEM SEE THE FRUITS OF THEIR LABOR

- Personal Interview with Jon Shapiro, August 30th, 2017.

- Kolb, David. "The Kolb Learning Cycle." 1985, *The Experiential Educator*, 2017.

- "Science of Paying it Forward" The New York Times, March 16th, 2014. https://www.nytimes.com/2014/03/16/opinion/sunday/the-science-of-paying-it-forward.html

BLESSING #6: PROMOTE COLLABORATION, END INCLUSION

- Personal Interview with Aliza Kline, September 19th, 2017.

- "Workplace Ostracism More Distressing Than Harassment" Psychological Science, January 30th, 2014. https://www.psychologicalscience.org/news/minds-business/workplace-ostracism-more-distressing-than-harassment.html

- OneTable Website: www.onetable.org

- Mogahaddam, Fathali M. & Taylor, Don. *Theories of Intergroup Relations: International Social Psychological Perspectives*, 2nd Edition, Praeger; 2 edition (June 30, 1994)

- Tajfel ,Turner. *Social Identity Theory*, organisationdevelopment.org https://www.learning-theories.com/social-identity-theory-tajfel-turner.html

- Mayim Chayim website: https://www.mayyimhayyim.org/

- Davidson, Steven. "How Much Do Top Jewish Non-Profit Leaders Make?" The Forward, December 11, 2017 https://forward.com/news/388240/how-much-do-top-jewish-non-profit-leaders-make/

- Centeno-Milton, Carolyn "What is Abundant Thinking?" Forbes Magazine, Apr. 4th, 2018.
https://www.forbes.com/sites/carolyncenteno/2018/04/04/what-is-abundant-thinking/#b8e16303a0c2

BLESSING #7: CUT THE BS

- Personal Interview with Graham Hoffman, September 20th, 2017

- Mandel, Mort. *It's All About Who You Hire, How They Lead...and Other Essential Advice from a Self-Made Leader,* Jossey-Bass; 1 edition (November 28, 2012)

- Welch, Jack. *Winning*. Harper Business; 1st edition (April 2005)

- "Study Looks at Why We All Spew So Much BS. Smithsonian.com, May 11th, 2018.
https://www.smithsonianmag.com/smart-news/study-looks-why-we-all-spew-so-much-bs-180969062/

- Resnick, Brian. "Why People Fall for Bullshit, According to a Scientist. Vox.com, Dec. 3, 2015.
https://www.vox.com/science-and-health/2015/12/3/9844480/why-people-believe-bullshit-science

- Thomas, AJ. "Culture Matters: How Leadership Enables Toxicity and Makes Way for Mediocrity." Forbes Magazine, July 16, 2018.
https://www.forbes.com/sites/forbeshumanresourcescouncil/2018/07/16/culture-matters-how-leadership-enables-toxicity-and-makes-way-for-mediocrity/#7775780632d0

- Weiss, Naomi Korb. "Measuring Nonprofits by Their Impact Not Their Overhead," 2013.
https://ejewishphilanthropy.com/measuring-nonprofits-by-their-impact-not-their-overhead/

- Ton, Zeynep. "Good Jobs Are Good for Retailers." *Harvard Business Review*, 2012.
https://hbr.org/2012/01/why-good-jobs-are-good-for-retailers

- Cancialosi, Chris. "Using Your Culture to Attract Top Talent." Forbes Magazine. Oct 20, 2014
https://www.forbes.com/sites/chriscancialosi/2014/10/20/using-your-culture-to-attract-top-talent/#460ed18cfe50

- Sinek, Simon "How Great Leaders Inspire Action" TED TALK, 2010.
https://www.ted.com/talks/simon_sinek_how_great_leaders_inspire_action?language=en

- Burton, Neel. "Our Hierarchy of Needs: True freedom is luxury of the mind." Psychology Today, May 23rd, 2012
https://www.psychologytoday.com/us/blog/hide-and-seek/201205/our-hierarchy-needs

- Ton, Zeynep. "Higher Wages Aren't Enough to Turn Mediocre Jobs into Good Ones." Harvard Business Review, 2018.
https://hbr.org/2018/10/higher-wages-arent-enough-to-turn-mediocre-jobs-into-good-ones

- Lencioni, Patrick. Death By Meeting: A Leadership Fable…About Solving the Most Painful Problem in Business, Jossey-Bass; 1 edition (March 4, 2004)

- Kanfer-Stewart, Mamie. *The Modern Manager Podcast*, episode #1
https://www.mamieks.com/podcast

BLESSING #8: EMPOWER THEM BY FOCUSING ON THE BIG PICTURE

- Personal Interview with Rabbi Laura Baum, September 25th, 2017.

- Heifetz, Ronald & and Linsky, Marty. Leadership On the Line: Staying Alive Through the Dangers of Leading, Harvard Business Review Press; 1 edition (April 18, 2002)

- Bronznick, Shifra & Goldenhar, Didi. Leveling the Playing Field: Advancing Women in Jewish Organizational Life, Cambridge Leadership Associates; 1st edition (March 5, 2008)

- Bernstein, Maya. "Let's Verb Leadership". Gleanings: the e-journal of the William Davidson Graduate School of Jewish Education, Volume 3, Issue 2. Fall 2016.
http://www.jtsa.edu/lets-verb-leadership

BLESSING #9: ENABLE THEM TO BRING THEIR WHOLE INTEGRATED SELVES TO WORK

- Personal Interview with Becky Voorwinde, October 19th, 2017.

- Robbins, Mike. Bring Your Whole Self to Work: How Vulnerability Unlocks Creativity, Connection, and Performance, Hay House Inc. (May 1, 2018).
"If you really knew me exercise" https://mike-robbins.com/express-yourself/

- Bronfman Youth Fellowships Website: http://www.bronfman.org/

- Maidment, Adam. "Study Finds People Who Shoe Their True Selves Work Are Happier and More Productive." Lifehack, accessed October 2018. https://www.lifehack.org/348765/study-finds-people-who-show-their-true-selves-work-are-happier-and-more-productive

- Covey, Stephen. The 7 Habits of Highly Effective People: Powerful Lessons in Personal Change Paperback – Free Press; Revised edition (November 9, 2004)

- Adams, Bryan. "How Google's 20 Percent Rule Can Make You More Productive and Energetic." Inc.com. Dec. 28, 2016. https://www.inc.com/bryan-adams/12-ways-to-encourage-more-free-thinking-and-innovation-into-any-business.html

- Beard, Mary. *Women in Power: A Manifesto*. Liveright; 1 edition (December 12, 2017)

BLESSING #10: SHOW THEM IT IS NOT ABOUT THEM AT ALL

- Personal Interview with Rachel Felber, November 1st, 2017.

- Etkes, Immanuel. *Rabbi Israel Salanter and the Mussar Movement*. The Jewish Publication Society; 1st English edition (May 1, 1993)

- Rabbi David Jaffe Personal Website http://www.Rabbidavidjaffe.com (accessed July 8th, 2019).

- Fisher, Roger and Ury, William. *Getting To Yes: Negotiating Agreement Without Giving In*. Penguin Books; Updated, Revised edition (May 3, 2011)

- Cain, Susan. *Quiet: The Power of Introverts in a World That Can't Stop Talking*, Broadway Books (January 29, 2013)

- "The Five Love Languages Defined." (Accessed July 8th, 2019). https://www.5lovelanguages.com/2018/06/the-five-love-languages-defined/

- Morinis, Alan. Everyday Holiness: The Jewish Spiritual Path of Mussar, Trumpeter; 2nd Printing edition (December 2, 2008)

BLESSING #11: MAKE IT ALL ABOUT THEM

- Personal Interview with Marc Fein, October 26th, 2017.

- Kok, Leonard. "The Emotional Bank Account (EBA)." Focus Adventure http://www.focusadventure.com/team-building/gallery/the-emotional-bank-account/

BLESSING #12: CHAMPION THEIR RELENTLESS PURSUIT

- Personal Interview with Carine Warsawski, November 16th, 2017.

- Upstart website: www.upstartlab.org

- Gasca, Peter "10 Tips to Help Entrepreneurs Motivated" Entrepreneur.com, May 3, 2016 https://www.entrepreneur.com/article/270443

- I-Center website: https://www.theicenter.org/

- Chamorro-Premuzic, Thomas. "The Five Characteristics Successful Innovators.", Harvard Business Review, October 25, 2013
  https://hbr.org/2013/10/the-five-characteristics-of-successful-innovators

- Warsawski, Carine. "The Power of No." Collabrastory. ELI Talk – Carine Warsawski, From the May 2018 Collaboratory presented by Upstart
  https://www.youtube.com/watch?v=DISoLH1eukA

- "Systematic Inventive Thinking" and the SIT Model Website: http://www.sitsite.com/

BLESSING #13: WHAT SUCCESS CAN LOOK LIKE

- Personal Interview with Evan Traylor, December 21st, 2018

- Jews of Color Field Building Initiative Website: https://jewsofcolorfieldbuilding.org/

BLESSING #14: AMPLIFY OUR STRENGTHENS

- Simon, Adam. "What Makes People Stand Up, Say Heneni, and Lead?" ELI Talk:
  https://elitalks.org/what-makes-people-stand-say-hineini-and-lead

- Dukes, Elizabeth. "Don't Assume Employees Care About Your Company's Mission, Inc.com, Oct 17, 2017.
  https://www.inc.com/elizabeth-dukes/how-to-get-employees-invested-in-your-mission-why-it-matters.html

BLESSING #15: ADJUST OUR IMPERFECTIONS

- Edelson, Harriet. "Social Security Benefit to Increase 2.8% in 2019." AARP, October 11th, 2018.
  https://www.aarp.org/retirement/social-security/info-2018/new-cola-benefit-2019.html

- Weiss, Naomi Korb. "Measuring Nonprofits by Their Impact, Not Their Overhead." Ejewishphilanthropy.com, April 3, 2013.
  https://ejewishphilanthropy.com/measuring-nonprofits-by-their-impact-not-their-overhead/

- Palotta, Dan. *The Way We Think About Charity is Dead Wrong.* TED TALK, 2013.
  https://www.ted.com/talks/dan_pallotta_the_way_we_think_about_charity_is_dead_wrong?language=en,

- Davidson, Steven. "How Much Do Top Jewish Non-Profit Leaders Make?" The Forward, December 11, 2017
  https://forward.com/news/388240/how-much-do-top-jewish-non-profit-leaders-make/

- "The State of the Gender Pay Gap 2019."
  https://www.payscale.com/data/gender-pay-gap (Accessed July 11th, 2019).

- Epstein, Shira and Jacobs, Andrea. "Gender Equity and Leadership Initiative:
  A Research and Planning Task Force of the Leadership Commons. The Jewish
  Theological Seminary, Spring 2019.
  http://www.jtsa.edu/stuff/contentmgr/files/0/7cf060c9b5ae1960b4e95024ef77e86a/
  misc/jts_genderequity_r4.pdf

- Shapiro-Plevan, Sara. Sirbu, Rebecca and Fine, Alison. "Who Do You Choose for
  Your Leadership Positions?" ejewishphilanthropy.com, February 27th, 2019.
  https://ejewishphilanthropy.com/who-do-you-choose-to-hire-for-leadership-positions/

- Finestone, Barry and Linden, Seth. Leadership Development: A Strategy Emerges,
  Investments Are Made, the Jim Joseph Foundation. October 26th, 2017.
  https://jimjosephfoundation.org/news-blogs/leadership-development-strategy-
  emerges-investments-made/

POST-BLESSING: BLESSING OUR WORKFORCE

- Young, Mark. Bar Mitzvah D'var Torah, June 25, 1994.

about mark s. young

Mark S. Young is passionate about strengthening the experience and opportunities for the professionals who help make thriving Jewish community a reality.

Mark joined the team at JCC Association of North America as director of its new signature program, JResponse in July 2019, and serves as an integral member of the program and talent team. Mark headed to JCC Association after serving the Jewish Theological Seminary for 8 1/2 years as Managing Director of its Leadership Commons at the William Davidson Graduate School of Jewish Education and previously as the school's Director of Alumni Engagement and Program Coordinator for its Experiential Learning Initiative.

Prior to joining JTS, Mark worked in Human Resources for Episcopal Social Services of New York and the 92nd Street Y. Mark is a board member of JPRO Network and a past board chair of Advancing Jewish Professionals of NYC (now JPRO NYC), and writes frequently on how to best invest in Jewish community professional talent, including his $54,000 Strategy series on ejewishphilanthropy and his 2016 ELI Talk: Mah Tovu.

Mark holds a BS in Psychology and Economics from McGill University, as well as an MPA in Nonprofit Management and an MA in Hebrew and Judaic Studies from New York University. Mark lives in Hartsdale, NY with his wife, Rabbi Mara Young, and two children, Noah Sadie (8) and Asher Russell (5).